Perfect Score. 33 | Name George Rodriguez

Deduct......... — | Date 4/15/91 Class

Your Score.... — | Checked by

1

UNIT A — Accounting Career Information

DIRECTIONS: Place a check mark (√) in the proper Answers column to show whether each of the following statements is true or false. Before you begin, read the example given as 0.

	Answers True	Answers False	For Scoring
0. Accounting knowledge is essential for an accounting career but not important for any other career		√	**0.** √
1. If owners and managers are to make good business decisions, they need good financial information			**1.**
2. A business may fail because of the types of accounting records kept			**2.**
3. Accounting is often referred to as the language of business			**3.**
4. Accounting knowledge may be used for earning a living, but is seldom used for personal affairs			**4.**
5. The four major accounting job categories are: accountants, bookkeepers, machine operators, and accounting clerks			**5.**
6. According to information reported in Chapter 1, about 20,000 persons are employed in various accounting positions in the United States			**6.**
7. In 1980, the U.S. Department of Labor estimated that the annual job openings for accountants and bookkeepers would be approximately 150,000			**7.**
8. Accountants often do secretarial work as part of their duties			**8.**
9. A four-year college degree is essential for finding a job in accounting			**9.**
10. Private accountants work for only one business			**10.**
11. Bookkeepers usually work for a single employer			**11.**
12. In small firms, bookkeepers may be required to do general office work			**12.**
13. Job titles for accounting clerks often describe the accounting records on which they work			**13.**
14. An accounting clerk should know the total accounting system			**14.**
15. Accounting tasks performed by general office clerks must follow basic accounting concepts and procedures			**15.**
16. A person with one year of high school accounting study usually starts work as an accountant		√	**16.**
17. A person with two years of high school accounting study usually starts work as an accounting clerk or a bookkeeper	√		**17.**
18. A person with accounting study in addition to high school usually starts work as a bookkeeper or an accountant	√		**18.**
19. The study of accounting by accounting clerks is basic background for earning a promotion	√		**19.**

UNIT B — Accounting Terms

DIRECTIONS: Select the one term in Column I that best fits each definition in Column II. Print the letter identifying your choice in the Answers column. Before you begin, read the example given as 0.

Column I

A. accountants
B. accounting
C. accounting clerks
D. accounting records
E. bookkeepers
F. entry-level jobs
G. general office clerks
H. public accounting firm

Column II	Answers	For Scoring
0. Planning, keeping, analyzing, and interpreting financial records	*B*	**0.** ✓
20. The first jobs that individuals get		**20.**
21. A business selling accounting services to the general public		**21.**
22. Persons doing general kinds of office tasks, including some accounting tasks		**22.**
23. Persons who do general accounting work plus some summarizing and analyzing		**23.**
24. Persons who record, sort, and file accounting information		**24.**
25. Persons who plan, summarize, analyze, and interpret accounting information		**25.**
26. Orderly records of businesses' financial activities		**26.**

UNIT C — Basic Accounting Concepts

DIRECTIONS: For each item below, select the choice that best completes the sentence. Print the letter identifying your choice in the Answers column. Before you begin, read the example given as 0.

	Answers	For Scoring
0. Reporting financial changes for a specific period of time in the form of financial statements is based on the concept (A) accounting period cycle (B) business entity (C) adequate disclosure (D) none of these	*A*	**0.** ✓
27. Assuring that all financial information is reported on financial statements is an application of the concept (A) business entity (B) conservatism (C) adequate disclosure (D) none of these		**27.**
28. Assets and the value of earnings should not be overstated is an application of the concept (A) accounting period cycle (B) objective evidence (C) conservatism (D) none of these		**28.**
29. The business entity concept means that (A) a business exists (B) the business' and owner's personal records should not be mixed (C) a business is successful (D) none of these		**29.**
30. The consistent reporting concept means that (A) financial statements are prepared at the same time each year (B) the same statement format is used each year (C) unless changes make information more easily understood, changes in accounting methods or statements are not made (D) none of these		**30.**
31. When Marilyn Feesler says that she expects her business to remain in operation indefinitely, she is referring to the accounting concept (A) business entity (B) going concern (C) objective evidence (D) none of these		**31.**
32. When a business records financial information in dollars and cents, it is using the accounting concept (A) historical cost (B) unit of measurement (C) consistent reporting (D) none of these		**32.**
33. When a business records only the actual amount paid or received, it is using the accounting concept (A) historical cost (B) unit of measurement (C) consistent reporting (D) none of these		**33.**

Perfect Score. 54 Name ____________

Deduct.......... ___ Date ____________ Class ____________

Your Score.... ___ Checked by ____________

STUDY GUIDE **2**

UNIT A — Analyzing a Beginning Balance Sheet

DIRECTIONS: Each part of the balance sheet at the right is identified by a capital letter. For each item below, decide which part(s) of the balance sheet are being described. Print the letter(s) identifying your choice in the Answers column.

A *Mendall Company*
B *Balance Sheet*
C *November 30, 1982*

Assets D		*Liabilities* L	
Cash	E 515 00	*Becker Supply Co.*	560 00 M
Supplies	F 550 00	*Wilson Equipment Co.*	O 440 00 N
Golf Equipment	G 3100 00	*Total Liabilities*	1000 00 P
Maintenance Equipment	H 1160 00	*Capital* Q	
	I	*Arnold Mendall, Capital*	S 4325 00 R
Total Assets	K J 5325 00	*Total Liab. and Capital*	U 5325 00 T

	Answers	For Scoring
0. The name of the business for which the balance sheet is prepared	*A*	**0.** ✓
1. The first asset item		**1.**
2. An amount owed to Becker Supply Company		**2.**
3. The value of supplies owned by the business		**3.**
4. The equity total for all liabilities		**4.**
5. The owner's equity		**5.**
6. The amounts proving that the balance sheet is in balance		**6.**
7. The total value of all things owned by the business		**7.**
8. The ruled lines showing that the balance sheet is in balance		**8.**
9. The total equity in the business		**9.**
10. The date of the balance sheet		**10.**

UNIT B — Recording an Opening Entry in a Journal

DIRECTIONS: A two-column general journal is at the right. The locations of parts of an opening entry are labeled with capital letters. For each item below, decide where the part of the entry described should be recorded. Print the letter identifying your choice in the Answers column.

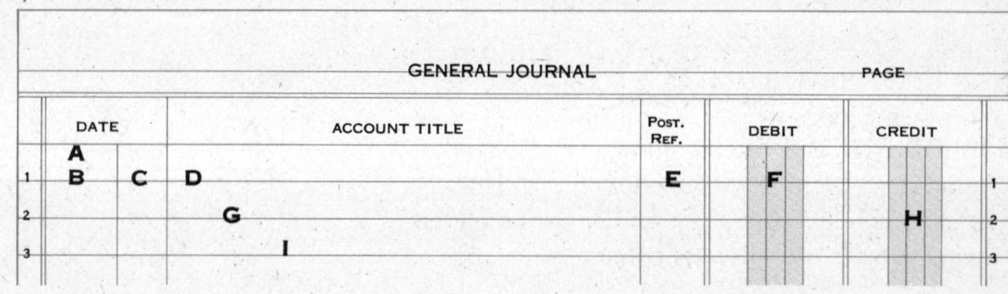

	Answers	For Scoring
0. Debit amount	*F*	**0.** ✓
11. Reason or source document for a journal entry		**11.**
12. Name of an account that is debited		**12.**
13. Day of the month for a journal entry		**13.**
14. Name of the month for a journal entry		**14.**
15. Year for a journal entry		**15.**
16. Credit amount for a journal entry		**16.**
17. Name of an account that is credited		**17.**
18. Account number to which an amount is posted		**18.**

UNIT C — Accounting Terms

DIRECTIONS: Select the one term in Column I that best fits each definition in Column II. Print the letter identifying your choice in the Answers column.

Column I

A. account
B. account number
C. account title
D. accounting equation
E. asset
F. balance sheet
G. capital
H. chart of accounts
I. credit side
J. debit side
K. entry
L. equities
M. flowchart
N. general journal
O. journal
P. ledger
Q. liability
R. opening an account
S. opening entry
T. posting
U. sole proprietorship
V. source document

Column II	Answers	For Scoring
0. Writing an account title and number on the heading of an account form	*R*	**0.** ✓
19. A group of accounts		**19.**
20. An equation showing the relationship between the assets and equities of a business		**20.**
21. Transferring information from journal entries to ledger accounts		**21.**
22. The record in which accounting information is recorded in chronological order		**22.**
23. An amount owed by a business		**23.**
24. Anything of value that a business owns		**24.**
25. The financial rights to the assets of a business		**25.**
26. A business owned by one person		**26.**
27. A business form that reports assets, liabilities, and capital on a specific date		**27.**
28. Each item recorded in a journal		**28.**
29. The left side of a two-column account form		**29.**
30. A name given to a separate ledger account		**30.**
31. The right side of a two-column account form		**31.**
32. A number given to an account		**32.**
33. An entry to record information from a beginning balance sheet		**33.**
34. A journal with two amount columns in which all kinds of entries can be recorded		**34.**
35. A list of account titles and numbers showing the location of the accounts in a ledger		**35.**
36. The business paper from which information is obtained for a journal entry		**36.**
37. An accounting form used to sort and summarize changes in a specific item		**37.**
38. A diagram showing the sequence of steps involved in a procedure		**38.**
39. The value of the owner's equity, or share of a business		**39.**

UNIT D — Analyzing a Two-column Ledger Account Form

DIRECTIONS: Each column of the ledger account at the right is identified with a capital letter. For each item in Parts 1 and 2, print the identifying letter in the Answers column.

ACCOUNT — ACCOUNT NO.

A B C D E F G H

I J K L

Part 1: The column *heading* for the following locations:

	Answers	For Scoring
0. Date (debit side)	*A*	**0.** ✓
40. Date (credit side)		**40.**
41. Credit amount		**41.**
42. Debit amount		**42.**
43. Post. Ref. (credit side)		**43.**
44. Post Ref. (debit side)		**44.**
45. Item (credit side)		**45.**
46. Item (debit side)		**46.**

Part 2: The *column* in which the following items are written:

	Answers	For Scoring
47. Year (credit side)		**47.**
48. Year (debit side)		**48.**
49. Day (debit side)		**49.**
50. Day (credit side)		**50.**
51. Debit amounts		**51.**
52. Credit amounts		**52.**
53. Month (debit side)		**53.**
54. Month (credit side)		**54.**

Name ______________________ Date __________ Class __________

DRILL 2-D 1, p. 32
[1–3]

Classifying assets, liabilities, and capital

1	2	3	4	5
	Balance Sheet		General Journal	
			Column in which amount in opening entry is recorded	
Balance Sheet Items	Left-hand side	Right-hand side	Debit column	Credit column
1. Delivery equipment	*Asset*		√	
2. Mannies Supply Company				
3. Cash				
4. Office Equipment				
5. Office Supplies				
6. Zapata Equipment Company				
7. Dry cleaning equipment				
8. Supplies				
9. Golf Equipment				
10. Any amount owed				
11. Anything owned				
12. Bryan Dooley, Capital				

Preparing a chart of accounts

DRILL 2-D 2, p. 32

Preparing a beginning balance sheet

PROBLEM 2-1, p. 33
[1, 2]

Recording an opening entry

PROBLEM 2-2, p. 33
[1, 2]

Problem 2-2 is continued in the next problem. Your teacher will return it to you before it is needed in Problem 2-3.

GENERAL JOURNAL PAGE

	DATE		ACCOUNT TITLE	POST. REF.	DEBIT	CREDIT	
1							1
2							2
3							3
4							4
5							5
6							6
7							7
8							8
9							9
10							10
11							11
12							12
13							13
14							14
15							15

Name ______________________ Date __________ Class __________

PROBLEM 2-3, p. 34
[1, 2]

Posting an opening entry

For Problem 2-3, use the general journal from Problem 2-2.

LEDGER

ACCOUNT ______________________ ACCOUNT NO. ______

DATE		ITEM	POST. REF.	DEBIT	DATE		ITEM	POST. REF.	CREDIT

ACCOUNT ______________________ ACCOUNT NO. ______

DATE		ITEM	POST. REF.	DEBIT	DATE		ITEM	POST. REF.	CREDIT

ACCOUNT ______________________ ACCOUNT NO. ______

DATE		ITEM	POST. REF.	DEBIT	DATE		ITEM	POST. REF.	CREDIT

ACCOUNT ______________________ ACCOUNT NO. ______

DATE		ITEM	POST. REF.	DEBIT	DATE		ITEM	POST. REF.	CREDIT

ACCOUNT ______________________ ACCOUNT NO. ______

DATE		ITEM	POST. REF.	DEBIT	DATE		ITEM	POST. REF.	CREDIT

ACCOUNT ______________________ ACCOUNT NO. ______

DATE		ITEM	POST. REF.	DEBIT	DATE		ITEM	POST. REF.	CREDIT

[1, 2]

LEDGER

ACCOUNT ACCOUNT NO.

DATE		ITEM	POST. REF.	DEBIT	DATE		ITEM	POST. REF.	CREDIT

ACCOUNT ACCOUNT NO.

DATE		ITEM	POST. REF.	DEBIT	DATE		ITEM	POST. REF.	CREDIT

Preparing a partial chart of accounts; preparing a beginning balance sheet; recording and posting an opening entry

PROBLEM 2-4, p. 34
[1]

[2]

[3, 5]

GENERAL JOURNAL

PAGE

	DATE		ACCOUNT TITLE	POST. REF.	DEBIT	CREDIT	
1							1
2							2
3							3
4							4
5							5
6							6
7							7
8							8
9							9
10							10
11							11
12							12
13							13
14							14

LEDGER

ACCOUNT ACCOUNT NO.

DATE		ITEM	POST. REF.	DEBIT	DATE		ITEM	POST. REF.	CREDIT

ACCOUNT ACCOUNT NO.

DATE		ITEM	POST. REF.	DEBIT	DATE		ITEM	POST. REF.	CREDIT

ACCOUNT ACCOUNT NO.

DATE		ITEM	POST. REF.	DEBIT	DATE		ITEM	POST. REF.	CREDIT

ACCOUNT ACCOUNT NO.

DATE		ITEM	POST. REF.	DEBIT	DATE		ITEM	POST. REF.	CREDIT

ACCOUNT ACCOUNT NO.

DATE		ITEM	POST. REF.	DEBIT	DATE		ITEM	POST. REF.	CREDIT

Name ______________________ Date __________ Class __________

PROBLEM 2-4, concluded
[4, 5]

LEDGER

ACCOUNT ACCOUNT NO.

DATE	ITEM	POST. REF.	DEBIT	DATE	ITEM	POST. REF.	CREDIT

ACCOUNT ACCOUNT NO.

DATE	ITEM	POST. REF.	DEBIT	DATE	ITEM	POST. REF.	CREDIT

ACCOUNT ACCOUNT NO.

DATE	ITEM	POST. REF.	DEBIT	DATE	ITEM	POST. REF.	CREDIT

ACCOUNT ACCOUNT NO.

DATE	ITEM	POST. REF.	DEBIT	DATE	ITEM	POST. REF.	CREDIT

ACCOUNT ACCOUNT NO.

DATE	ITEM	POST. REF.	DEBIT	DATE	ITEM	POST. REF.	CREDIT

Preparing a beginning balance sheet;
recording and posting an opening entry

MASTERY PROBLEM 2-M, p. 34

[1]

[2, 4]

GENERAL JOURNAL

PAGE

	DATE		ACCOUNT TITLE	POST. REF.	DEBIT	CREDIT	
1							1
2							2
3							3
4							4
5							5
6							6
7							7
8							8
9							9
10							10
11							11
12							12
13							13
14							14
15							15

Name ______________ Date ________ Class ________

MASTERY PROBLEM 2-M, concluded

[3, 4]

LEDGER

ACCOUNT ACCOUNT NO.

DATE		ITEM	POST. REF.	DEBIT	DATE		ITEM	POST. REF.	CREDIT

ACCOUNT ACCOUNT NO.

DATE		ITEM	POST. REF.	DEBIT	DATE		ITEM	POST. REF.	CREDIT

ACCOUNT ACCOUNT NO.

DATE		ITEM	POST. REF.	DEBIT	DATE		ITEM	POST. REF.	CREDIT

ACCOUNT ACCOUNT NO.

DATE		ITEM	POST. REF.	DEBIT	DATE		ITEM	POST. REF.	CREDIT

ACCOUNT ACCOUNT NO.

DATE		ITEM	POST. REF.	DEBIT	DATE		ITEM	POST. REF.	CREDIT

ACCOUNT ACCOUNT NO.

DATE		ITEM	POST. REF.	DEBIT	DATE		ITEM	POST. REF.	CREDIT

ACCOUNT ACCOUNT NO.

DATE		ITEM	POST. REF.	DEBIT	DATE		ITEM	POST. REF.	CREDIT

[1]

[2]

GENERAL JOURNAL PAGE

	DATE		ACCOUNT TITLE	POST. REF.	DEBIT	CREDIT	
1							1
2							2
3							3
4							4
5							5
6							6
7							7
8							8
9							9
10							10
11							11
12							12
13							13
14							14

Perfect Score. 41	Name ______________________________
Deduct.......... ___	Date ________________ Class ____________
Your Score .... ___	Checked by ______________________________

STUDY GUIDE 3

UNIT A — Analyzing Transactions' Effects on an Expanded Accounting Equation

DIRECTIONS: For each transaction below, select the two items on the expanded accounting equation that are affected. Print the letters identifying your choices in the proper Answers column(s) to show whether the items are increased or decreased.

Expanded Accounting Equation

Assets				= Liabilities		+ Capital
Cash	Supplies	Office Equipment	Delivery Equipment	Maple Supply Company	Settle Equip. Company	
A	B	C	D	E	F	G

Transactions	Answers: Increase	Answers: Decrease	For Scoring	
0–0. Received cash for sale of office equipment	*A*	*C*	**0.** ✓	**0.** ✓
1–2. Paid cash to Maple Supply Company for amount owed.............			**1.**	**2.**
3–4. Paid cash for month's rent			**3.**	**4.**
5–6. Received cash from owner as additional investment..................			**5.**	**6.**
7–8. Received cash from week's sales..			**7.**	**8.**
9–10. Paid cash to Settle Equipment Company for amount owed			**9.**	**10.**
11–12. Paid cash for supplies			**11.**	**12.**
13–14. Paid cash for telephone bill			**13.**	**14.**
15–16. Paid cash for new delivery equipment			**15.**	**16.**
17–18. Paid cash to owner for personal use.......................................			**17.**	**18.**
19–20. Paid cash for miscellaneous repairs to the office			**19.**	**20.**

UNIT B — Analyzing a Balance Sheet

DIRECTIONS: Use the balance sheet at the right. For each statement that follows, select the choice that best completes the sentence. Print the letter identifying your choice in the Answers column.

Mendall Company
Balance Sheet
November 30, 1982

Assets		*Liabilities*	
Cash	515 00	*Becker Supply Co.*	560 00
Supplies	550 00	*Wilson Equipment Co.*	440 00
Golf Equipment	3100 00	*Total Liabilities*	1000 00
Maintenance Equipment	1160 00	*Capital*	
		Arnold Mendall, Capital	4325 00
Total Assets	5325 00	*Total Liab. and Capital*	5325 00

	Answers	For Scoring
0. The balance sheet's date is **(A)** November 30, 1982 **(B)** Month ending November 30, 1982 **(C)** unknown **(D)** none of these............	*A*	**0.** ✓
21. If the capital on October 31, 1982 was $2,800.00, the amount of capital has **(A)** increased **(B)** decreased (C) stayed the same **(D)** none of these............		**21.**
22. Mendall Company's total equity is **(A)** $1,000.00 **(B)** $4,325.00 **(C)** $5,325.00 **(D)** none of these		**22.**
23. The total amount that Mendall Company owes to others is **(A)** $5,325.00 **(B)** $4,325.00 **(C)** $1,000.00 **(D)** none of these.....................		**23.**
24. The amount that proves the balance sheet is in balance is **(A)** $4,325.00 **(B)** $1,000.00 **(C)** $5,325.00 **(D)** none of these		**24.**
25. Arnold Mendall's equity is **(A)** $5,325.00 **(B)** $1,000.00 **(C)** $4,325.00 **(D)** none of these		**25.**

UNIT C — Accounting Terms

DIRECTIONS: Select the one term in Column I that best fits each definition in Column II. Print the letter identifying your choice in the Answers Column.

Column I	Column II	Answers	For Scoring
A. balance sheet	0. A business form that reports assets, liabilities, and capital on a specific date	A	0. √
B. expense	26. Assets taken out of a business for the personal use of the owner		26.
C. revenue	27. An increase in capital resulting from the operation of a business		27.
D. transaction	28. A normal business activity that changes assets, liabilities, or owner's equity		28.
E. withdrawals	29. A decrease in capital resulting from the operation of a business		29.

UNIT D — Accounting Facts

DIRECTIONS: For each item below, select the choice that best completes the sentence. Print the letter identifying your choice in the Answers column.

	Answers	For Scoring
0. Each time a business activity occurs, amounts are changed in the (A) accounting equation (B) assets (C) capital (D) none of these	A	0. √
30. For every transaction, one or more of the amounts in the basic accounting equation (A) increases (B) decreases (C) changes (D) none of these		30.
31. After a transaction's effect is shown on the basic accounting equation, the equation should be (A) incorrect (B) in balance (C) recorded (D) none of these		31.
32. If a basic equation's left side is decreased, the right side should be (A) in balance (B) increased (C) decreased (D) none of these		32.
33. If a basic equation's left side is both increased and decreased for the same amount, the right side should be (A) increased (B) decreased (C) ruled with double lines (D) none of these		33.
34. When cash is paid for a liability (A) assets increase and liabilities decrease (B) liabilities and assets decrease (C) liabilities decrease and capital increases (D) none of these		34.
35. When cash is received from sales (A) assets and capital increase (B) assets increase and liabilities decrease (C) assets both increase and decrease (D) none of these		35.
36. When cash is paid for an expense (A) liabilities are not affected (B) assets increase and capital decreases (C) assets decrease and capital increases (D) none of these		36.
37. When cash is received from an owner's additional investment (A) assets and capital increase (B) assets and capital decrease (C) assets decrease and capital increases (D) none of these		37.
38. When cash is paid for supplies (A) assets and capital decrease (B) assets both increase and decrease (C) capital both increases and decreases (D) none of these		38.
39. When cash is paid for new equipment (A) assets increase and liabilities decrease (B) assets and capital decrease (C) capital both increases and decreases (D) none of these		39.
40. With each increase in total assets there must also be (A) an increase in liabilities (B) an increase in capital (C) an increase in total equity (D) none of these		40.
41. When there is an increase in cash and a decrease in equipment (A) there must also be a decrease in capital (B) there must also be an increase in liabilities (C) there is no change in equities (D) none of these		41.

DRILL 3-D 1, p. 46

Name ______________________ Date __________ Class __________

Determining how transactions change the basic accounting equation

TRANS. NO.	ASSETS		= LIABILITIES		+ CAPITAL	
	Increased	Decreased	Increased	Decreased	Increased	Decreased
1.	√	√				
2.						
3.						
4.						
5.						
6.						
7.						
8.						
9.						
10.						

Determining how transactions change the expanded accounting equation

DRILL 3-D 2, p. 47

TRANS. NO.	ASSETS						= LIABILITIES				+ CAPITAL	
	Cash		Supplies		Equipment		Mizer Co.		Seitz Co.			
	+	−	+	−	+	−	+	−	+	−	+	−
1.	√					√						
2.												
3.												
4.												
5.												
6.												
7.												
8.												
9.												
10.												

TRANS. NO.	ASSETS				=	LIABILITIES		+	CAPITAL
	Cash	Supplies	Truck Equip.	Office Equip.		Sayles Equip. Co.	Truck Supply Co.		
Bal. 1.	1,200 *+100*	100	7,000	300 *−100*	=	200	50	+	8,350
Bal. 2.	*1,300*	*100*	*7,000*	*200*	=	*200*	*50*	+	*8,350*
Bal. 3.									
Bal. 4.									
Bal. 5.									
Bal. 6.									
Bal. 7.									
Bal. 8.									
Bal. 9.									
Bal. 10.									
Bal. 11.									
Bal.									

Name________________________Date__________Class__________ *PROBLEM 3-2, p. 48*

Determining how transactions change the expanded accounting equation

The solution to Problem 3-2 is needed to complete Problem 3-3.

TRANS. NO.	ASSETS				=	LIABILITIES		+	CAPITAL
	Cash	Supplies	Motel Equip.	Maint. Equip.		Motel Supply Co.	Melmer Laundry		
Bal. 1.	4,200 *−700*	500	8,000	2,000	=	4,000	1,000	+	9,700 *−700*
Bal. 2.	*3,500*	*500*	*8,000*	*2,000*	=	*4,000*	*1,000*	+	*9,000*
Bal. 3.									
Bal. 4.									
Bal. 5.									
Bal. 6.									
Bal. 7.									
Bal. 8.									
Bal. 9.									
Bal. 10.									
Bal. 11.									
Bal. 12.									
Bal. 13.									
Bal. 14.									
Bal. 15.									
Bal. 16.									
Bal. 17.									
Bal. 18.									
Bal.									

Preparing a balance sheet based on a changed accounting equation

PROBLEM 3-3, p. 49

The solution to Problem 3-2 is needed to complete Problem 3-3.

Extra form

Name ______________________ Date __________ Class __________

MASTERY PROBLEM 3-M, p. 49

[1]

Determining how transactions change the expanded accounting equation

TRANS. NO.	ASSETS			=	LIABILITIES	+	CAPITAL
	Cash	Supplies	Equipment		Gates Supply Co.		
Bal. 1.	3,000 *–300*	200	600	=	100	+	3,700 *–300*
Bal. 2.	*2,700*	*200*	*600*	=	*100*	+	*3,400*
Bal. 3.							
Bal. 4.							
Bal. 5.							
Bal. 6.							
Bal. 7.							
Bal. 8.							
Bal. 9.							
Bal. 10.							
Bal. 11.							
Bal. 12.							
Bal. 13.							
Bal. 14.							
Bal. 15.							
Bal.							

[2]

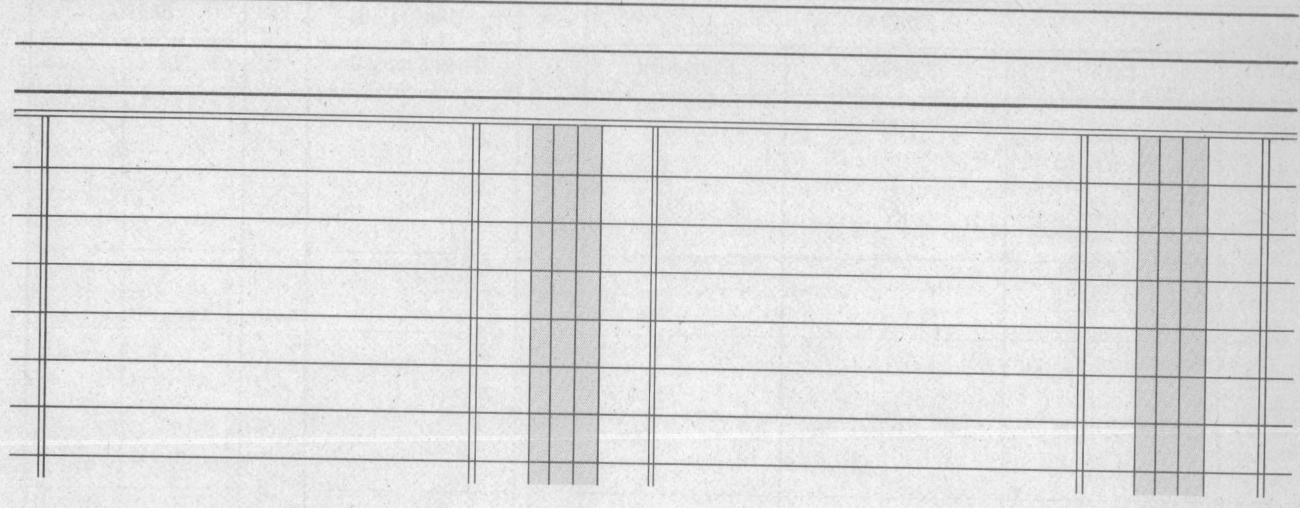

Figuring the missing amounts in the basic accounting equation

CHALLENGE PROBLEM 3-C, p. 50

[1–3]

Line	ASSETS	=	LIABILITIES	+	CAPITAL
1.	*5,500.00*		1,000.00		4,500.00
2.					
3.					
4.					
5.					
6.					
7.					
8.					
9.					
10.					
11.					
12.					
13.					
14.					
15.					

Perfect Score. 49 Name ______________________

Deduct......... ___ Date ______________ Class ____________

Your Score.... ___ Checked by ______________________

STUDY GUIDE 4

UNIT A — Analyzing Changes in Accounts

DIRECTIONS: For each item below, select the choice that best completes the sentence. Print the letter identifying your choice in the Answers column.

Question	Answers	For Scoring
0. The left hand side of any account is the **(A)** debit side **(B)** credit side **(C)** balance side **(D)** none of these	*A*	**0.** ✓
1. An account balance is decreased by recording an amount on the **(A)** balance side **(B)** side opposite the balance side **(C)** debit side **(D)** none of these...............		**1.**
2. Increases in any account are recorded on the **(A)** debit side **(B)** credit side **(C)** balance side **(D)** none of these		**2.**
3. When cash is paid out, the amount is recorded in the cash account on the **(A)** left hand side as a debit **(B)** left hand side as a credit **(C)** right hand side as a debit **(D)** none of these...............		**3.**
4. When cash is received, the amount is recorded in the cash account on the **(A)** left hand side as a debit **(B)** left hand side as a credit **(C)** right hand side as a debit **(D)** none of these...............		**4.**
5. When cash is paid out for supplies, the transaction causes **(A)** an increase in cash **(B)** an increase in supplies **(C)** both A and B **(D)** none of these...............		**5.**
6. When cash is paid out for a telephone bill, the transaction causes **(A)** an increase in cash **(B)** a decrease in utilities expense **(C)** both A and B **(D)** none of these...............		**6.**
7. When cash is paid out for an amount owed, the transaction causes **(A)** a decrease in cash **(B)** a decrease in liabilities **(C)** both A and B **(D)** none of these...............		**7.**
8. When cash is received for a week's sales, the transaction causes **(A)** a decrease in expenses **(B)** an increase in revenue **(C)** both A and B **(D)** none of these...............		**8.**
9. When cash is paid to an owner for personal use, the transaction causes **(A)** a decrease in equity **(B)** a decrease in cash **(C)** both A and B **(D)** none of these...............		**9.**
10. When cash is paid for new equipment, the transaction causes **(A)** an increase in cash **(B)** an increase in an asset **(C)** both A and B **(D)** none of these...............		**10.**
11. When cash is received from an owner's additional investment, the transaction causes **(A)** an increase in the owner's equity **(B)** an increase in total equities **(C)** both A and B **(D)** none of these		**11.**
12. When cash is received from the sale of equipment, the transaction causes **(A)** an increase in equipment **(B)** a decrease in cash **(C)** both A and B **(D)** none of these...............		**12.**
13. The debit side of any account is the **(A)** balance side **(B)** left hand side **(C)** right hand side **(D)** none of these.....		**13.**
14. The credit side of any asset account is the **(A)** balance side **(B)** increase side **(C)** decrease side **(D)** none of these........		**14.**
15. The credit side of any liability account is the **(A)** balance side **(B)** decrease side **(C)** side opposite the balance side **(D)** none of these		**15.**
16. The credit side of any revenue account is the **(A)** increase side **(B)** decrease side **(C)** side opposite the balance side **(D)** none of these		**16.**
17. The credit side of any expense account is the **(A)** increase side **(B)** side opposite the balance side **(C)** debit side **(D)** none of these..................		**17.**

UNIT B — Accounting Terms

DIRECTIONS: Select the one term in Column I that best fits each definition in Column II. Print the letter identifying your choice in the Answers column.

Column I

A. account balance
B. credit
C. credit balance
D. debit
E. debit balance
F. T account
G. temporary capital accounts

Column II

Column II	Answers	For Scoring
0. Revenue and expense accounts used to store information until transferred to the capital account..........................	*G*	**0.** ✓
18. The account balance when the total debits exceed the total credits		**18.**
19. An entry made on the right side of an account...............		**19.**
20. The account balance when the total credits exceed the total debits		**20.**
21. A skeleton form of account showing the account title and the debit and credit sides..		**21.**
22. An entry made on the left side of an account.................		**22.**
23. The difference between the totals of the amounts recorded on the two sides of an account		**23.**

UNIT C — Principles of Debit and Credit

DIRECTIONS: Place a check mark (√) in one of the Answers columns to show which word, *Debit* or *Credit*, best completes each statement.

	Answers		For Scoring
	Debit	Credit	
0. An increase in any asset account is recorded as a	√		**0.** ✓
24. The balance of any asset account is a			**24.**
25. The balance of any liability account is a..			**25.**
26. The balance of an owner's capital account is a			**26.**
27. The balance of any revenue account is a			**27.**
28. The balance of any expense account is a..			**28.**
29. An increase in an owner's capital account is recorded as a			**29.**
30. An increase in any revenue account is recorded as a			**30.**
31. A decrease in any expense account is recorded as a			**31.**
32. A decrease in an owner's capital account is recorded as a			**32.**
33. A decrease in any liability account is recorded as a..................................			**33.**

UNIT D — Debit and Credit Parts of Transactions

DIRECTIONS: Analyze each of the transactions below into debit and credit parts. Print the letter identifying the debited account in the Debit Answers column. Print the letter identifying the credited account in the Credit Answers column.

Account Titles

A. Cash
B. Supplies
C. Equipment
D. Otto Supply Company (liability)
E. Westlake Equipment Company (liability)
F. Mannie Chon, Capital
G. Mannie Chon, Drawing
H. Sales
I. Miscellaneous Expense
J. Rent Expense
K. Utilities Expense

Transactions	Answers		For Scoring	
	Debit	Credit	Debit	Credit
0–0. Paid cash to owner for personal use.......................................	*G*	*A*	**0.** ✓	**0.** ✓
34–35. Paid cash for new equipment...			**34.**	**35.**
36–37. Received cash for week's sales			**36.**	**37.**
38–39. Paid cash to Otto Supply Company for amount owed			**38.**	**39.**
40–41. Paid cash for having walk in front of business swept			**40.**	**41.**
42–43. Paid cash for supplies to be used in the business			**42.**	**43.**
44–45. Paid cash for the electric bill			**44.**	**45.**
46–47. Received cash from owner as an additional investment.............			**46.**	**47.**
48–49. Paid cash for month's rent			**48.**	**49.**

Name ______________________ Date __________ Class __________

DRILL 4-D 1, p. 63
[1–4]

Determining the balance side, increase side, and decrease side of ledger accounts

Cash	
Debit side *Balance side* +	*Credit side* –

Analyzing the effect of transactions on ledger accounts

DRILL 4-D 2, p. 64
[1–4]

1	2	3	4	5	6	7	8	9
Trans. No.	Account Title	Change in Account	Account Classifications					Debit or Credit
			Assets	Liabilities	Capital	Revenue	Expenses	
1.	*Cash*	+	√					*Dr.*
	Golf Equipment	–	√					*Cr.*
2.								
3.								
4.								
5.								
6.								
7.								
8.								
9.								
10.								

Analyzing transactions into debit and credit parts

1.

Cash	
50.00	

Office Machines	
	50.00

2.

3.

4.

5.

6.

7.

8.

9.

10.

11.

12.

13.

14.

15.

[1–3]

Analyzing transactions into debit and credit parts

1	2	3	4	5	6	7	8
Trans. No.	**ACCOUNT DEBITED**			**ACCOUNT CREDITED**			**DESCRIPTION OF THE TRANSACTION**
	Title	**Classification**	**Effect**	**Title**	**Classification**	**Effect**	
1.	*Advertising Expense*	*Expense*	+	*Cash*	*Asset*	–	*Paid cash for advertising expense*
2.							
3.							
4.							
5.							
6.							
7.							
8.							
9.							
10.							
11.							
12.							

Perfect Score. 42	Name ______________________
Deduct.......... ___	Date ______________ Class ______________
Your Score.... ___	Checked by ______________________

STUDY GUIDE 5

UNIT A — Proving and Ruling a Cash Journal

DIRECTIONS: For each item below, select the choice that best completes the sentence. Print the letter identifying your choice in the Answers column.

	Answers	For Scoring
0. Actual count of cash on hand is $550.00; beginning cash balance is $1,489.00; total of the journal's Cash Debit column is $2,039.00; total of the journal's Cash Credit column is $943.00; therefore **(A)** cash proves **(B)** cash does not prove **(C)** the cash journal's column totals are wrong **(D)** none of these	*B*	**0.** √
1. The cash journal's amount column totals are: Cash Debit, $993.00; Cash Credit, $629.00; General Debit, $629.00; General Credit, $183.00; Sales Credit, $810.00; therefore **(A)** the journal proves **(B)** the journal does not prove **(C)** the cash balance is incorrect **(D)** none of these		**1.**
2. Single lines drawn across all cash journal amount columns **(A)** show that work for the month is completed **(B)** show that the journal is in balance **(C)** show that the columns are to be added **(D)** none of these		**2.**
3. Double lines drawn across all cash journal amount columns **(A)** show that totaling is completed **(B)** show that ruling is completed **(C)** both A and B **(D)** none of these		**3.**
4. When a cash journal page is filled and the work is continued on the next page **(A)** the amount columns are totaled **(B)** the amount columns are totaled and the equality of debits and credits is proved **(C)** the amount columns are totaled, equality of debits and credits is proved, and the totals are carried forward to the first line of the next page **(D)** none of these		**4.**
5. When an error is made in recording an amount in a cash journal **(A)** the error is erased **(B)** a line is drawn through the error and the correct amount is written immediately above **(C)** the error is erased and the correct amount is written in its place **(D)** none of these		**5.**
6. On each page of a cash journal, the year is written **(A)** once **(B)** for each entry **(C)** never **(D)** none of these		**6.**
7. On each page of a cash journal, the name of the month is written **(A)** once **(B)** for each entry **(C)** never **(D)** none of these		**7.**
8. On each page of a cash journal, the day of the month is written **(A)** once **(B)** for each entry **(C)** never **(D)** none of these		**8.**
9. For a cash sales transaction, check marks are placed in the cash journal's Account Title column to show **(A)** that the entry has been recorded **(B)** that no source document is used **(C)** that no account title needs to be written for this entry **(D)** none of these		**9.**

UNIT B — Accounting Terms

DIRECTIONS: Select the one term from Column I that best fits each definition in Column II. Print the letter identifying your choice in the Answers column.

Column I

A. cash journal
B. check
C. detail tape
D. double-entry accounting
E. journalizing
F. proving cash
G. receipt
H. special amount column
I. special journal

Column II	Answers	For Scoring
0. The recording of the debit and credit parts of a transaction..................	*D*	**0.** √
10. A journal used to record only one kind of transaction		**10.**
11. A journal amount column headed with an account title		**11.**
12. Recording a business transaction in a journal		**12.**
13. A written acknowledgment given when cash is received...		**13.**
14. A business form ordering a bank to pay cash from a depositor's bank account..................		**14.**
15. A paper tape inside a cash register on which details of transactions are printed		**15.**
16. Determining that the amount of cash on hand agrees with the accounting records		**16.**
17. A special journal used only for cash transactions..................		**17.**

UNIT C — Using Cash Journal Columns

DIRECTIONS: The columns of the cash journal below are identified with capital letters. For each item below, decide which column is being described. Print the letter identifying your choice in the Answers column.

	Answers	For Scoring
0. Where to write the year for the first entry on a journal page..................	*C*	**0.** √
18. Where to write the name of the month..................		**18.**
19. Where to write the day of the month for each transaction..................		**19.**
20. Where to write the account title for an amount in the General Debit column		**20.**
21. Where to place a check mark for an entry in which no account title needs to be written .		**21.**
22. Where to indicate the source document for an entry..................		**22.**
23. Where to write a check number for a cash payments entry		**23.**
24. Where to place a check mark when recording cash on hand at the beginning of a month.		**24.**

CASH JOURNAL — PAGE

	1 CASH DEBIT	2 CASH CREDIT	DATE		ACCOUNT TITLE	DOC. NO.	POST. REF.	3 GENERAL DEBIT	4 GENERAL CREDIT	5 SALES CREDIT	
1	A	B	C	D	E	F	G	H	I	J	1

UNIT D — Recording Entries in a Cash Journal

DIRECTIONS: The columns of the cash journal above are identified with capital letters. For each transaction below, decide which debit and credit amount columns will be used. Print the letters identifying your choices in the proper Answers columns.

	Answers Debit	Answers Credit	For Scoring Debit	For Scoring Credit
0–0. Paid cash for telephone bill	*H*	*B*	**0.** √	**0.** √
25–26. Received cash from the sale of old equipment..................			**25.**	**26.**
27–28. Paid cash to a liability for part of amount owed..................			**27.**	**28.**
29–30. Received cash from weekly sales			**29.**	**30.**
31–32. Paid cash for month's rent			**31.**	**32.**
33–34. Received cash from owner as additional investment..................			**33.**	**34.**
35–36. Paid cash for supplies			**35.**	**36.**
37–38. Paid cash for new equipment..................			**37.**	**38.**
39–40. Paid cash to owner for personal use..................			**39.**	**40.**
41–42. Paid cash for minor window repairs			**41.**	**42.**

Name ______________________ Date __________ Class __________

DRILL 5-D 1, p. 88
[1, 2]

Analyzing transactions

1.

Cash	
100.00	

Sales	
	100.00

2.

3.

4.

5.

6.

7.

8.

9.

10.

11.

[1–4]

	1	2	3	4	5	6
Trans. No.	Account Titles Affected	Account Classification	Account is		Balance of Account is	
			Debited	Credited	Increased	Decreased
1.	*Cash*	*Asset*	√		√	
	Fees Revenue	*Revenue*		√	√	
2.						
3.						
4.						
5.						
6.						
7.						
8.						
9.						
10.						
11.						
12.						
13.						

Name ______________ Date ________ Class ________

PROBLEM 5-2, p. 90
[1–3]

Recording transactions in a cash journal

CASH JOURNAL

PAGE

	1	2					3	4	5	
	CASH		DATE	ACCOUNT TITLE	DOC. NO.	POST. REF.	GENERAL		SALES CREDIT	
	DEBIT	CREDIT					DEBIT	CREDIT		
1										1
2										2
3										3
4										4
5										5
6										6
7										7
8										8
9										9
10										10
11										11
12										12
13										13
14										14
15										15
16										16
17										17
18										18
19										19
20										20
21										21
22										22
23										23
24										24
25										25

[3] *Prove equality of debits and credits in the journal:*

Cash Debit column .... $ ________

General Debit column .... ________

Total debits .... $ ________

Cash Credit column .... $ ________

General Credit column............................... ________

Sales Credit column .... ________

Total credits .... $ ________

[4–8]

CASH JOURNAL

PAGE

	1	2					3	4	5	
	CASH		DATE	ACCOUNT TITLE	DOC. NO.	POST. REF.	GENERAL		SALES CREDIT	
	DEBIT	CREDIT					DEBIT	CREDIT		
1										1
2										2
3										3
4										4
5										5
6										6
7										7
8										8
9										9
10										10
11										11
12										12
13										13
14										14
15										15
16										16
17										17
18										18
19										19
20										20
21										21
22										22
23										23
24										24
25										25

[6] *Prove cash:*

Beginning cash balance .... $__________

Plus cash received during the month .... __________

Equals total .... $__________

Less cash paid out during the month .... __________

Equals cash on hand at the end of the month .... $__________

[7] *Prove equality of debits and credits in the journal:*

Cash Debit column .... $__________

General Debit column .... __________

Total debits .... $__________

Cash Credit column .... $__________

General Credit column.............................. __________

Sales Credit column .... __________

Total credits .... $__________

Name ______________________ Date __________ Class __________

MASTERY PROBLEM 5-M, p. 91

[1–5]

Recording transactions in a cash journal

CASH JOURNAL PAGE

	1	2					3	4	5	
	CASH		DATE	ACCOUNT TITLE	DOC. NO.	POST. REF.	GENERAL		FARES EARNED CREDIT	
	DEBIT	CREDIT					DEBIT	CREDIT		
1										1
2										2
3										3
4										4
5										5
6										6
7										7
8										8
9										9
10										10
11										11
12										12
13										13
14										14
15										15
16										16
17										17
18										18
19										19
20										20
21										21
22										22
23										23
24										24
25										25

[3] *Prove cash:*

Beginning cash balance .... $__________

Plus cash received during the month .... __________

Equals total .... $__________

Less cash paid out during the month .... __________

Equals cash on hand at the end of the month .... $__________

[4] *Prove equality of debits and credits in the journal:*

Cash Debit column .... $__________

General Debit column .... __________

Total debits .... $__________

Cash Credit column .... $__________

General Credit column.............................. __________

Fares Earned Credit column .... __________

Total credits .... $__________

CHALLENGE PROBLEM 5-C, p. 92
[1–5]

CASH JOURNAL — PAGE

	DATE		ACCOUNT TITLE	DOC. NO.	POST. REF.	1 GENERAL DEBIT	2 GENERAL CREDIT	3 CASH DEBIT	4 CASH CREDIT	5 COMMISSIONS REVENUE CREDIT	
1											1
2											2
3											3
4											4
5											5
6											6
7											7
8											8
9											9
10											10
11											11
12											12
13											13
14											14
15											15
16											16
17											17
18											18
19											19
20											20
21											21
22											22
23											23
24											24

[3] *Prove cash:*

Beginning cash balance ....$________

Plus cash received during the month........... ________

Equals total ....$________

Less cash paid out during the month .... ________

Equals cash on hand at the end of the month ....$________

[4] *Prove equality of debits and credits in the journal:*

Cash Debit column ....$________

General Debit column .... ________

Total debits ....$________

Cash Credit column ....$________

General Credit column............................... ________

Commissions Revenue Credit column......... ________

Total credits ....$________

Perfect Score. 44 Name ____________________

Deduct......... ___ Date ______________ Class ______________

Your Score.... ___ Checked by ____________________

STUDY GUIDE 6

UNIT A — Posting from a Cash Journal

DIRECTIONS: In the cash journal below, some items are identified with capital letters. In the ledger accounts, locations to which items are to be posted are identified with numbers. For each number in a ledger account, select the item in the journal that will be posted to that numbered location. Print the letter identifying your choice in the Answers column.

CASH JOURNAL — PAGE 10 **A**

	Cash Debit	Cash Credit	Date	Account Title	Doc. No.	Post. Ref.	General Debit	General Credit	Sales Credit	
1			1982 Aug. 1	Balance on hand, $925.00		✓				1
2	**B** 5000		**C** 1	Office Equipment	R25			**D** 5000		2
3		**E** 10000	**F** 1	Melcor Supply Co.	C105		**G** 10000			3
25	190000	160000	31	Totals			185000	5000	160000	25
26	**H**	**I**	**J**				**K**	**L**	**M**	26

ACCOUNT Cash — ACCOUNT NO. 11

Date	Item	Post. Ref.	Debit	Date	Item	Post. Ref.	Credit
1982 Aug. 1	Balance	✓	92500	3		4	5
0		1	2				

ACCOUNT Office Equipment — ACCOUNT NO. 14

Date	Item	Post. Ref.	Debit	Date	Item	Post. Ref.	Credit
1982 Aug. 1	Balance	✓	50000	6		7	8

ACCOUNT Melcor Supply Co. — ACCOUNT NO. 21

Date	Item	Post. Ref.	Debit	Date	Item	Post. Ref.	Credit
9		10	11	1982 Aug. 1	Balance	✓	30000

Color Numbers in Ledger Accounts	Answers	For Scoring
0	J	0. ✓
1		1.
2		2.
3		3.
4		4.
5		5.
6		6.
7		7.
8		8.
9		9.
10		10.
11		11.

UNIT B — Review of Account Balances and Increases or Decreases

DIRECTIONS: For each question in Column II, select the one item in Column I that best answers each question in Column II. Print the letter identifying your choice in the Answers column.

Column I

A. credit balance
B. credit side
C. debit balance
D. debit side

Column II

Question	Answers	For Scoring
0. What kind of balance does Cash have?	C	0. ✓
12. What kind of balance does Office Equipment have?		12.
13. What kind of balance does Sales have?		13.
14. What kind of balance does a liability account have?		14.
15. What kind of balance does an owner's capital account have?		15.
16. What kind of balance does Rent Expense have?		16.
17. On which side of a cash account is an increase shown?		17.
18. On which side of a sales account is an increase shown?		18.
19. On which side of a liability account is an increase shown?		19.
20. On which side of an expense account is an increase shown?		20.
21. On which side of an owner's capital account is an increase shown?		21.
22. On which side of an owner's drawing account is an increase shown?		22.
23. On which side of an asset account is a decrease shown?		23.
24. On which side of a liability account is a decrease shown?		24.
25. On which side of a revenue account is a decrease shown?		25.
26. On which side of an expense account is a decrease shown?		26.

UNIT C — Principles of Posting

DIRECTIONS: For each item below, select the choice that best completes the sentence. Print the letter identifying your choice in the Answers column.

0. The first entry on line 1 of a cash journal for each month is
(A) for a business transaction **(B)** posted to the cash account
(C) not posted to any account **(D)** none of these ....

27. The procedure of transferring information from a journal to a ledger is known as
(A) footing **(B)** journalizing **(C)** posting **(D)** none of these ....

28. In Putt Around's ledger, the first division contains the
(A) asset accounts **(B)** liability accounts **(C)** revenue accounts **(D)** none of these ..

29. The second division of Putt Around's ledger contains the
(A) asset accounts **(B)** revenue accounts **(C)** capital accounts **(D)** none of these ...

30. The fifth division of Putt Around's ledger contains the
(A) asset accounts **(B)** revenue accounts **(C)** expense accounts **(D)** none of these .

31. Each account in Putt Around's ledger is assigned
(A) a division title **(B)** a two-digit account number
(C) to the ledger in alphabetical order **(D)** none of these ....

32. The first digit of Putt Around's account number 53 shows that the account is
(A) a revenue account **(B)** in the fifth division of the ledger
(C) both A and B **(D)** none of these ....

33. The second digit of Putt Around's account number 54 shows that the account is
(A) an expense account **(B)** the fourth expense account
(C) a capital account **(D)** none of these ....

34. When both the debit and credit amounts for an entry are recorded in a cash journal's special amount columns
(A) only the amount in the General Debit column is posted
(B) neither amount is posted separately
(C) both amounts are posted separately to the accounts in the Account Title column
(D) none of these..

35. When posting an entry from a cash journal to a ledger account, the first step is
(A) to record the amount in the account **(B)** to record the date in the account
(C) to record the account number in the journal **(D)** none of these ....

36. When posting an entry from a cash journal to a ledger, the last step is to
(A) record the amount in the account **(B)** record the date in the account
(C) record the account number in the journal **(D)** none of these ....

37. An account number written in parentheses under a cash journal's column total shows
(A) the total has already been posted **(B)** the total needs to be posted
(C) the total is to be posted at the end of the next month **(D)** none of these.........

38. If an amount is posted from page 1 of a cash journal, the abbreviation placed in the ledger account's Post. Ref. column is
(A) CJ1 **(B)** C1 **(C)** CJP1 **(D)** none of these ....

39. If an amount is posted from page 1 of a general journal, the abbreviation placed in the ledger account's Post. Ref. column is
(A) C1 **(B)** CJ1 **(C)** G1 **(D)** none of these ....

40. The total of a cash journal's Cash Debit column is
(A) posted **(B)** not posted **(C)** double posted **(D)** none of these.................

41. The total of a cash journal's General Debit column is
(A) posted **(B)** not posted **(C)** double posted **(D)** none of these.................

42. The individual amounts in a cash journal's General Credit column are
(A) posted **(B)** not posted **(C)** double posted **(D)** none of these.................

43. The individual amounts in a cash journal's Cash Credit column are
(A) posted **(B)** not posted **(C)** double posted **(D)** none of these.................

44. A check mark in a cash journal's posting reference column shows that
(A) an amount has already been posted **(B)** nothing on that line needs to be posted
(C) no account titles need to be written in the journal **(D)** none of these ....

Answers	For Scoring
C	0. ✓
	27.
	28.
	29.
	30.
	31.
	32.
	33.
	34.
	35.
	36.
	37.
	38.
	39.
	40.
	41.
	42.
	43.
	44.

Name ______________________ Date __________ Class __________

DRILL 6-D 1, p. 104
[1–3]

Assigning account numbers

Item	Account Number
1. The first asset account	11
2. The first liability account	
3. The owner's capital account	
4. The first revenue account	
5. The first expense account	
6. The third asset account	
7. The second liability account	
8. The owner's drawing account	
9. The fourth expense account	
10. The second asset account	
11. The third expense account	

Analyzing posting from a cash journal

DRILL 6-D 2, p. 105

1. ______________________

2. ______________________

3. ______________________

4. ______________________

5. ______________________

6. ______________________

7. ______________________

8. ______________________

9. ______________________

Posting from a cash journal

PROBLEM 6-1. p. 105
[1, 2, 3]

The cash journal prepared in Problem 5-1 is needed to complete Problem 6-1.

LEDGER

ACCOUNT ACCOUNT NO.

DATE		ITEM	POST. REF.	DEBIT	DATE		ITEM	POST. REF.	CREDIT

ACCOUNT ACCOUNT NO.

DATE		ITEM	POST. REF.	DEBIT	DATE		ITEM	POST. REF.	CREDIT

ACCOUNT ACCOUNT NO.

DATE		ITEM	POST. REF.	DEBIT	DATE		ITEM	POST. REF.	CREDIT

ACCOUNT ACCOUNT NO.

DATE		ITEM	POST. REF.	DEBIT	DATE		ITEM	POST. REF.	CREDIT

ACCOUNT ACCOUNT NO.

DATE		ITEM	POST. REF.	DEBIT	DATE		ITEM	POST. REF.	CREDIT

ACCOUNT ACCOUNT NO.

DATE		ITEM	POST. REF.	DEBIT	DATE		ITEM	POST. REF.	CREDIT

ACCOUNT ACCOUNT NO.

DATE		ITEM	POST. REF.	DEBIT	DATE		ITEM	POST. REF.	CREDIT

[1, 2, 3]

LEDGER

ACCOUNT ACCOUNT NO.

DATE		ITEM	POST. REF.	DEBIT	DATE		ITEM	POST. REF.	CREDIT

ACCOUNT ACCOUNT NO.

DATE		ITEM	POST. REF.	DEBIT	DATE		ITEM	POST. REF.	CREDIT

ACCOUNT ACCOUNT NO.

DATE		ITEM	POST. REF.	DEBIT	DATE		ITEM	POST. REF.	CREDIT

ACCOUNT ACCOUNT NO.

DATE		ITEM	POST. REF.	DEBIT	DATE		ITEM	POST. REF.	CREDIT

ACCOUNT ACCOUNT NO.

DATE		ITEM	POST. REF.	DEBIT	DATE		ITEM	POST. REF.	CREDIT

ACCOUNT ACCOUNT NO.

DATE		ITEM	POST. REF.	DEBIT	DATE		ITEM	POST. REF.	CREDIT

ACCOUNT ACCOUNT NO.

DATE		ITEM	POST. REF.	DEBIT	DATE		ITEM	POST. REF.	CREDIT

The solution to Problem 6-1 is needed to complete Problem 7-1.

CASH JOURNAL

PAGE 6

	1	2					3	4	5
	CASH						GENERAL		
	DEBIT	CREDIT	DATE	ACCOUNT TITLE	DOC. NO.	POST. REF.	DEBIT	CREDIT	SALES CREDIT
1			19-- June 1	Balance on hand, $1,430.00					
2		66000	2	Michael's Tool Company	C101		66000		
3		78000	3	Rent Expense	C102		78000		
4	70500		5	✓	T5				70500
5		3250	8	Utilities Expense	C103		3250		
6		52000	8	Repair Equipment	C104		52000		
7		1300	9	Miscellaneous Expense	C105		1300		
8		3000	10	Advertising Expense	C106		3000		
9	75400		12	✓	T12				75400
10		9750	15	Supplies	C107		9750		
11	6500		16	Office Equipment	R10			6500	
12		7800	18	Utilities Expense	C108		7800		
13		7500	19	George Robinson, Drawing	C109		7500		
14	89100		19	✓	T19				89100
15		13000	22	Supplies	C110		13000		
16		1500	23	Miscellaneous Expense	C111		1500		
17		5160	25	Utilities Expense	C112		5160		
18		650	25	Miscellaneous Expense	C113		650		
19	93700		26	✓	T26				93700
20	36100		30	✓	T30				36100
21		50000	30	Post Equipment and Supply Co.	C114		50000		
22									
23									
24									
25									

[1] *Prove cash:*

Beginning cash balance .... $__________

Plus cash received during the month .... __________

Equals total .... $__________

Less cash paid out during the month .... __________

Equals cash on hand at the end of the month .... $__________

[2] *Prove equality of debits and credits in the journal:*

Cash Debit column .... $__________

General Debit column .... __________

Total debits .... $__________

Cash Credit column .... $__________

General Credit column .... __________

Sales Credit column .... __________

Total credits .... $__________

Name ________________ Date ________ Class ________

PROBLEM 6-2, continued
[3, 4]

LEDGER

ACCOUNT *Cash* ACCOUNT NO. *11*

DATE		ITEM	POST. REF.	DEBIT	DATE		ITEM	POST. REF.	CREDIT
19-- *June*	*1*	*Balance*	*✓*	*1430 00*					

ACCOUNT *Supplies* ACCOUNT NO. *12*

DATE		ITEM	POST. REF.	DEBIT	DATE		ITEM	POST. REF.	CREDIT
19-- *June*	*1*	*Balance*	*✓*	*650 00*					

ACCOUNT *Repair Equipment* ACCOUNT NO. *13*

DATE		ITEM	POST. REF.	DEBIT	DATE		ITEM	POST. REF.	CREDIT
19-- *June*	*1*	*Balance*	*✓*	*2600 00*					

ACCOUNT *Office Equipment* ACCOUNT NO. *14*

DATE		ITEM	POST. REF.	DEBIT	DATE		ITEM	POST. REF.	CREDIT
19-- *June*	*1*	*Balance*	*✓*	*1430 00*					

ACCOUNT *Michael's Tool Company (Liability)* ACCOUNT NO. *21*

DATE		ITEM	POST. REF.	DEBIT	DATE		ITEM	POST. REF.	CREDIT
					19-- *June*	*1*	*Balance*	*✓*	*840 00*

ACCOUNT *Post Equipment and Supply Company (Liability)* ACCOUNT NO. *22*

DATE		ITEM	POST. REF.	DEBIT	DATE		ITEM	POST. REF.	CREDIT
					19-- *June*	*1*	*Balance*	*✓*	*715 00*

ACCOUNT *George Robinson, Capital* ACCOUNT NO. *31*

DATE		ITEM	POST. REF.	DEBIT	DATE		ITEM	POST. REF.	CREDIT
					19-- *June*	*1*	*Balance*	*✓*	*4555 00*

LEDGER

ACCOUNT George Robinson, Drawing ACCOUNT NO. 32

DATE		ITEM	POST. REF.	DEBIT	DATE		ITEM	POST. REF.	CREDIT

ACCOUNT Sales ACCOUNT NO. 41

DATE		ITEM	POST. REF.	DEBIT	DATE		ITEM	POST. REF.	CREDIT

ACCOUNT Advertising Expense ACCOUNT NO. 51

DATE		ITEM	POST. REF.	DEBIT	DATE		ITEM	POST. REF.	CREDIT

ACCOUNT Miscellaneous Expense ACCOUNT NO. 52

DATE		ITEM	POST. REF.	DEBIT	DATE		ITEM	POST. REF.	CREDIT

ACCOUNT Rent Expense ACCOUNT NO. 53

DATE		ITEM	POST. REF.	DEBIT	DATE		ITEM	POST. REF.	CREDIT

ACCOUNT Utilities Expense ACCOUNT NO. 54

DATE		ITEM	POST. REF.	DEBIT	DATE		ITEM	POST. REF.	CREDIT

Name ____________________ Date ________ Class ________

MASTERY PROBLEM 6-M, p. 106
[1, 5]

Journalizing and posting using a cash journal

LEDGER

ACCOUNT ____________________ ACCOUNT NO. ______

DATE		ITEM	POST. REF.	DEBIT	DATE		ITEM	POST. REF.	CREDIT

ACCOUNT ____________________ ACCOUNT NO. ______

DATE		ITEM	POST. REF.	DEBIT	DATE		ITEM	POST. REF.	CREDIT

ACCOUNT ____________________ ACCOUNT NO. ______

DATE		ITEM	POST. REF.	DEBIT	DATE		ITEM	POST. REF.	CREDIT

ACCOUNT ____________________ ACCOUNT NO. ______

DATE		ITEM	POST. REF.	DEBIT	DATE		ITEM	POST. REF.	CREDIT

ACCOUNT ____________________ ACCOUNT NO. ______

DATE		ITEM	POST. REF.	DEBIT	DATE		ITEM	POST. REF.	CREDIT

ACCOUNT ____________________ ACCOUNT NO. ______

DATE		ITEM	POST. REF.	DEBIT	DATE		ITEM	POST. REF.	CREDIT

MASTERY PROBLEM 6-M, continued
[1, 5]

LEDGER

ACCOUNT ACCOUNT NO.

DATE	ITEM	POST. REF.	DEBIT	DATE	ITEM	POST. REF.	CREDIT

ACCOUNT ACCOUNT NO.

DATE	ITEM	POST. REF.	DEBIT	DATE	ITEM	POST. REF.	CREDIT

ACCOUNT ACCOUNT NO.

DATE	ITEM	POST. REF.	DEBIT	DATE	ITEM	POST. REF.	CREDIT

ACCOUNT ACCOUNT NO.

DATE	ITEM	POST. REF.	DEBIT	DATE	ITEM	POST. REF.	CREDIT

ACCOUNT ACCOUNT NO.

DATE	ITEM	POST. REF.	DEBIT	DATE	ITEM	POST. REF.	CREDIT

ACCOUNT ACCOUNT NO.

DATE	ITEM	POST. REF.	DEBIT	DATE	ITEM	POST. REF.	CREDIT

ACCOUNT ACCOUNT NO.

DATE	ITEM	POST. REF.	DEBIT	DATE	ITEM	POST. REF.	CREDIT

[2–5]

CASH JOURNAL

PAGE

1	2					3	4	5
CASH		DATE	ACCOUNT TITLE	DOC. NO.	POST. REF.	GENERAL		PROFESSIONAL FEES CREDIT
DEBIT	CREDIT					DEBIT	CREDIT	

[3] *Prove cash:*

Beginning cash balance ....$__________

Plus cash received during the month........... __________

Equals total ....$__________

Less cash paid out during the month .... __________

Equals cash on hand at the end of the month ....$__________

[4] *Prove equality of debits and credits in the journal:*

Cash Debit column ....$__________

General Debit column .... __________

Total debits ....$__________

Cash Credit column ....$__________

General Credit column............................... __________

Professional Fees Credit column................. __________

Total credits ....$__________

[1–5]

CASH JOURNAL

PAGE

	1	2					3	4	5	
	CASH DEBIT	GENERAL DEBIT	DATE	ACCOUNT TITLE	DOC. NO.	POST. REF.	GENERAL CREDIT	SALES CREDIT	CASH CREDIT	
1										1
2										2
3										3
4										4
5										5
6										6
7										7
8										8
9										9
10										10
11										11
12										12
13										13
14										14
15										15
16										16
17										17
18										18
19										19
20										20
21										21
22										22
23										23
24										24
25										25

[3] *Prove cash:*

Beginning cash balance .... $ __________

Plus cash received during the month .... __________

Equals total .... $ __________

Less cash paid out during the month .... __________

Equals cash on hand at the end of the month .... $ __________

[4] *Prove equality of debits and credits in the journal:*

Cash Debit column .... $ __________

General Debit column .... __________

Total debits .... $ __________

General Credit column .... $ __________

Sales Credit column .... __________

Cash Credit column .... __________

Total credits .... $ __________

[5]

LEDGER

ACCOUNT *Cash* ACCOUNT NO. *11*

DATE		ITEM	POST. REF.	DEBIT	DATE		ITEM	POST. REF.	CREDIT
19-- Aug.	1	Balance	✓	4631 00					

ACCOUNT *Delivery Truck* ACCOUNT NO. *12*

DATE		ITEM	POST. REF.	DEBIT	DATE		ITEM	POST. REF.	CREDIT
19-- Aug.	1	Balance	✓	4200 00					

ACCOUNT *Office Furniture* ACCOUNT NO. *13*

DATE		ITEM	POST. REF.	DEBIT	DATE		ITEM	POST. REF.	CREDIT
19-- Aug.	1	Balance	✓	3696 00					

ACCOUNT *Delivery Equipment Company (Liability)* ACCOUNT NO. *21*

DATE		ITEM	POST. REF.	DEBIT	DATE		ITEM	POST. REF.	CREDIT
					19-- Aug.	1	Balance	✓	3762 00

ACCOUNT *Holliday Supply Company (Liability)* ACCOUNT NO. *22*

DATE		ITEM	POST. REF.	DEBIT	DATE		ITEM	POST. REF.	CREDIT
					19-- Aug.	1	Balance	✓	4950 00

ACCOUNT *Peter Roselle, Capital* ACCOUNT NO. *31*

DATE		ITEM	POST. REF.	DEBIT	DATE		ITEM	POST. REF.	CREDIT
					19-- Aug.	1	Balance	✓	3815 00

[5]

LEDGER

ACCOUNT Peter Roselle, Drawing — ACCOUNT NO. 32

DATE		ITEM	POST. REF.	DEBIT	DATE		ITEM	POST. REF.	CREDIT

ACCOUNT Sales — ACCOUNT NO. 41

DATE		ITEM	POST. REF.	DEBIT	DATE		ITEM	POST. REF.	CREDIT

ACCOUNT Delivery Expense — ACCOUNT NO. 51

DATE		ITEM	POST. REF.	DEBIT	DATE		ITEM	POST. REF.	CREDIT

ACCOUNT Miscellaneous Expense — ACCOUNT NO. 52

DATE		ITEM	POST. REF.	DEBIT	DATE		ITEM	POST. REF.	CREDIT

ACCOUNT Rent Expense — ACCOUNT NO. 53

DATE		ITEM	POST. REF.	DEBIT	DATE		ITEM	POST. REF.	CREDIT

ACCOUNT Utilities Expense — ACCOUNT NO. 54

DATE		ITEM	POST. REF.	DEBIT	DATE		ITEM	POST. REF.	CREDIT

Name ____________________ Date __________ Class __________

REINFORCEMENT ACTIVITY 1
PART A – p. 109

AN ACCOUNTING CYCLE FOR A SOLE PROPRIETORSHIP
USING A CASH JOURNAL

[1, 3, 17, 18]

GENERAL JOURNAL

PAGE

DATE		ACCOUNT TITLE	POST. REF.	DEBIT	CREDIT

The general journal used in Reinforcement Activity 1, Part A, is needed to complete Part D.

LEDGER

ACCOUNT ACCOUNT NO.

DATE		ITEM	POST. REF.	DEBIT	DATE		ITEM	POST. REF.	CREDIT

ACCOUNT ACCOUNT NO.

DATE		ITEM	POST. REF.	DEBIT	DATE		ITEM	POST. REF.	CREDIT

ACCOUNT ACCOUNT NO.

DATE		ITEM	POST. REF.	DEBIT	DATE		ITEM	POST. REF.	CREDIT

ACCOUNT ACCOUNT NO.

DATE		ITEM	POST. REF.	DEBIT	DATE		ITEM	POST. REF.	CREDIT

ACCOUNT ACCOUNT NO.

DATE		ITEM	POST. REF.	DEBIT	DATE		ITEM	POST. REF.	CREDIT

LEDGER

ACCOUNT ACCOUNT NO.

DATE		ITEM	POST. REF.	DEBIT	DATE		ITEM	POST. REF.	CREDIT

ACCOUNT ACCOUNT NO.

DATE		ITEM	POST. REF.	DEBIT	DATE		ITEM	POST. REF.	CREDIT

ACCOUNT ACCOUNT NO.

DATE		ITEM	POST. REF.	DEBIT	DATE		ITEM	POST. REF.	CREDIT

ACCOUNT ACCOUNT NO.

DATE		ITEM	POST. REF.	DEBIT	DATE		ITEM	POST. REF.	CREDIT

ACCOUNT ACCOUNT NO.

DATE		ITEM	POST. REF.	DEBIT	DATE		ITEM	POST. REF.	CREDIT

LEDGER

ACCOUNT ACCOUNT NO.

DATE	ITEM	POST. REF.	DEBIT	DATE	ITEM	POST. REF.	CREDIT

ACCOUNT ACCOUNT NO.

DATE	ITEM	POST. REF.	DEBIT	DATE	ITEM	POST. REF.	CREDIT

ACCOUNT ACCOUNT NO.

DATE	ITEM	POST. REF.	DEBIT	DATE	ITEM	POST. REF.	CREDIT

ACCOUNT ACCOUNT NO.

DATE	ITEM	POST. REF.	DEBIT	DATE	ITEM	POST. REF.	CREDIT

ACCOUNT ACCOUNT NO.

DATE	ITEM	POST. REF.	DEBIT	DATE	ITEM	POST. REF.	CREDIT

The ledger prepared in Reinforcement Activity 1, Part A, is used to complete Parts B and D.

Name ______________________ Date __________ Class __________

REINFORCEMENT ACTIVITY 1
PART A – continued
[4–6]

CASH JOURNAL

PAGE

	1	2					3	4	5	
	CASH		DATE	ACCOUNT TITLE	DOC. NO.	POST. REF.	GENERAL		SECRETARIAL FEES CREDIT	
	DEBIT	CREDIT					DEBIT	CREDIT		
1										1
2										2
3										3
4										4
5										5
6										6
7										7
8										8
9										9
10										10
11										11
12										12
13										13
14										14
15										15
16										16
17										17
18										18
19										19
20										20
21										21
22										22
23										23
24										24

CASH JOURNAL

PAGE

1	2					3	4	5
CASH		DATE	ACCOUNT TITLE	DOC. NO.	POST. REF.	GENERAL		SECRETARIAL FEES CREDIT
DEBIT	CREDIT					DEBIT	CREDIT	

[8] *Prove cash:*

Beginning cash balance .... $__________

Plus cash received during the month .... __________

Equals total .... $__________

Less cash paid out during the month .... __________

Equals cash on hand at the end of the month .... $__________

[9] *Prove equality of debits and credits in the journal:*

Cash Debit column .... $__________

General Debit column .... __________

Total debits .... $__________

Cash Credit column .... $__________

General Credit column............................... __________

Secretarial Fees Credit column .... __________

Total credits .... $__________

Perfect Score. 42 Name ______

Deduct......... ___ Date ______ Class ______

Your Score.... ___ Checked by ______

STUDY GUIDE 7

UNIT A — Accounting Terms

DIRECTIONS: Select the one term in Column I that best fits each definition in Column II. Print the letter identifying your choice in the Answers column.

Column I

- **A.** analysis paper
- **B.** fiscal period
- **C.** net income
- **D.** net loss
- **E.** trial balance
- **F.** work sheet

Column II

	Answers	For Scoring
0. Analysis paper on which the financial condition of a business is summarized	*F*	**0.** ✓
1. The difference when the amount of revenue is greater than the total expenses		**1.**
2. The length of time for which a business analyzes business information		**2.**
3. The difference when the total expenses are greater than the revenue		**3.**
4. Proof of the equality of debits and credits in a ledger		**4.**
5. Accounting paper with a number of amount columns used in analyzing ledger accounts		**5.**

UNIT B — Preparing a Trial Balance on a Work Sheet

DIRECTIONS: Decide whether the balance of each of the following accounts will appear in a work sheet's trial balance debit or credit column. Place a check mark (√) in the proper Answers column to show your answer.

	Trial Balance Debit	Trial Balance Credit	For Scoring
0. Advertising Expense	√		**0.** ✓
6. Cash			**6.**
7. Golf Equipment			**7.**
8. Harry Rossi, Capital			**8.**
9. Harry Rossi, Drawing			**9.**
10. Maintenance Equipment			**10.**
11. Melcor Equipment Company (liability)			**11.**
12. Miscellaneous Expense			**12.**
13. Rent Expense			**13.**
14. Sales			**14.**
15. Sasson Supply Company (liability)			**15.**
16. Supplies			**16.**
17. Utilities Expense			**17.**

UNIT C — Extending Account Balances on a Work Sheet

DIRECTIONS: For each of the following accounts, determine to which work sheet column the balance will be extended. Place a check mark (√) in the proper Answers column to show your answer.

	Income Statement Debit	Income Statement Credit	Balance Sheet Debit	Balance Sheet Credit	For Scoring
0. Advertising Expense	√				**0.** ✓
18. Cash					**18.**
19. Golf Equipment					**19.**
20. Harry Rossi, Capital					**20.**
21. Harry Rossi, Drawing					**21.**
22. Maintenance Equipment					**22.**
23. Melcor Equipment Company (liability)					**23.**
24. Miscellaneous Expense					**24.**
25. Rent Expense					**25.**
26. Sales					**26.**
27. Sasson Supply Company (liability)					**27.**
28. Supplies					**28.**
29. Utilities Expense					**29.**

UNIT D — Preparing a Work Sheet

DIRECTIONS: For each item below, select the choice that best completes the sentence. Print the letter identifying your choice in the Answers column.

Item	Answers	For Scoring
0. The information written on the second line of a work sheet's heading is the **(A)** name of the report **(B)** fiscal period **(C)** name of a business **(D)** none of these	*A*	**0.** ✓
30. A work sheet summarizes the financial condition of a business for a **(A)** future fiscal period **(B)** current fiscal period **(C)** specific date **(D)** none of these		**30.**
31. Putt Around's cash account balance is figured **(A)** by pencil footing the amount columns and subtracting the smaller total from the larger total **(B)** by ruling the cash account and writing the account balance in the Items column **(C)** by comparing the account balance with the last check stub **(D)** none of these		**31.**
32. On July 31, Putt Around's cash account has a debit balance because **(A)** the first ledger account always has a debit balance **(B)** more cash was paid out than received **(C)** the account's debits are greater than the credits **(D)** none of these		**32.**
33. The columns of a work sheet in which each expense account's balance is listed are **(A)** Trial Balance Debit and Balance Sheet Debit **(B)** Trial Balance Debit and Income Statement Debit **(C)** Trial Balance Debit and Income Statement Credit **(D)** none of these		**33.**
34. When the total of the Income Statement Debit column is larger than the Income Statement Credit column total, the difference is a **(A)** net income **(B)** net loss **(C)** net result **(D)** none of these		**34.**
35. A net loss amount is entered in the two work sheet columns titled **(A)** Income Statement Credit and Balance Sheet Debit **(B)** Income Statement Debit and Balance Sheet Credit **(C)** Income Statement Credit and Balance Sheet Credit **(D)** none of these		**35.**
36. When the Income Statement Credit column total is larger than the Income Statement Debit column total, the difference is a **(A)** net income **(B)** net loss **(C)** net result **(D)** none of these		**36.**
37. The final step in completing a six-column work sheet is to **(A)** rule a single line across all amount columns and add the columns **(B)** rule double lines below final totals of the Income Statement and Balance Sheet columns **(C)** write *net income* in the Account Title column **(D)** none of these		**37.**
38. If the Trial Balance columns on a work sheet do not balance, and the difference between the totals is $1.00, then the error is most often **(A)** a transposition **(B)** in addition **(C)** in posting **(D)** none of these		**38.**
39. If the Trial Balance columns do not balance, and the difference between the totals is $45.00, the error most likely is **(A)** a transposition **(B)** in addition **(C)** in posting **(D)** none of these		**39.**
40. If the Trial Balance columns do not balance, and the difference between the totals is $32.00, the error most likely is **(A)** an omission of an amount in the trial balance or in posting **(B)** a slide in writing amounts **(C)** in addition **(D)** none of these		**40.**
41. When any pair of work sheet columns does not balance, the error is most often **(A)** in addition **(B)** in posting **(C)** in copying amounts **(D)** none of these		**41.**
42. A net income amount figured for the Income Statement columns is extended to the **(A)** Balance Sheet Debit column **(B)** Balance Sheet Credit column **(C)** Income Statement Credit column **(D)** none of these		**42.**

Name ______________________ Date __________ Class __________

DRILL 7-D 1, p. 125
[1–3]

Sorting account balances on a work sheet

	1	2	3	4	5	6
Account Title	**Trial Balance**		**Income Statement**		**Balance Sheet**	
	Debit	**Credit**	**Debit**	**Credit**	**Debit**	**Credit**
1. *Advertising Expense*	√		√			
2.						
3.						
4.						
5.						
6.						
7.						
8.						
9.						
10.						
11.						

DRILL 7-D 2, p. 126
[1–5]

Figuring net income or net loss on a work sheet

	Income Statement		**Balance Sheet**	
	Debit	**Credit**	**Debit**	**Credit**
COMPANY 1				
1.	*$4,500.00*	*$5,300.00*	*$36,670.00*	*$35,870.00*
2. *Net Income*	*800.00*			*800.00*
3.	*$5,300.00*	*$5,300.00*	*$36,670.00*	*$36,670.00*
COMPANY 2				
1.				
2.				
3.				
COMPANY 3				
1.				
2.				
3.				
COMPANY 4				
1.				
2.				
3.				

PROBLEM 7-1, p. 126 **[2–4]** Preparing a trial balance on a work sheet

PROBLEM 7-2, p. 127 **[1–6]** Completing a work sheet

The ledger prepared for Problem 6-1 is needed to complete Problem 7-1.

	ACCOUNT TITLE	1 TRIAL BALANCE DEBIT	2 TRIAL BALANCE CREDIT	3 INCOME STATEMENT DEBIT	4 INCOME STATEMENT CREDIT	5 BALANCE SHEET DEBIT	6 BALANCE SHEET CREDIT	
1								1
2								2
3								3
4								4
5								5
6								6
7								7
8								8
9								9
10								10
11								11
12								12
13								13
14								14
15								15
16								16
17								17
18								18
19								19
20								20
21								21
22								22
23								23
24								24
25								25

The solution to Problem 7-2 is needed to complete Problem 8-1.

Extra form

	ACCOUNT TITLE	1 TRIAL BALANCE DEBIT	2 TRIAL BALANCE CREDIT	3 INCOME STATEMENT DEBIT	4 INCOME STATEMENT CREDIT	5 BALANCE SHEET DEBIT	6 BALANCE SHEET CREDIT	
1								1
2								2
3								3
4								4
5								5
6								6
7								7
8								8
9								9
10								10
11								11
12								12
13								13
14								14
15								15
16								16
17								17
18								18
19								19
20								20
21								21
22								22
23								23
24								24
25								25

Finding errors in accounting records [1]

Window Kleen
Work Sheet
For Month Ended July 31, 19--

	ACCOUNT TITLE	TRIAL BALANCE DEBIT (1)	TRIAL BALANCE CREDIT (2)	INCOME STATEMENT DEBIT (3)	INCOME STATEMENT CREDIT (4)	BALANCE SHEET DEBIT (5)	BALANCE SHEET CREDIT (6)	
1	Cash	87780				87780		1
2	Supplies	29000				29000		2
3	Equipment	110500				110500		3
4	Middletown Company		40000				40000	4
5	Robert Evans, Capital		115750				115750	5
6	Robert Evans, Drawing		6000				6000	6
7	Income Summary							7
8	Sales		108910				108910	8
9	Miscellaneous Expense	2800		2800				9
10	Rent Expense	24000		24000				10
11		254000	254000	26800	—	227280	270660	11
12	Net Loss				26800	26800		12
13				26800	26800	254000	270660	13

[2]

The ledger for this problem begins on the next page.

	ACCOUNT TITLE	1 TRIAL BALANCE DEBIT	2 TRIAL BALANCE CREDIT	3 INCOME STATEMENT DEBIT	4 INCOME STATEMENT CREDIT	5 BALANCE SHEET DEBIT	6 BALANCE SHEET CREDIT	
1								1
2								2
3								3
4								4
5								5
6								6
7								7
8								8
9								9
10								10
11								11
12								12
13								13
14								14
15								15
16								16
17								17
18								18
19								19
20								20
21								21
22								22
23								23
24								24
25								25

[1]

LEDGER

ACCOUNT Cash — ACCOUNT NO. 11

DATE		ITEM	POST. REF.	DEBIT	DATE		ITEM	POST. REF.	CREDIT
19-- July	1	Balance	✓	942 50	19-- July	31		C1	1,243 70
	31	877.80	C1	1,178 00 2,120 50					

ACCOUNT Supplies — ACCOUNT NO. 12

DATE		ITEM	POST. REF.	DEBIT	DATE		ITEM	POST. REF.	CREDIT
19-- July	1	Balance	✓	250 00					
	8		C1	40 00 290 00					

ACCOUNT Equipment — ACCOUNT NO. 13

DATE		ITEM	POST. REF.	DEBIT	DATE		ITEM	POST. REF.	CREDIT
19-- July	1	Balance	✓	1,105 00					

ACCOUNT Middletown Company — ACCOUNT NO. 21

DATE		ITEM	POST. REF.	DEBIT	DATE		ITEM	POST. REF.	CREDIT
19-- July	15		C1	200 00	19-- July	1	Balance 400.00	✓	600 00

ACCOUNT Robert Evans, Capital — ACCOUNT NO. 31

DATE		ITEM	POST. REF.	DEBIT	DATE		ITEM	POST. REF.	CREDIT
					19-- July	1	Balance	✓	1,000 00
						31		C1	157 50 1,157 50

ACCOUNT Robert Evans, Drawing — ACCOUNT NO. 32

DATE		ITEM	POST. REF.	DEBIT	DATE		ITEM	POST. REF.	CREDIT
19-- July	5		C1	60 00					

ACCOUNT Income Summary — ACCOUNT NO. 33

DATE		ITEM	POST. REF.	DEBIT	DATE		ITEM	POST. REF.	CREDIT

Name ______________________ Date __________ Class __________

PROBLEM 7-3, concluded
[1]

LEDGER

ACCOUNT *Sales* ACCOUNT NO. *41*

DATE		ITEM	POST. REF.	DEBIT	DATE		ITEM	POST. REF.	CREDIT
					19-- July	31		C1	108910

ACCOUNT *Miscellaneous Expense* ACCOUNT NO. *51*

DATE		ITEM	POST. REF.	DEBIT	DATE		ITEM	POST. REF.	CREDIT
19-- July	2		C1	500					
	9		C1	1100					
	24		C1	800					
	30		C1	400 2800					

ACCOUNT *Rent Expense* ACCOUNT NO. *52*

DATE		ITEM	POST. REF.	DEBIT	DATE		ITEM	POST. REF.	CREDIT
19-- July	2		C1	24000					

ACCOUNT *Utilities Expense* ACCOUNT NO. *53*

DATE		ITEM	POST. REF.	DEBIT	DATE		ITEM	POST. REF.	CREDIT
19-- July	2		C1	1000					
	15		C1	2050					
	28		C1	1630 4680					

ERRORS

Completing a work sheet [1–3]

	ACCOUNT TITLE	1 TRIAL BALANCE	2	3 INCOME STATEMENT	4	5 BALANCE SHEET	6	
		DEBIT	CREDIT	DEBIT	CREDIT	DEBIT	CREDIT	
1								1
2								2
3								3
4								4
5								5
6								6
7								7
8								8
9								9
10								10
11								11
12								12
13								13
14								14
15								15
16								16
17								17
18								18
19								19
20								20
21								21
22								22
23								23
24								24
25								25

Name ______________________ Date __________ Class __________ *MASTERY PROBLEM 7-M, p. 128*

Completing a work sheet

	ACCOUNT TITLE	1 TRIAL BALANCE DEBIT	2 TRIAL BALANCE CREDIT	3 INCOME STATEMENT DEBIT	4 INCOME STATEMENT CREDIT	5 BALANCE SHEET DEBIT	6 BALANCE SHEET CREDIT	
1								1
2								2
3								3
4								4
5								5
6								6
7								7
8								8
9								9
10								10
11								11
12								12
13								13
14								14
15								15
16								16
17								17
18								18
19								19
20								20
21								21
22								22
23								23
24								24
25								25

Preparing a trial balance and a work sheet [1, 2]

	ACCOUNT TITLE	1 TRIAL BALANCE	2	3 INCOME STATEMENT	4	5 BALANCE SHEET	6	
		DEBIT	CREDIT	DEBIT	CREDIT	DEBIT	CREDIT	
1								1
2								2
3								3
4								4
5								5
6								6
7								7
8								8
9								9
10								10
11								11
12								12
13								13
14								14
15								15
16								16
17								17
18								18
19								19
20								20
21								21
22								22
23								23
24								24
25								25

Name ______________ Date ________ Class ________

REINFORCEMENT ACTIVITY 1
PART B – p. 129

AN ACCOUNTING CYCLE FOR A SOLE PROPRIETORSHIP USING A CASH JOURNAL [13, 14]

The ledger used in Part A is needed to complete Part B.

	ACCOUNT TITLE	1 TRIAL BALANCE	2	3 INCOME STATEMENT	4	5 BALANCE SHEET	6	
		DEBIT	CREDIT	DEBIT	CREDIT	DEBIT	CREDIT	
1								1
2								2
3								3
4								4
5								5
6								6
7								7
8								8
9								9
10								10
11								11
12								12
13								13
14								14
15								15
16								16
17								17
18								18
19								19
20								20
21								21
22								22
23								23
24								24
25								25

The work sheet used in Part B is needed to complete Parts C and D of this reinforcement activity. The ledger is needed to complete Part D.

	ACCOUNT TITLE	1 TRIAL BALANCE DEBIT	2 TRIAL BALANCE CREDIT	3 INCOME STATEMENT DEBIT	4 INCOME STATEMENT CREDIT	5 BALANCE SHEET DEBIT	6 BALANCE SHEET CREDIT	
1								1
2								2
3								3
4								4
5								5
6								6
7								7
8								8
9								9
10								10
11								11
12								12
13								13
14								14
15								15
16								16
17								17
18								18
19								19
20								20
21								21
22								22
23								23
24								24
25								25

Perfect Score. 42 Name ______________________

Deduct.......... ___ Date ______________ Class ______________

Your Score.... ___ Checked by ______________________

STUDY GUIDE 8

UNIT A — Accounting Terms

DIRECTIONS: Select the one term in Column I that best fits each definition in Column II. Print the letter identifying your choice in the Answers column.

Column I	*Column II*	Answers	For Scoring
A. fiscal period statements	**0.** Analysis paper on which the financial condition of a business is summarized	*D*	**0.** √
B. income statement	**1.** Financial statements prepared at the end of a fiscal period		**1.**
C. interim statements	**2.** A financial statement showing the revenue, expenses, and net income or net loss of a business		**2.**
D. work sheet	**3.** Financial statements prepared for periods shorter than a fiscal period		**3.**

UNIT B — Income Statement

DIRECTIONS: The capital letters on the form below show the location of items on an income statement. Decide the location of each item listed below. Print the letter identifying your choice in the Answers column.

A
B
C
D E J
F G K
H L
I M

	Answers	For Scoring
0. Period of time covered.......	*C*	**0.** √
4. Expense account titles		**4.**
5. Revenue account titles.......		**5.**
6. Heading for *Expense* section		**6.**
7. Heading for *Revenue* section		**7.**
8. Statement name...............		**8.**
9. Words *Total Expenses*		**9.**
10. Words *Net Income*...........		**10.**
11. Expense account balances ..		**11.**
12. Net income or loss amount .		**12.**
13. Total expense amount........		**13.**
14. Total revenue amount........		**14.**
15. Name of business.............		**15.**

UNIT C — Balance Sheet

DIRECTIONS: The capital letters on the form below show the location of items on a balance sheet. Decide the location of each item listed below. Print the letter identifying your choice in the Answers column.

A
B
C
D I
E G J O
K P
L
M Q
F H N R

	Answers	For Scoring
16. Heading for *Capital* section		**16.**
17. Heading for *Liabilities* section		**17.**
18. Heading for *Assets* section..		**18.**
19. Words *Total Assets*		**19.**
20. Words *Total Liab. and Capital*		**20.**
21. Words *Total Liabilities*		**21.**
22. Capital account title		**22.**
23. Liability account titles		**23.**
24. Asset account titles		**24.**
25. Total amount of assets		**25.**
26. Total amount of liabilities ...		**26.**
27. Total of liabilities and capital..................................		**27.**
28. Asset account balances		**28.**
29. Liability account balances ..		**29.**
30. Capital account balance		**30.**

UNIT D — Preparing Financial Statements

DIRECTIONS: For each item below, select the choice that best completes the sentence. Print the letter identifying your choice in the Answers column.

	Answers	For Scoring
0. Amounts needed to complete an income statement are obtained from the **(A)** ledger accounts **(B)** work sheet's Trial Balance columns **(C)** work sheet's Income Statement columns **(D)** none of these..........................	*C*	**0.** √
31. An income statement reports the **(A)** financial progress of a business for a fiscal period **(B)** financial condition of a business on a specific date **(C)** total capital of a business **(D)** none of these		**31.**
32. The last section on an income statement is the **(A)** Total Liabilities and Capital **(B)** Revenue **(C)** Net Worth **(D)** none of these..........................		**32.**
33. The revenue amounts needed for an income statement are obtained from the **(A)** work sheet's Trial Balance columns **(B)** work sheet's Income Statement Debit column **(C)** work sheet's Income Statement Credit column **(D)** none of these..........................		**33.**
34. The expense amounts needed for an income statement are obtained from the **(A)** work sheet's Trial Balance Credit column **(B)** work sheet's Income Statement Debit column **(C)** work sheet's Income Statement Credit column **(D)** none of these..........................		**34.**
35. Income statement figures are assumed to be correct when the net income or loss on the statement is the same as the **(A)** work sheet's Income Statement Credit column total **(B)** net income or loss on the work sheet **(C)** work sheet's Balance Sheet Debit column total **(D)** none of these..........................		**35.**
36. A balance sheet shows the financial condition of a business **(A)** on a specific date **(B)** for a fiscal period **(C)** since the business was started **(D)** none of these..........................		**36.**
37. Amounts needed to prepare a balance sheet's liabilities section are obtained from the **(A)** work sheet's Balance Sheet Credit column **(B)** liabilities ledger accounts **(C)** work sheet's Balance Sheet Debit column **(D)** none of these		**37.**
38. Amounts needed to prepare a balance sheet's assets section are obtained from the **(A)** work sheet's Balance Sheet Credit column **(B)** assets ledger accounts **(C)** work sheet's Balance Sheet Debit column **(D)** none of these		**38.**
39. Amounts needed to prepare a balance sheet's capital section are obtained from the **(A)** work sheet's Balance Sheet Credit column **(B)** capital ledger accounts **(C)** work sheet's Balance Sheet Debit column **(D)** none of these		**39.**
40. Net loss is the difference that results when **(A)** revenue is greater than total expenses **(B)** expenses are greater than total revenue **(C)** more is invested than is withdrawn **(D)** none of these..........................		**40.**
41. The capital amount to be shown on Putt Around's balance sheet is figured by **(A)** adding capital account balance *plus* net income *less* drawing account balance **(B)** using the capital account balance in the ledger **(C)** subtracting total liabilities from total assets on a balance sheet **(D)** none of these..........................		**41.**
42. A balance sheet is assumed to be correct when **(A)** beginning capital *plus* net income *equals* ending capital **(B)** total liabilities and capital *equal* the total assets as shown on the balance sheet **(C)** amounts on a balance sheet agree with amounts on a work sheet **(D)** none of these..........................		**42.**

Name ____________ Date ________ Class ________

DRILL 8-D 1, p. 139
[1–3]

Classifying accounts

1	2	3	4	5	6	7	8
	Kind of Account					**Financial Statement**	
Account Title	**Asset**	**Liab.**	**Capital**	**Revenue**	**Expense**	**Income Statement**	**Balance Sheet**
1. *Cash*	√						√
2.							
3.							
4.							
5.							
6.							
7.							
8.							
9.							
10.							
11.							
12.							
13.							

Figuring net income or net loss

	1	2	3	4	5	6	7	8	9
Business	Total Assets	Total Liabilities	Balance of Capital	Balance of Drawing	Total Revenue	Total Expenses	Net Income	Net Loss	Ending Capital
A	$2,500.00	$ 900.00	$1,050.00	$ 50.00	$1,000.00	$ 400.00	*$600.00*		*$1,600.00*
B	3,250.00	1,170.00	1,265.00	65.00	1,400.00	520.00			
C	[illegible],750.00	1,440.00	2,430.00	80.00	1,600.00	640.00			
D	[illegible],250.00	1,260.00	2,220.00	70.00	1,400.00	560.00			
E	[illegible],750.00	1,710.00	1,795.00	95.00	2,100.00	760.00			
F	[illegible],125.00	2,565.00	2,567.00	142.00	3,275.00	1,140.00			
G	[illegible],056.00	2,180.00	2,185.00	120.00	2,780.00	969.00			
H	[illegible],690.00	3,500.00	6,432.00	190.00	4,448.00	4,500.00			

Use the space below for your calculations.

Name ______________________ Date __________ Class __________

Preparing an income statement

The solution to Problem 7-2 is needed to complete Problem 8-1.

Preparing a balance sheet

The solution to Problem 7-2 is needed to complete Problem 8-2.

Westside Bowling Lanes
Work Sheet
For Month Ended November 30, 19--

ACCOUNT TITLE	TRIAL BALANCE (1) DEBIT	TRIAL BALANCE (2) CREDIT	INCOME STATEMENT (3) DEBIT	INCOME STATEMENT (4) CREDIT	BALANCE SHEET (5) DEBIT	BALANCE SHEET (6) CREDIT
Cash	341250				341250	
Supplies	371860				371860	
Equipment	5951440				5951440	
Ledle Supply Company		252000				252000
Garbonia Equipment Company		571075				571075
Weston Repair Company		41300				41300
Wes Miller, Capital		5348325				5348325
Wes Miller, Drawing	120000				120000	
Income Summary						
Sales		747450		747450		
Advertising Expense	17400		17400			
Maintenance Expense	28200		28200			
Miscellaneous Expense	6840		6840			
Rent Expense	95000		95000			
Utilities Expense	28160		28160			
	6960150	6960150	175600	747450	6784550	6212700
Net Income			571850			571850
			747450	747450	6784550	6784550

[1]

[2]

Preparing a work sheet and financial statements [1]

	ACCOUNT TITLE	1 TRIAL BALANCE	2	3 INCOME STATEMENT	4	5 BALANCE SHEET	6	
		DEBIT	CREDIT	DEBIT	CREDIT	DEBIT	CREDIT	
1								1
2								2
3								3
4								4
5								5
6								6
7								7
8								8
9								9
10								10
11								11
12								12
13								13
14								14
15								15
16								16
17								17
18								18
19								19
20								20
21								21
22								22
23								23
24								24
25								25

[2]

[3]

Preparing a work sheet and financial statements [2]

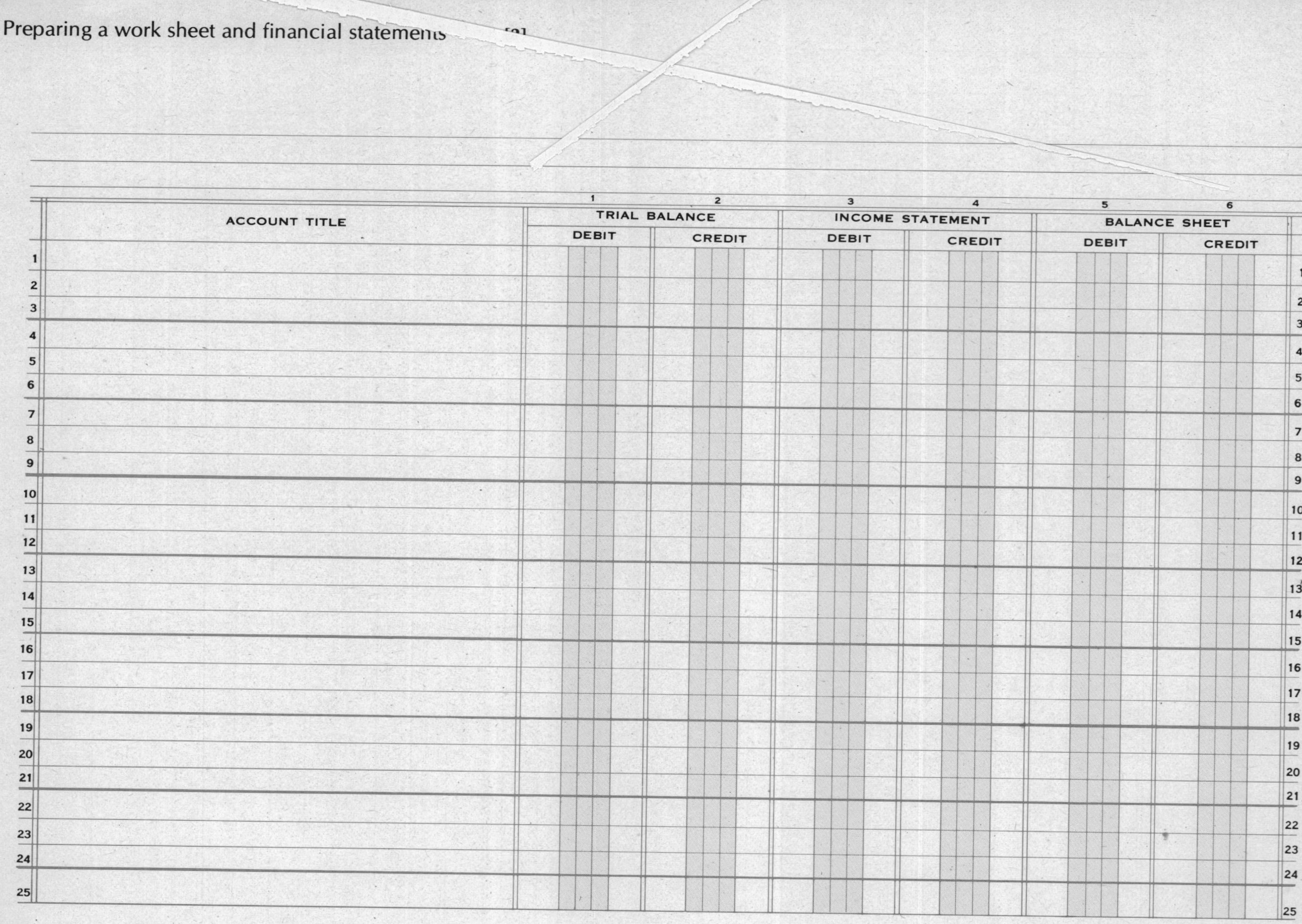

	ACCOUNT TITLE	TRIAL BALANCE 1 DEBIT	TRIAL BALANCE 2 CREDIT	INCOME STATEMENT 3 DEBIT	INCOME STATEMENT 4 CREDIT	BALANCE SHEET 5 DEBIT	BALANCE SHEET 6 CREDIT	
1								1
2								2
3								3
4								4
5								5
6								6
7								7
8								8
9								9
10								10
11								11
12								12
13								13
14								14
15								15
16								16
17								17
18								18
19								19
20								20
21								21
22								22
23								23
24								24
25								25

Use space below to figure the balance of the owner's capital account.

[1]

[3]

[4]

Name ______________________ Date __________ Class __________

REINFORCEMENT ACTIVITY 1
PART C – p. 142

[15]

AN ACCOUNTING CYCLE FOR A SOLE PROPRIETORSHIP USING A CASH JOURNAL

The work sheet prepared for Part B is needed to complete Part C.

The work sheet used in Part C is needed to complete Part D of this reinforcement activity.

Perfect Score. 38 Name ______________________

Deduct.......... ___ Date ______________ Class ______________

Your Score .... ___ Checked by ______________________

STUDY GUIDE 9

UNIT A — Accounting Terms

DIRECTIONS: Select the one term in Column I that best fits each definition in Column II. Print the letter identifying your choice in the Answers column.

Column I

A. accounting cycle
B. balance sheet
C. closed account
D. closing entries
E. combined entry
F. post-closing trial balance

Column II	Answers	For Scoring
0. A business form that reports assets, liabilities, and capital on a specific date	*B*	**0.** ✓
1. An entry that contains two or more debits or two or more credits		**1.**
2. The complete series of accounting activities followed in recording financial information for a fiscal period		**2.**
3. An account that has its balance transferred to another account		**3.**
4. A trial balance prepared after the closing entries are posted		**4.**
5. Journal entries used to prepare temporary capital accounts for a new fiscal period		**5.**

UNIT B — Accounts Affected by Closing Entries

DIRECTIONS: Decide which accounts listed below at the left are affected by each of the following closing entries. Print the account numbers identifying your choices in the proper Answers columns.

Partial Chart of Accounts

ACCOUNT TITLE	ACCT. NO.
Wilson Brown, Capital	31
Wilson Brown, Drawing	32
Income Summary	33
Sales	41
Advertising Expense	51
Miscellaneous Expense	52
Rent Expense	53
Utilities Expense	54

	Accounts to be Debited	Accounts to be Credited	For Scoring Debit	For Scoring Credit
0–0. Closing entry for revenue account ...	*41*	*33*	**0.** ✓	**0.** ✓
6–7. Closing entry for all expense accounts			**6.**	**7.**
8–9. Closing entry for Income Summary with a net income..			**8.**	**9.**
10–11. Closing entry for Income Summary with a net loss			**10.**	**11.**
12–13. Closing entry for drawing account ...			**12.**	**13.**

UNIT C — Analyzing Accounts after Closing Entries Are Posted

DIRECTIONS: Decide which accounts listed below will have balances and which will have zero balances after closing entries are posted. Place a check mark (✓) in the proper column to show your decisions.

	Accounts will have a balance	Accounts will have a zero balance	For Scoring
0. Advertising Expense		✓	**0.** ✓
14. Cash			**14.**
15. Golf Equipment			**15.**
16. Harry Rossi, Capital			**16.**
17. Harry Rossi, Drawing			**17.**
18. Maintenance Equipment			**18.**
19. Melcor Equipment Company (liability)			**19.**
20. Miscellaneous Expense			**20.**
21. Rent Expense			**21.**
22. Sales			**22.**
23. Sasson Supply Company (liability)			**23.**
24. Supplies			**24.**
25. Utilities Expense			**25.**
26. Income Summary			**26.**

UNIT D — Analyzing Closing Entries

DIRECTIONS: For each item below, select the choice that best completes the sentence. Write the letter identifying your choice in the Answers column.

Item	Answers	For Scoring
0. Income Summary is (A) a revenue account (B) a temporary capital account (C) a liability account (D) none of these	*B*	0. ✓
27. After closing entries are posted, the net income amount usually appears (A) in Income Summary as a credit (B) in the owner's capital account as a credit (C) in the owner's drawing account as a debit (D) none of these		27.
28. After closing entries are posted, a net loss amount would usually appear (A) in Income Summary as a debit (B) in the owner's capital account as a credit (C) in the owner's drawing account as a debit (D) none of these		28.
29. The information needed for closing all revenue accounts is obtained from the work sheet's (A) Trial Balance Debit column (B) Income Statement Debit column (C) Income Statement Credit column (D) none of these		29.
30. The information needed for closing all expense accounts is obtained from the work sheet's (A) Trial Balance Credit column (B) Income Statement Credit column (C) Balance Sheet Debit column (D) none of these		30.
31. The information needed for closing the owner's drawing account is obtained from the work sheet's (A) Trial Balance Credit column (B) Income Statement Credit column (C) Balance Sheet Debit column (D) none of these		31.
32. The information needed for closing the income summary account is obtained from the work sheet's (A) Income Statement Credit column total (B) Trial Balance columns (C) heading (D) none of these		32.
33. The income summary account balance represents a net income when (A) credits are larger than debits in the account (B) debits are larger then credits in the account (C) the business receives more cash than it pays out (D) none of these		33.
34. If the income summary account has a debit balance before the account is closed to the owner's capital account, the business has (A) a net income (B) a net loss (C) too much business (D) none of these		34.
35. After closing entries are posted, the owner's capital account balance should be the same as (A) capital shown on the balance sheet (B) revenue for the fiscal period (C) net income for the fiscal period (D) none of these		35.
36. The accounts listed on a post-closing trial balance are (A) those that have balances after closing entries are posted (B) those that have no balances after closing entries are posted (C) all accounts in the ledger (D) none of these		36.
37. A post-closing trial balance is prepared to show (A) the owner's capital account balance (B) the net income for the fiscal period (C) that debits still equal credits in the ledger after closing entries are posted (D) none of these		37.
38. The first step in Putt Around's accounting cycle is to (A) record transactions in a journal (B) prepare financial statements (C) verify and analyze source documents for transactions (D) none of these		38.

Name ____________ Date ________ Class ________

DRILL 9-D 1, p. 156
[1–3]

Identifying accounts affected by closing entries

1	2	3	4
Account Title	Account is affected by a closing entry	After closing entries are posted, account has	
		a zero balance	a balance
1. *Advertising Expense*	✓	✓	
2.			
3.			
4.			
5.			
6.			
7.			
8.			
9.			
10.			
11.			
12.			
13.			
14.			
15.			
16.			

Analyzing the effect of net income or net loss and withdrawals on capital

DRILL 9-D 2, p. 156

1	2	3	4	5
Business	Account balances on trial balance		Net income or loss for fiscal period	Balance of capital account on post-closing trial balance
	Capital	Drawing		
1	$ 18,000.00	$ 500.00	$5,568.00	*$ 23,068.00*
2	33,600.00	none	*–1,860.00*	31,740.00
3	54,720.00	2,000.00	7,740.00	
4	24,960.00	800.00	4,056.00	
5	67,800.00	2,500.00		63,800.00
6	46,620.00	none		51,840.00
7	44,256.00		3,168.00	43,824.00
8	111,000.00	5,000.00		106,144.00
9		500.00	2,844.00	31,696.00
10	5,600.00	250.00	750.00	

Recording closing entries

PROBLEM 9-1, p. 157

The solution to Problem 7-2 is needed to complete Problem 9-1.

GENERAL JOURNAL PAGE

	DATE		ACCOUNT TITLE	POST. REF.	DEBIT	CREDIT	
1							1
2							2
3							3
4							4
5							5
6							6
7							7
8							8
9							9
10							10
11							11
12							12

Posting closing entries

PROBLEM 9-2, p. 157

Use the solutions to Problems 7-1 and 9-1 for Problem 9-2. The solution to Problem 9-2 is needed to complete Problem 9-3.

Preparing a post-closing trial balance

PROBLEM 9-3, p. 158
[2]

ACCOUNT TITLE	DEBIT	CREDIT

Name ______________ Date __________ Class __________

PROBLEM 9-4, p. 158
[1–4]

Recording closing entries

GENERAL JOURNAL

PAGE

DATE		ACCOUNT TITLE	POST. REF.	DEBIT	CREDIT

Recording closing entries

MASTERY PROBLEM 9-M, p. 158

GENERAL JOURNAL

PAGE

DATE		ACCOUNT TITLE	POST. REF.	DEBIT	CREDIT

LEDGER

ACCOUNT *Cash* ACCOUNT NO. 11

DATE		ITEM	POST. REF.	DEBIT	DATE		ITEM	POST. REF.	CREDIT
19--					19--				
Nov.	1	Balance	✓	104557	Nov.	30		C2	428886
	30		C2	612120					

ACCOUNT *Delivery Equipment* ACCOUNT NO. 12

DATE		ITEM	POST. REF.	DEBIT	DATE		ITEM	POST. REF.	CREDIT
19--					19--				
Nov.	1	Balance	✓	872000	Nov.	5		C1	50800
	18		C1	118400					

ACCOUNT *Office Equipment* ACCOUNT NO. 13

DATE		ITEM	POST. REF.	DEBIT	DATE		ITEM	POST. REF.	CREDIT
19--									
Nov.	1	Balance	✓	62200					

ACCOUNT *Cook Equipment Company* ACCOUNT NO. 21

DATE		ITEM	POST. REF.	DEBIT	DATE		ITEM	POST. REF.	CREDIT
19--					19--				
Nov.	1		C1	16000	Nov.	1	Balance	✓	64000

ACCOUNT *Mott Supply Company* ACCOUNT NO. 22

DATE		ITEM	POST. REF.	DEBIT	DATE		ITEM	POST. REF.	CREDIT
19--					19--				
Nov.	22		C2	100000	Nov.	1	Balance	✓	186000

ACCOUNT *Durwood Manby, Capital* ACCOUNT NO. 31

DATE		ITEM	POST. REF.	DEBIT	DATE		ITEM	POST. REF.	CREDIT
					19--				
					Nov.	1	Balance	✓	788757
						1		C1	200000

[1, 4, 5]

LEDGER

ACCOUNT Durwood Manby, Drawing — ACCOUNT NO. 32

DATE		ITEM	POST. REF.	DEBIT	DATE		ITEM	POST. REF.	CREDIT
19-- Nov.	30		C2	100000					

ACCOUNT Income Summary — ACCOUNT NO. 33

DATE		ITEM	POST. REF.	DEBIT	DATE		ITEM	POST. REF.	CREDIT

ACCOUNT Sales — ACCOUNT NO. 41

DATE		ITEM	POST. REF.	DEBIT	DATE		ITEM	POST. REF.	CREDIT
					19-- Nov.	30		C2	486800

ACCOUNT Delivery Expense — ACCOUNT NO. 51

DATE		ITEM	POST. REF.	DEBIT	DATE		ITEM	POST. REF.	CREDIT
19-- Nov.	30		C2	150400					

ACCOUNT Miscellaneous Expense — ACCOUNT NO. 52

DATE		ITEM	POST. REF.	DEBIT	DATE		ITEM	POST. REF.	CREDIT
19-- Nov.	15		C1	7400					
	30		C2	6166					

ACCOUNT Rent Expense — ACCOUNT NO. 53

DATE		ITEM	POST. REF.	DEBIT	DATE		ITEM	POST. REF.	CREDIT
19-- Nov.	2		C1	56000					

[1, 2]

	ACCOUNT TITLE	TRIAL BALANCE		INCOME STATEMENT		BALANCE SHEET		
		1	2	3	4	5	6	
		DEBIT	CREDIT	DEBIT	CREDIT	DEBIT	CREDIT	
1								1
2								2
3								3
4								4
5								5
6								6
7								7
8								8
9								9
10								10
11								11
12								12
13								13
14								14
15								15
16								16
17								17
18								18
19								19
20								20
21								21
22								22
23								23
24								24
25								25

[3, 4]

GENERAL JOURNAL

PAGE

	DATE		ACCOUNT TITLE	POST. REF.	DEBIT	CREDIT	
1							1
2							2
3							3
4							4
5							5
6							6
7							7
8							8
9							9
10							10
11							11
12							12
13							13

[5]

ACCOUNT TITLE	DEBIT	CREDIT

GENERAL JOURNAL

PAGE

DATE		ACCOUNT TITLE	POST. REF.	DEBIT	CREDIT

Name ______________________ Date __________ Class __________

REINFORCEMENT ACTIVITY 1
PART D – p. 160
[20]

AN ACCOUNTING CYCLE FOR A SOLE PROPRIETORSHIP USING A CASH JOURNAL

The work sheet prepared in Part B and used in Part C is needed to complete Part D. Also, the ledger used in Parts A and B is needed. In addition, the general journal used in Part A is needed.

ACCOUNT TITLE	DEBIT	CREDIT

ACCOUNT TITLE	DEBIT	CREDIT

Perfect Score. 46 Name ____________________

Deduct.......... ___ Date ____________ Class ____________

Your Score .... ___ Checked by ____________________

UNIT A — Accounting Terms

DIRECTIONS: Select the one term in Column I that best fits each definition in Column II. Print the letter identifying your choice in the Answers column.

Column I	Column II	Answers	For Scoring
A. ABA numbers	**0.** Placing cash in a bank account	*N*	**0.** ✓
B. bank balance	**1.** A bank account from which payments can be ordered by a depositor		**1.**
C. bank service charge	**2.** The person or business in whose name cash is deposited		**2.**
D. bank statement	**3.** A check that a bank refuses to pay		**3.**
E. blank endorsement	**4.** A bank account on which a bank pays interest to a depositor		**4.**
F. canceled checks	**5.** A form on which a brief message is written		**5.**
G. checking account	**6.** A form signed by each person authorized to sign checks		**6.**
H. deposit slip	**7.** Bringing bank statement and checkbook balances into agreement		**7.**
I. depositor	**8.** A bank form on which a depositor lists all cash and checks being deposited		**8.**
J. dishonored check	**9.** A charge made by a bank for maintaining a checking account		**9.**
K. drawee	**10.** Identification numbers assigned to banks by the American Bankers Association		**10.**
L. drawer	**11.** Deposits made but not yet shown on a bank statement		**11.**
M. endorsement	**12.** An endorsement restricting transfer of a check		**12.**
N. making a deposit	**13.** A signature or stamp on a check's back transferring ownership		**13.**
O. memorandum	**14.** An endorsement stating to whom a check is to be paid		**14.**
P. outstanding checks	**15.** An endorsement consisting only of the endorser's signature		**15.**
Q. outstanding deposits	**16.** An endorsement showing that the endorser assumes no responsibility for payment		**16.**
R. payee	**17.** Checks issued by a depositor but not yet received by a bank		**17.**
S. qualified endorsement	**18.** A person or business issuing a check		**18.**
T. reconciling a bank statement	**19.** Checks paid by a bank and returned to a depositor		**19.**
U. restrictive endorsement	**20.** A person or business to whom a check is issued		**20.**
V. savings account	**21.** A bank on which a check is drawn		**21.**
W. signature card	**22.** The up-to-date balance appearing on a depositor's bank records		**22.**
X. special endorsement	**23.** A report of deposits, withdrawals, and bank balance sent to a depositor by a bank		**23.**
Y. voiding a check	**24.** Marking a check so that it cannot be used		**24.**

UNIT B — Analyzing a Bank Statement

DIRECTIONS: Parts of a bank statement are identified with capital letters on the form at the right. Determine which part answers each of the questions below. Write the letter identifying your choice in the Answers column.

CBO
CITIZENS BANK OF OHIO
Columbus, OH 43226-4520

STATEMENT OF ACCOUNT FOR	ACCOUNT NUMBER	STATEMENT DATE
A	B	C

BALANCE FROM PREVIOUS STATEMENT	NO. OF CHECKS	AMOUNT OF CHECKS	NO. OF DEPOSITS	AMOUNT OF DEPOSITS	SERVICE CHARGES	STATEMENT BALANCE
D	E	F	G	H	I	J

DATE	CHECKS	DEPOSITS	BALANCE
K	L	M	N

Question	Answers	For Scoring
0. Where is the amount of each deposit shown?	*M*	**0.** ✓
25. Where is the total amount of all checks paid by the bank shown?		**25.**
26. Where is the name and address of the depositor shown?		**26.**
27. Where is the depositor's account number shown?		**27.**
28. Where is the amount shown for each check paid by the bank?		**28.**
29. Where is the daily balance of the account shown?		**29.**
30. Where is the time covered by the bank statement shown?		**30.**
31. Where is the beginning balance of the account shown?		**31.**
32. Where is the ending balance of the account shown?		**32.**
33. Where is the total amount of service charge shown?		**33.**
34. Where is the date on which each deposit is received by the bank shown?		**34.**
35. Where is the date on which each check is received by the bank shown?		**35.**

UNIT C — Analyzing Bank Services

DIRECTIONS: Place a check mark (✓) in the proper Answers column to show whether each of the following statements is true or false.

Statement	Answers: True	Answers: False	For Scoring
0. A deposit slip is sometimes known as a deposit ticket	✓		**0.** ✓
36. A lost check with a restrictive endorsement can be cashed by anyone finding the check			**36.**
37. A check made payable to Joan Risner should be endorsed as *Mrs. Donald Risner*			**37.**
38. Each time Putt Around makes a deposit, the amount of the deposit should be recorded in the cash journal as a debit to Cash			**38.**
39. If the ABA number is $\frac{18\text{-}523}{1322}$, only one specific bank in the area assigned the number *18* has the number *523* assigned to it			**39.**
40. A stamped endorsement, with no written signature, is not accepted by most banks			**40.**
41. Putt Around uses a check stub as the source document for the entry to record a dishonored check			**41.**
42. A record of a voided check is not made in Putt Around's cash journal because no check is written for the payment			**42.**
43. A bank service charge should be recorded in the cash journal and on the next unused check stub			**43.**
44. Putt Around's entry to record a bank service charge is a debit to Miscellaneous Expense and a credit to Cash			**44.**
45. Putt Around's entry to record a dishonored check is a debit to Miscellaneous Expense and a credit to Cash			**45.**
46. Putt Around's entry to record a voided check is a debit to Miscellaneous Expense and a credit to Cash			**46.**

Name ______________________ Date __________ Class __________

DRILL 10-D 1, p. 176

Reconciling a bank statement

DRILL 10-D 2, p. 176

Reconciling a bank statement

Reconciling a bank statement

DRILL 10-D 3, p. 176

Preparing a deposit slip

PROBLEM 10-1, p. 177
[1]

For deposit to the account of:

96-525
1230

____
Please print exact title of account

Account Number: ___ ___ — ___ ___ ___ ___ ___ — ___ ___

FARMERS STATE BANK

Medford, OR 97501-2714

Date ______________ 19 ___

Currency		
Coin		
Checks		
TOTAL		

[2]

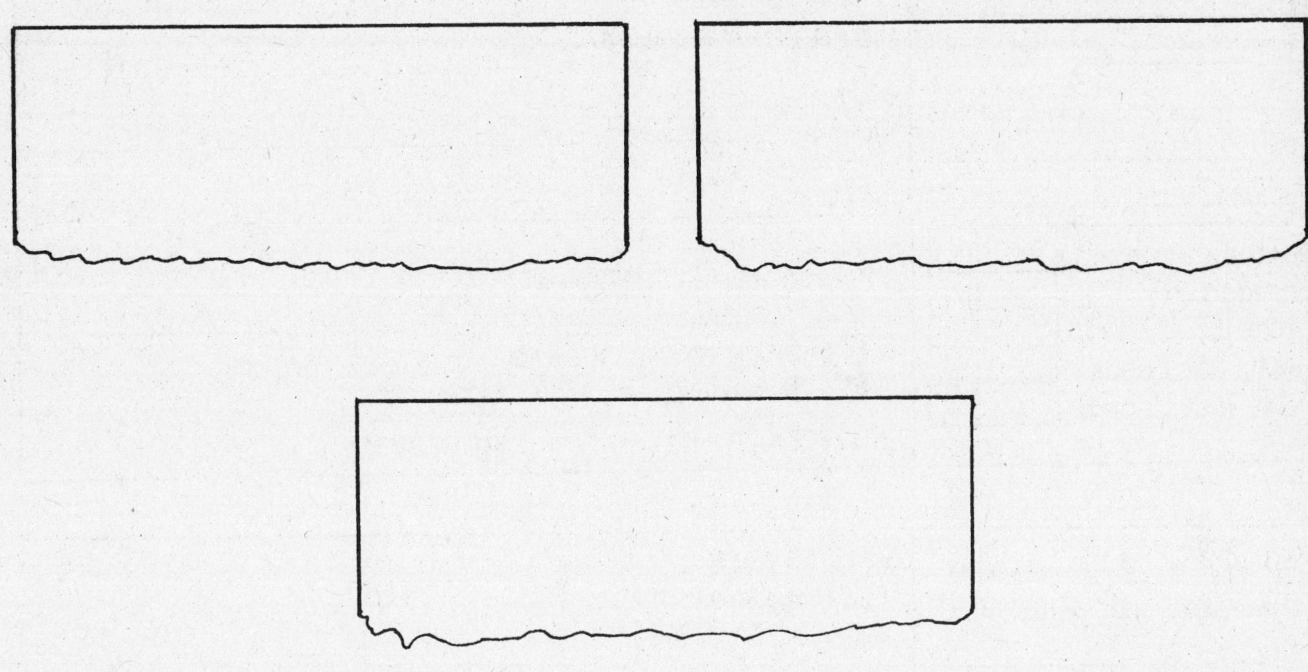

Preparing check stubs and writing checks

PROBLEM 10-2, p. 177

[1, 2]

NO. **21** $ __________

Date __________________ 19 ____

To ______________________

____

For ______________________

____

BAL. BR'T FOR'D......		
DEPOSITED.. [ ] [ ] [ ] Date		
TOTAL....................		
AM'T THIS CHECK....		
BAL. CAR'D FOR'D...		

KEY CAR WASH
1150 Hinkle Street
Bakersfield, CA 93305-5742

16-479
1220

NO. **21**

____________________ 19 ____

Pay to the
Order of ________________________________ $ __________

____ Dollars

For ____________________

____________________ ____________________

P PACIFIC STATE BANK
Bakersfield, CA 93305-5387

⑆122004793⑆ 79⑈ 00468787⑈

NO. 22 $ ________

Date ________ 19 ___

To ________

____

For ________

____

BAL. BR'T FOR'D......		
DEPOSITED.. Date		
TOTAL....................		
AM'T THIS CHECK....		
BAL. CAR'D FOR'D...		

KEY CAR WASH
1150 Hinkle Street
Bakersfield, CA 93305-5742

16-479
1220

NO. 22

________ 19 ___

Pay to the
Order of ________ $ ________

________ Dollars

For ________

________ ________

P PACIFIC STATE BANK
Bakersfield, CA 93305-5387

⑆1220047931⑆ 79⑈ 00468787⑈

NO. 23 $ ________

Date ________ 19 ___

To ________

____

For ________

____

BAL. BR'T FOR'D......		
DEPOSITED.. Date		
TOTAL....................		
AM'T THIS CHECK....		
BAL. CAR'D FOR'D...		

KEY CAR WASH
1150 Hinkle Street
Bakersfield, CA 93305-5742

16-479
1220

NO. 23

________ 19 ___

Pay to the
Order of ________ $ ________

________ Dollars

For ________

________ ________

P PACIFIC STATE BANK
Bakersfield, CA 93305-5387

⑆1220047931⑆ 79⑈ 00468787⑈

NO. 24 $ ________

Date ________ 19 ___

To ________

____

For ________

____

BAL. BR'T FOR'D......		
DEPOSITED.. Date		
TOTAL....................		
AM'T THIS CHECK....		
BAL. CAR'D FOR'D...		

KEY CAR WASH
1150 Hinkle Street
Bakersfield, CA 93305-5742

16-479
1220

NO. 24

________ 19 ___

Pay to the
Order of ________ $ ________

________ Dollars

For ________

________ ________

P PACIFIC STATE BANK
Bakersfield, CA 93305-5387

⑆1220047931⑆ 79⑈ 00468787⑈

Reconciling a bank statement and recording a bank service charge [1]

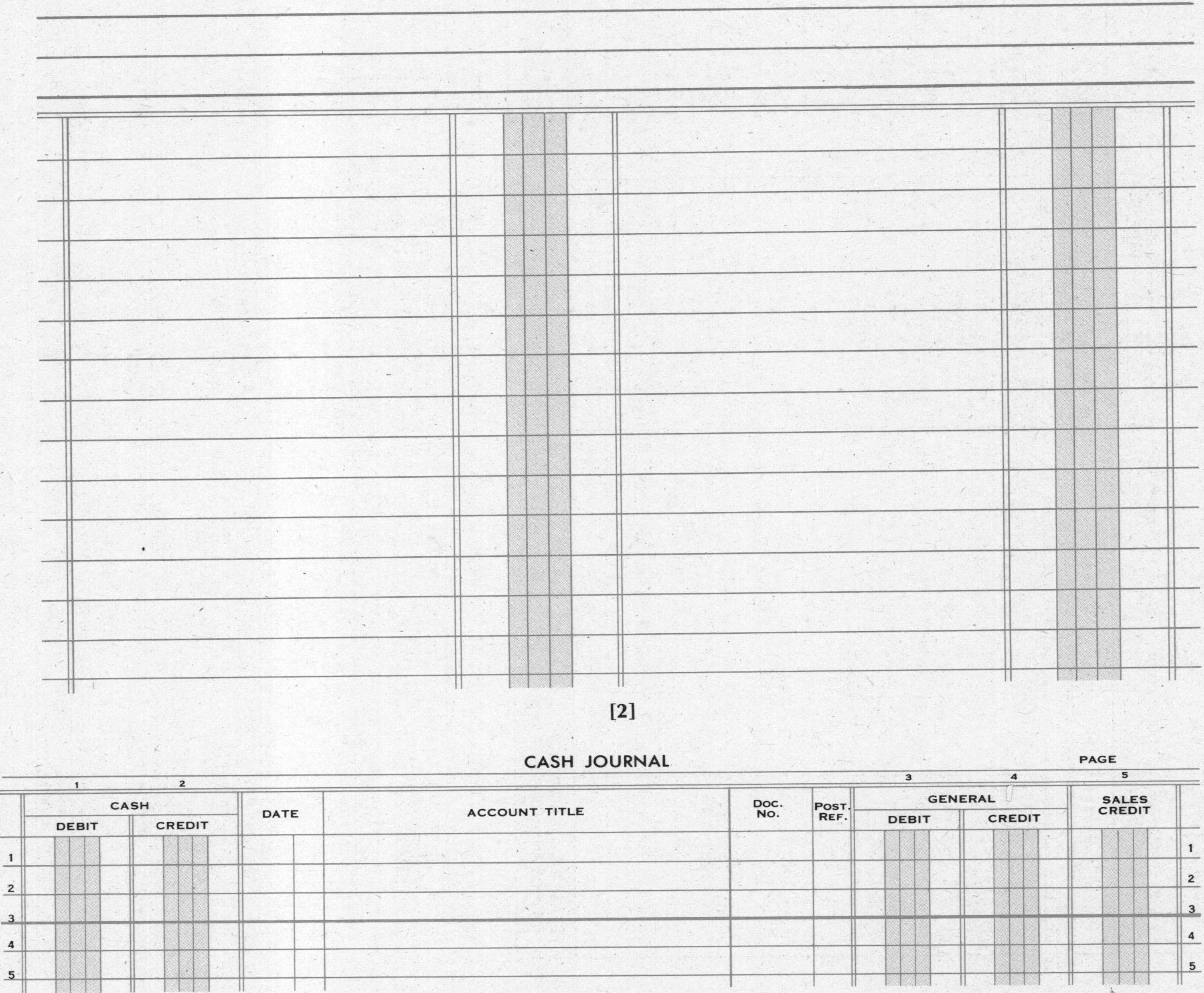

[1–3]

CBO

CITIZENS BANK OF OHIO
Columbus, OH 43226-4520

STATEMENT OF ACCOUNT FOR
LANES SERVICE COMPANY
715 PUTNAM DRIVE
COLUMBUS OH 43226-4379

ACCOUNT NUMBER
323-464777

STATEMENT DATE
9/30/--

BALANCE FROM PREVIOUS STATEMENT	NO. OF CHECKS	AMOUNT OF CHECKS	NO. OF DEPOSITS	AMOUNT OF DEPOSITS	SERVICE CHARGES	STATEMENT BALANCE
431.20	11	1,200.25	2	927.60	1.50	157.05

DATE	CHECKS		DEPOSITS	BALANCE
8/31/--				431.20
8/31/--			512.00	943.20
9/5/--	500.00			443.20
9/8/--	37.50	5.50		400.20
9/9/--	50.00			350.20
9/12/--	25.00		415.60	740.80
9/17/--	30.00			710.80
9/24/--	12.50	14.75		683.55
9/25/--	20.00	500.00		163.55
9/30/--	5.00			158.55
9/30/--	SC 1.50			157.05

PLEASE EXAMINE AT ONCE -- IF NO ERROR IS REPORTED WITHIN 10 DAYS THE ACCOUNT WILL BE CONSIDERED CORRECT AND VOUCHERS GENUINE. REFER ANY DISCREPANCY TO OUR ACCOUNTING DEPARTMENT IMMEDIATELY.

LANES SERVICE COMPANY, 715 Putnam Drive, Columbus, OH 43226-4379 — 25-317/440 — NO. 791 — August 31 19-- — Pay to the Order of Betty Lane $ 500.00

LANES SERVICE COMPANY, 715 Putnam Drive, Columbus, OH 43226-4379 — 25-317/440 — NO. 792 — September 4 19-- — Pay to the Order of Miller and Dolby $ 37.50

LANES SERVICE COMPANY, 715 Putnam Drive, Columbus, OH 43226-4379 — 25-317/440 — NO. 793 — September 6 19-- — Pay to the Order of Jack Willington $ 5.50

LANES SERVICE COMPANY, 715 Putnam Drive, Columbus, OH 43226-4379 — 25-317/440 — NO. 794 — September 8 19-- — Pay to the Order of Doyle Company $ 50.00

LANES SERVICE COMPANY, 715 Putnam Drive, Columbus, OH 43226-4379 — 25-317/440 — NO. 796 — September 12 19-- — Pay to the Order of Tripp Company $ 25.00

LANES SERVICE COMPANY
715 Putnam Drive
Columbus, OH 43226-4379
25-317/440 NO. 798
September 15 19--
Pay to the Order of Jodi's Drapery Shop $ 30.00
Thirty and no/100 Dollars
For Payment on account
Betty Lane

LANES SERVICE COMPANY, 715 Putnam Drive, Columbus, OH 43226-4379 — 25-317/440 — NO. 799 — September 20 19-- — Pay to the Order of J. A. Black $ 12.50

LANES SERVICE COMPANY, 715 Putnam Drive, Columbus, OH 43226-4379 — 25-317/440 — NO. 800 — September 20 19-- — Pay to the Order of Pat's Garage $ 14.75

LANES SERVICE COMPANY, 715 Putnam Drive, Columbus, OH 43226-4379 — 25-317/440 — NO. 801 — September 21 19-- — Pay to the Order of Malloy Printers $ 20.00

LANES SERVICE COMPANY, 715 Putnam Drive, Columbus, OH 43226-4379 — 25-317/440 — NO. 802 — September 22 19-- — Pay to the Order of Betty Lane $ 500.00

LANES SERVICE COMPANY
715 Putnam Drive
Columbus, OH 43226-4379
25-317/440 NO. 803
September 28 19--
Pay to the Order of John Wilson $ 5.00
Five and no/100 Dollars
For Miscellaneous
Betty Lane
CBO CITIZENS BANK OF OHIO, Columbus, OH 43226-4520
⑆044003173⑆ 323⑈464777⑈

[1–3, 6]

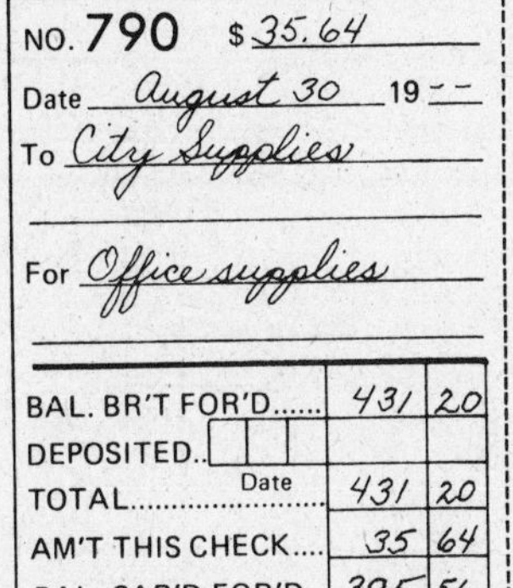

NO. 790 $ 35.64
Date August 30 19 --
To City Supplies
For Office supplies

BAL. BR'T FOR'D	431	20
DEPOSITED (Date)		
TOTAL	431	20
AM'T THIS CHECK	35	64
BAL. CAR'D FOR'D	395	56

NO. 791 $ 500.00
Date August 31 19 --
To Betty Lane
For Withdrawal

BAL. BR'T FOR'D	395	56
DEPOSITED 8/31/-- (Date)	512	00
TOTAL	907	56
AM'T THIS CHECK	500	00
BAL. CAR'D FOR'D	407	56

NO. 792 $ 37.50
Date September 4 19 --
To Miller and Dolby
For Repairs

BAL. BR'T FOR'D	407	56
DEPOSITED (Date)		
TOTAL	407	56
AM'T THIS CHECK	37	50
BAL. CAR'D FOR'D	370	06

NO. 793 $ 5.50
Date September 6 19 --
To Jack Willington
For Miscellaneous

BAL. BR'T FOR'D	370	06
DEPOSITED (Date)		
TOTAL	370	06
AM'T THIS CHECK	5	50
BAL. CAR'D FOR'D	364	56

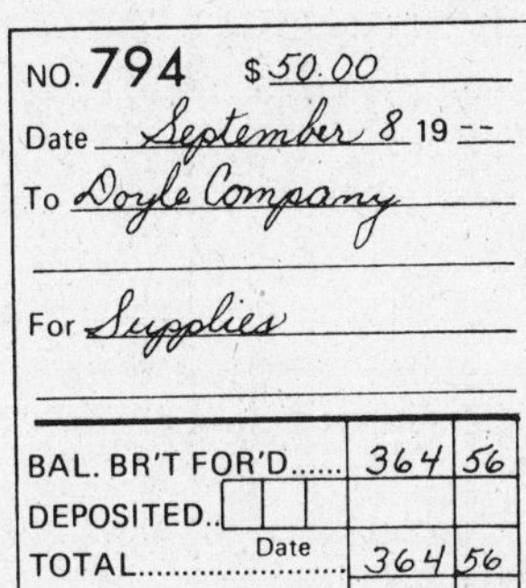

NO. 794 $ 50.00
Date September 8 19 --
To Doyle Company
For Supplies

BAL. BR'T FOR'D	364	56
DEPOSITED (Date)		
TOTAL	364	56
AM'T THIS CHECK	50	00
BAL. CAR'D FOR'D	314	56

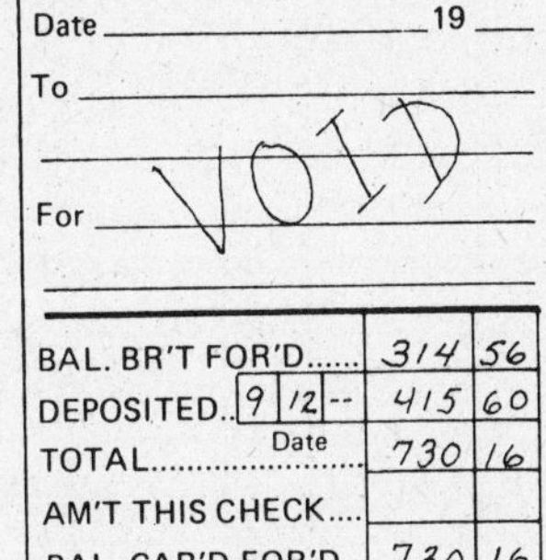

NO. 795 $ 2.50
Date ______ 19 __
To ______
For ______ VOID

BAL. BR'T FOR'D	314	56
DEPOSITED 9/12/-- (Date)	415	60
TOTAL	730	16
AM'T THIS CHECK		
BAL. CAR'D FOR'D	730	16

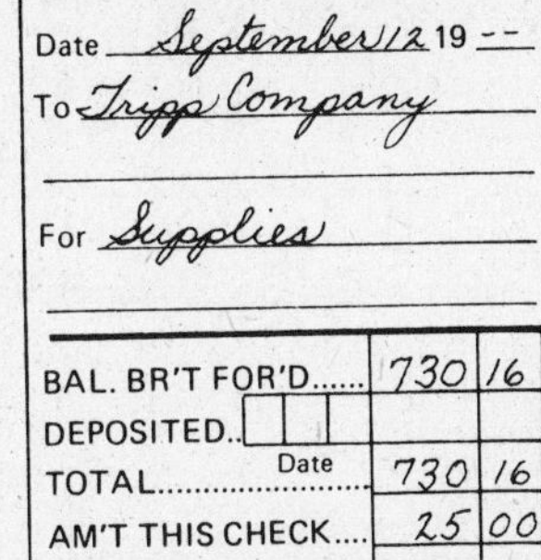

NO. 796 $ 25.00
Date September 12 19 --
To Tripp Company
For Supplies

BAL. BR'T FOR'D	730	16
DEPOSITED (Date)		
TOTAL	730	16
AM'T THIS CHECK	25	00
BAL. CAR'D FOR'D	705	16

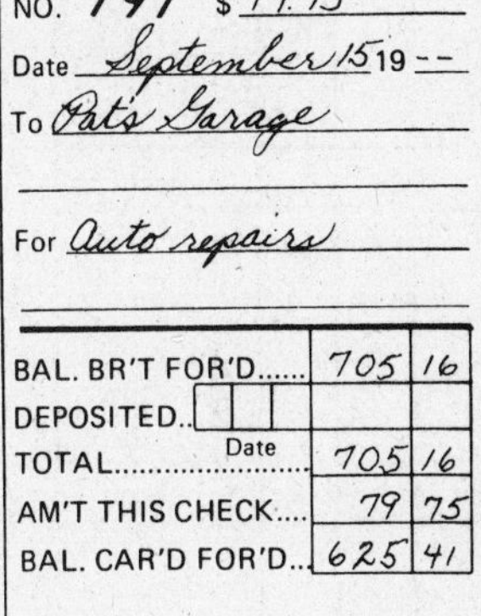

NO. 797 $ 79.75
Date September 15 19 --
To Pat's Garage
For Auto repairs

BAL. BR'T FOR'D	705	16
DEPOSITED (Date)		
TOTAL	705	16
AM'T THIS CHECK	79	75
BAL. CAR'D FOR'D	625	41

NO. 798 $ 30.00
Date September 15 19 --
To Jodi's Drapery Shop
For Payment on account

BAL. BR'T FOR'D	625	41
DEPOSITED (Date)		
TOTAL	625	41
AM'T THIS CHECK	30	00
BAL. CAR'D FOR'D	595	41

NO. 799 $ 12.50
Date September 20 19 --
To J. A. Black
For Miscellaneous

BAL. BR'T FOR'D	595	41
DEPOSITED (Date)		
TOTAL	595	41
AM'T THIS CHECK	12	50
BAL. CAR'D FOR'D	582	91

NO. 800 $ 14.75
Date September 20 19 --
To Pat's Garage
For Gasoline

BAL. BR'T FOR'D	582	91
DEPOSITED (Date)		
TOTAL	582	91
AM'T THIS CHECK	14	75
BAL. CAR'D FOR'D	568	16

NO. 801 $ 20.00
Date September 21 19 --
To Malloy Printers
For Stationery

BAL. BR'T FOR'D	568	16
DEPOSITED (Date)		
TOTAL	568	16
AM'T THIS CHECK	20	00
BAL. CAR'D FOR'D	548	16

NO. 802 $ 500.00
Date September 22 19 --
To Betty Lane
For Withdrawal

BAL. BR'T FOR'D	548	16
DEPOSITED (Date)		
TOTAL	548	16
AM'T THIS CHECK	500	00
BAL. CAR'D FOR'D	48	16

NO. 803 $ 5.00
Date September 28 19 --
To John Wilson
For Miscellaneous

BAL. BR'T FOR'D	48	16
DEPOSITED (Date)		
TOTAL	48	16
AM'T THIS CHECK	5	00
BAL. CAR'D FOR'D	43	16

NO. 804 $ 48.35
Date October 1 19 --
To Sylvia Brown
For Miscellaneous

BAL. BR'T FOR'D	43	16
DEPOSITED 10/1/-- (Date)	807	51
TOTAL	850	67
AM'T THIS CHECK	48	35
BAL. CAR'D FOR'D	802	32

NO. 805 $ ______
Date ______ 19 __
To ______
For ______

BAL. BR'T FOR'D	802	32
DEPOSITED (Date)		
TOTAL		
AM'T THIS CHECK		
BAL. CAR'D FOR'D		

[4]

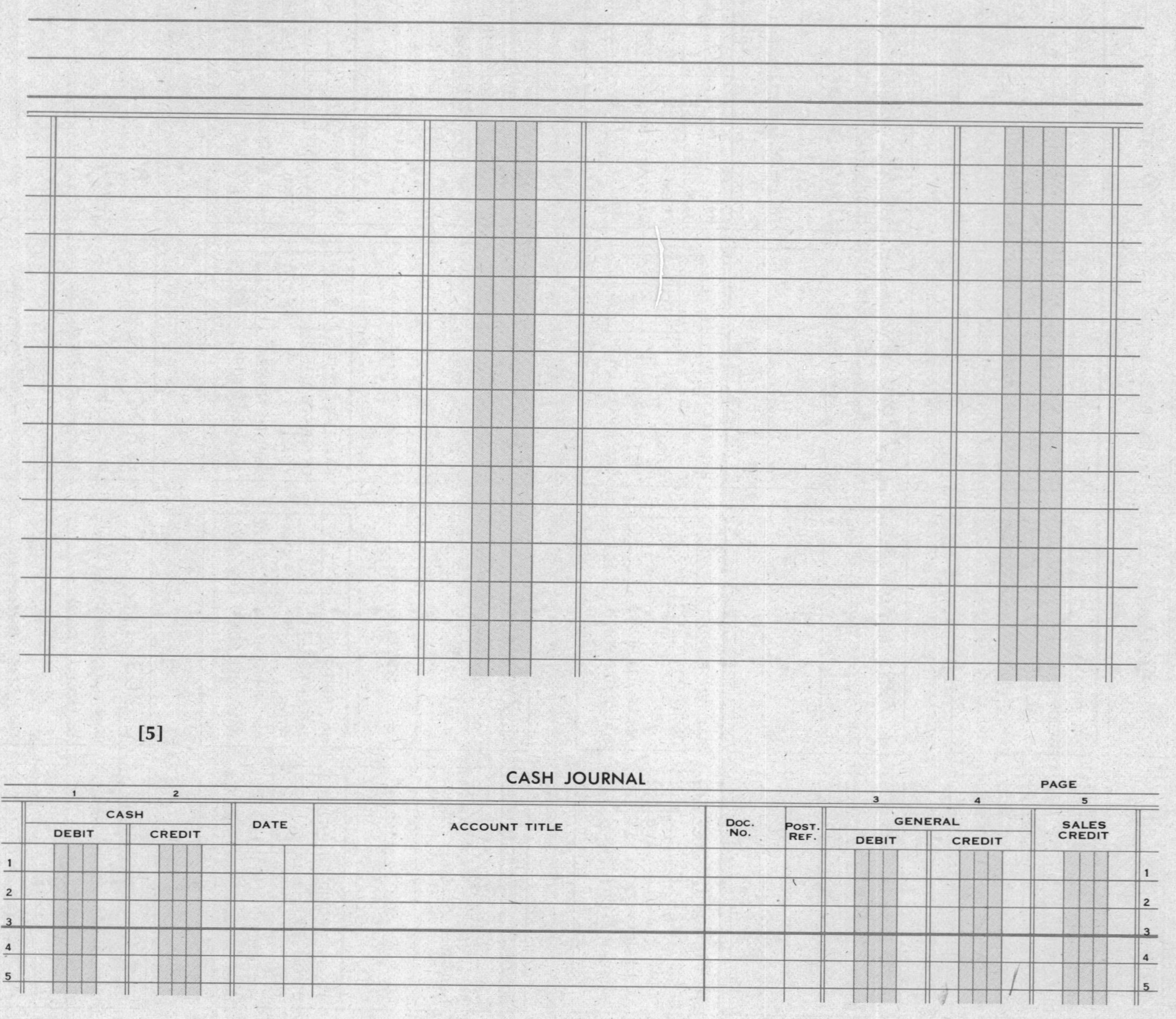

[5]

CASH JOURNAL PAGE

	1	2					3	4	5	
	CASH		DATE	ACCOUNT TITLE	DOC. NO.	POST. REF.	GENERAL		SALES CREDIT	
	DEBIT	CREDIT					DEBIT	CREDIT		
1										1
2										2
3										3
4										4
5										5

Writing checks; reconciling a bank statement; recording a bank service charge and a dishonored check

NO. 53 $ ________
Date ________ 19 ___
To ________
____
For ________
____

BAL. BR'T FOR'D......		
DEPOSITED.. (Date)		
TOTAL........		
AM'T THIS CHECK....		
BAL. CAR'D FOR'D...		

KRADDOCK'S SERVICE COMPANY
1693 Farley Court
Baltimore, MD 21203-2715

7-820
520

NO. 53

________ 19 ___

Pay to the
Order of ________ $ ________

________ Dollars

For ________

________ ________

INDUSTRIAL BANK OF MARYLAND
Baltimore, MD 21203-1567

⑆052008209⑆ 294⑈46⑈9081⑈

NO. 54 $ ________
Date ________ 19 ___
To ________
____
For ________
____

BAL. BR'T FOR'D......		
DEPOSITED.. (Date)		
TOTAL........		
AM'T THIS CHECK....		
BAL. CAR'D FOR'D...		

KRADDOCK'S SERVICE COMPANY
1693 Farley Court
Baltimore, MD 21203-2715

7-820
520

NO. 54

________ 19 ___

Pay to the
Order of ________ $ ________

________ Dollars

For ________

________ ________

INDUSTRIAL BANK OF MARYLAND
Baltimore, MD 21203-1567

⑆052008209⑆ 294⑈46⑈9081⑈

NO. 55 $ ________
Date ________ 19 ___
To ________
____
For ________
____

BAL. BR'T FOR'D......		
DEPOSITED.. (Date)		
TOTAL........		
AM'T THIS CHECK....		
BAL. CAR'D FOR'D...		

KRADDOCK'S SERVICE COMPANY
1693 Farley Court
Baltimore, MD 21203-2715

7-820
520

NO. 55

________ 19 ___

Pay to the
Order of ________ $ ________

________ Dollars

For ________

________ ________

INDUSTRIAL BANK OF MARYLAND
Baltimore, MD 21203-1567

⑆052008209⑆ 294⑈46⑈9081⑈

[3]

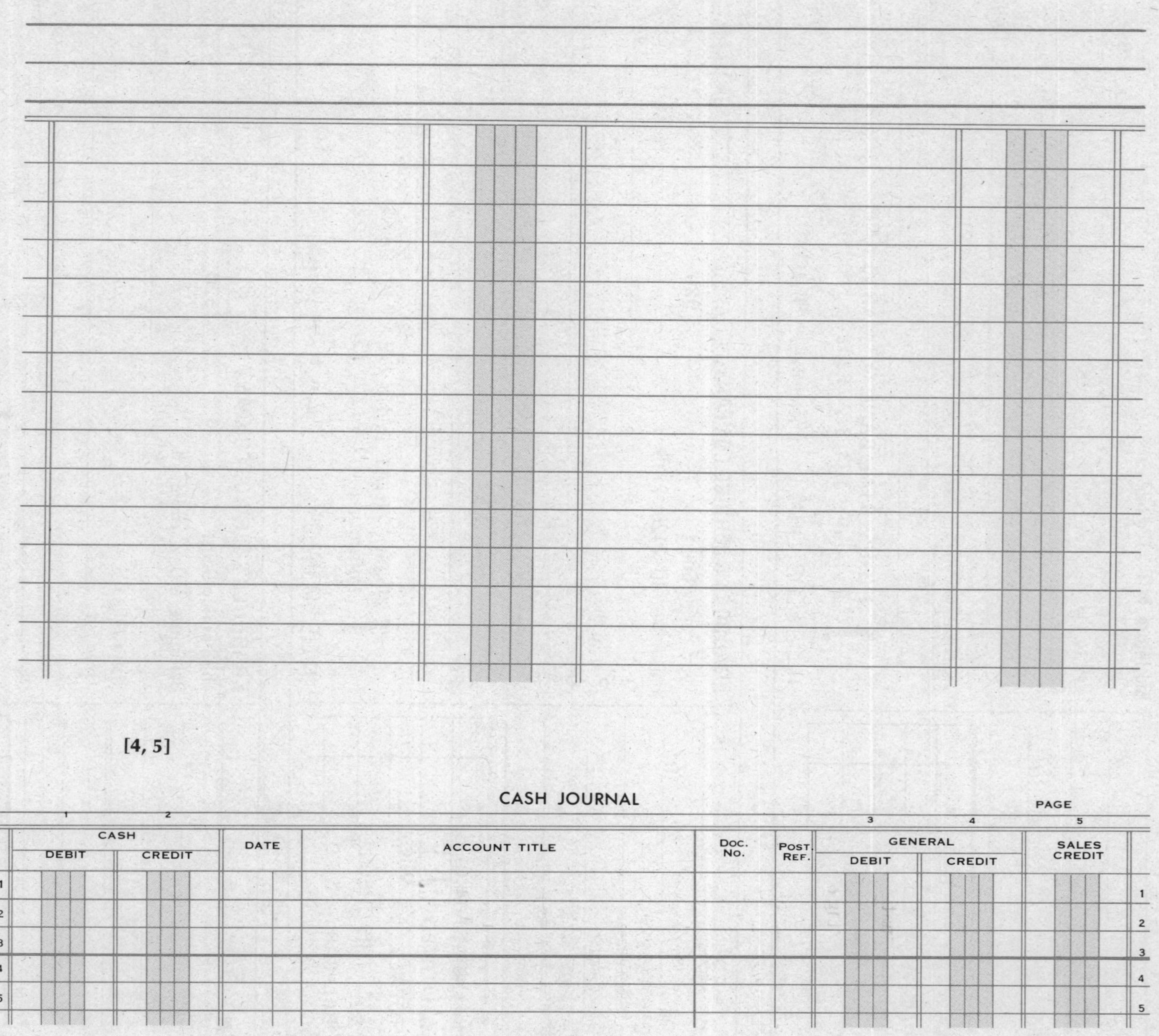

[4, 5]

CASH JOURNAL PAGE 5

	1	2					3	4	5	
	CASH		DATE	ACCOUNT TITLE	DOC. NO.	POST. REF.	GENERAL		SALES	
	DEBIT	CREDIT					DEBIT	CREDIT	CREDIT	
1										1
2										2
3										3
4										4
5										5

Perfect Score. 45	Name ______________________	
Deduct.......... ___	Date ______________	Class ______________
Your Score .... ___	Checked by ______________________	

UNIT A — Accounting Terms

DIRECTIONS: Select the one term in Column I that best fits each definition in Column II. Print the letter identifying your choice in the Answers column.

Column I	Column II	Answers	For Scoring
A. combination journal	**0.** The amount added to the cost of merchandise to establish the selling price	*F*	**0.** ✓
B. correcting entry	**1.** Goods that a merchandising business purchases to sell		**1.**
C. cost of merchandise	**2.** Each member of a partnership		**2.**
D. creditor	**3.** An invoice used as a source document for recording a purchase on account transaction........		**3.**
E. invoice	**4.** A multicolumn journal in which all transactions of a business are recorded		**4.**
F. markon	**5.** A business to which payment is owed........		**5.**
G. merchandise	**6.** A business in which two or more persons combine their assets and abilities		**6.**
H. merchandising business	**7.** An agreement between a buyer and a seller about payment for merchandise........		**7.**
I. partner	**8.** The price of merchandise a business purchases to sell		**8.**
J. partnership	**9.** A journal entry made to correct an error in the ledger		**9.**
K. purchase invoice	**10.** A transaction in which the merchandise purchased is to be paid for later........		**10.**
L. purchase on account	**11.** A form describing the goods shipped, the quantity, and the price........		**11.**
M. terms of sale	**12.** A business that purchases and sells goods........		**12.**

PAGE		COMBINATION JOURNAL							FOR MONTH OF			19			PAGE
1	2					3	4		5	6	7	8	9	10	11
CASH		DATE	ACCOUNT TITLE	DOC. NO.	POST. REF.	GENERAL			ACCOUNTS RECEIVABLE		SALES CREDIT	SALES TAX PAYABLE CREDIT	ACCOUNTS PAYABLE		PURCHASES DEBIT
DEBIT	CREDIT					DEBIT	CREDIT		DEBIT	CREDIT			DEBIT	CREDIT	
A	B	C	D	E	F	G	H		I	J	K	L	M	N	O

DIRECTIONS: Each column of the left and right pages of the combination journal above is identified with a capital letter. Print the letter identifying the column of the combination journal in which each of the following items should be recorded. The first five answers are supplied as examples.

A purchase on account transaction is recorded by writing the	Answers	For Scoring
0. date in	C	0. ✓
0. debit amount in	O	0. ✓
0. credit amount in	N	0. ✓
0. creditor name in	D	0. ✓
0. purchase invoice number in	E	0. ✓
A cash purchase transaction is recorded by writing the		
13. date in		13.
14. debit amount in		14.
15. credit amount in		15.
16. check mark in (to show that no account title needs to be written)		16.
17. check mark in (to show that no individual amounts on this line need to be posted)		17.
18. check number in		18.
A buying of supplies on account transaction is recorded by writing the		
19. date in		19.
20. debit amount in		20.
21. credit amount in		21.
22. title of the account debited in		22.
23. creditor name in		23.
24. brace ({) in		24.
25. memorandum number in		25.

A buying of supplies for cash transaction is recorded by writing the	Answers	For Scoring
26. date in		26.
27. debit amount in		27.
28. credit amount in		28.
29. account title debited in		29.
30. check number in		30.
A cash payment on account transaction is recorded by writing the		
31. date in		31.
32. debit amount in		32.
33. credit amount in		33.
34. creditor name in		34.
35. check number in		35.
A cash payment of expense transaction is recorded by writing the		
36. date in		36.
37. debit amount in		37.
38. credit amount in		38.
39. account title in		39.
40. check number in		40.
A cash withdrawal transaction is recorded by writing the		
41. date in		41.
42. debit amount in		42.
43. credit amount in		43.
44. account title in		44.
45. check number in		45.

Name ______________________ Date __________ Class __________

Analyzing transactions into debit and credit parts

1.

Purchases	
800.00	

Accounts Payable	
	800.00

2. supplies

150	

3.

4.

5.

6.

7.

8.

9.

10.

11.

12.

13.

14.

15.

17.

16.

18.

The solution to Drill 11-D1 is needed to complete Drill 11-D2.

Recording transactions using a combination journal

DRILL 11-D 2, p. 207

Transaction	Cash		General		Accounts Payable		Purchases
	Debit	Credit	Debit	Credit	Debit	Credit	Debit
1. Debit amount							✓
Credit amount						✓	
2. Debit amount							
Credit amount							
3. Debit amount							
Credit amount							
4. Debit amount							
Credit amount							
5. Debit amount							
Credit amount							
6. Debit amount							
Credit amount							
7. Debit amount							
Credit amount							
8. Debit amount							
Credit amount							
9. Debit amount							
Credit amount							
10. Debit amount							
Credit amount							
11. Debit amount							
Credit amount							
12. Debit amount							
Credit amount							
13. Debit amount							
Credit amount							
14. Debit amount							
Credit amount							
15. Debit amount							
Credit amount							
16. Debit amount							
Credit amount							
17. Debit amount							
Credit amount							
18. Debit amount							
Credit amount							

FOR MONTH OF 19 PAGE

5	6	7	8	9	10	11
ACCOUNTS RECEIVABLE		SALES CREDIT	SALES TAX PAYABLE CREDIT	ACCOUNTS PAYABLE		PURCHASES DEBIT
DEBIT	CREDIT			DEBIT	CREDIT	

Journalizing transactions for purchases, supplies, and cash payments in a combination journal

PROBLEM 11-1, p. 207
[1, 2]

PAGE 12

COMBINATION JOURNAL

1	2					3	4	
CASH						GENERAL		
DEBIT	CREDIT	DATE	ACCOUNT TITLE	Doc. No.	Post. Ref.	DEBIT	CREDIT	
		1991 Nov 1	Balance on hand $4,750		✓			1

Name ______________________ Date __________ Class __________

PROBLEM 11-1, concluded
[1, 2]

FOR MONTH OF Nov 19 1991 PAGE 12

	5	6	7	8	9	10	11	
	ACCOUNTS RECEIVABLE		SALES CREDIT	SALES TAX PAYABLE CREDIT	ACCOUNTS PAYABLE		PURCHASES DEBIT	
	DEBIT	CREDIT			DEBIT	CREDIT		
1								1
2								2
3								3
4								4
5								5
6								6
7								7
8								8
9								9
10								10
11								11
12								12
13								13
14								14
15								15
16								16
17								17
18								18
19								19
20								20
21								21
22								22
23								23
24								24
25								25
26								26
27								27
28								28
29								29
30								30
31								31
32								32
33								33

Journalizing transactions for purchases, supplies, and cash payments in a combination journal

MASTERY PROBLEM 11-M, p. 208
[1, 2]

PAGE

COMBINATION JOURNAL

	1	2					3	4	
	CASH		DATE	ACCOUNT TITLE	DOC. NO.	POST. REF.	GENERAL		
	DEBIT	CREDIT					DEBIT	CREDIT	
1									1
2									2
3									3
4									4
5									5
6									6
7									7
8									8
9									9
10									10
11									11
12									12
13									13
14									14
15									15
16									16
17									17
18									18
19									19
20									20
21									21
22									22
23									23
24									24
25									25
26									26
27									27
28									28
29									29
30									30
31									31
32									32
33									33

Name ______________ Date ________ Class ________ *MASTERY PROBLEM 11-M, concluded*

[1, 2]

FOR MONTH OF ______ 19 ___ PAGE ___

5	6	7	8	9	10	11
ACCOUNTS RECEIVABLE		SALES CREDIT	SALES TAX PAYABLE CREDIT	ACCOUNTS PAYABLE		PURCHASES DEBIT
DEBIT	CREDIT			DEBIT	CREDIT	

COMBINATION JOURNAL

PAGE

	1	2					3	4	
	CASH		DATE	ACCOUNT TITLE	DOC. NO.	POST. REF.	GENERAL		
	DEBIT	CREDIT					DEBIT	CREDIT	
1									1
2									2
3									3
4									4
5									5
6									6
7									7
8									8
9									9
10									10
11									11
12									12
13									13
14									14
15									15
16									16
17									17
18									18
19									19
20									20
21									21
22									22
23									23
24									24
25									25
26									26
27									27
28									28
29									29
30									30
31									31
32									32
33									33

FOR MONTH OF 19 PAGE

	5	6	7	8	9	10	11	
	ACCOUNTS RECEIVABLE		SALES CREDIT	SALES TAX PAYABLE CREDIT	ACCOUNTS PAYABLE		PURCHASES DEBIT	
	DEBIT	CREDIT			DEBIT	CREDIT		
1								1
2								2
3								3
4								4
5								5
6								6
7								7
8								8
9								9
10								10
11								11
12								12
13								13
14								14
15								15
16								16
17								17
18								18
19								19
20								20
21								21
22								22
23								23
24								24
25								25
26								26
27								27
28								28
29								29
30								30
31								31
32								32
33								33

PAGE

COMBINATION JOURNAL

	1	2					3	4	
	CASH		DATE	ACCOUNT TITLE	DOC. NO.	POST. REF.	GENERAL		
	DEBIT	CREDIT					DEBIT	CREDIT	
1									1
2									2
3									3
4									4
5									5
6									6
7									7
8									8
9									9
10									10
11									11
12									12
13									13
14									14
15									15
16									16
17									17
18									18
19									19
20									20
21									21
22									22
23									23
24									24
25									25
26									26
27									27
28									28
29									29
30									30
31									31
32									32
33									33

Perfect Score. 44 Name ____________

Deduct......... ___ Date ____________ Class ____________

Your Score.... ___ Checked by ____________

STUDY GUIDE 12

UNIT A — Accounting Terms

DIRECTIONS: Select the one term in Column I that best fits each definition in Column II. Print the letter identifying your choice in the Answers column.

Column I

A. cash sale
B. charge customer
C. credit card
D. customer
E. sale
F. sale on account
G. sales invoice
H. sales tax

Column II	Answers	For Scoring
0. A sale for which payment will be made at a later date	*F*	**0.** ✓
1. An embossed card used by a customer with an approved charge account..		**1.**
2. A person or firm to whom a business sells merchandise ...		**2.**
3. A person or firm to whom a sale on account is made		**3.**
4. A tax on a sale of goods..		**4.**
5. A sale in which cash is received for the total amount of sale at the time of the transaction..............................		**5.**
6. A form issued to a charge customer describing the goods sold, the quantity, and the price		**6.**
7. The transfer of merchandise to a customer in exchange for cash or a promise to pay..		**7.**

UNIT B — Debit and Credit Parts of Sales and Cash Receipts Transactions

DIRECTIONS: Sales and cash receipts transactions are given below. Print in the proper Answers columns the capital letters identifying the general ledger accounts to be debited and credited.

Account Title

A. Cash
B. Accounts Receivable
C. Sales
D. Sales Tax Payable

Transaction	Answers Debit	Answers Credit	For Scoring Debit	For Scoring Credit
0–0. Cash sales for the week	*A*	*C D*	**0.**✓	**0.**✓
8–9. Sold merchandise on account..............			**8.**	**9.**
10–11. Credit card sales for the week			**10.**	**11.**
12–13. Received cash on account			**12.**	**13.**

PAGE		COMBINATION JOURNAL						FOR MONTH OF				19		PAGE
1	2					3	4	5	6	7	8	9	10	11
CASH		DATE	ACCOUNT TITLE	DOC. NO.	POST. REF.	GENERAL		ACCOUNTS RECEIVABLE		SALES CREDIT	SALES TAX PAYABLE CREDIT	ACCOUNTS PAYABLE		PURCHASES DEBIT
DEBIT	CREDIT					DEBIT	CREDIT	DEBIT	CREDIT			DEBIT	CREDIT	
A	B	C	D	E	F	G	H	I	J	K	L	M	N	O

DIRECTIONS: Each column of the left and right pages of the combination journal above is identified with a capital letter. Print the letter identifying the column of the combination journal in which each of the following items should be recorded. The first two answers are supplied as examples.

A cash sales transaction is recorded by writing the

	Answers	For Scoring
0. date in	*C*	**0.** ✓
0. debit amount in	*A*	**0.** ✓
14. credit amount in		**14.**
15. credit amount in		**15.**
16. check mark in (to show that no account title needs to be written)		**16.**
17. check mark in (to show that no individual amounts on this line need to be posted)		**17.**
18. cash register tape number in		**18.**

A cash received on account transaction is recorded by writing the

	Answers	For Scoring
19. date in		**19.**
20. debit amount in		**20.**
21. credit amount in		**21.**
22. customer name in		**22.**
23. receipt number in		**23.**

A sale on account transaction is recorded by writing the

	Answers	For Scoring
24. date in		**24.**
25. debit amount in		**25.**
26. credit amount in		**26.**
27. credit amount in		**27.**
28. customer name in		**28.**
29. sales invoice number in		**29.**

A credit card sales transaction is recorded by writing the

	Answers	For Scoring
30. date in		**30.**
31. debit amount in		**31.**
32. credit amount in		**32.**
33. credit amount in		**33.**
34. check mark in (to show that no account title needs to be written)		**34.**
35. check mark in (to show that no individual amounts on this line need to be posted)		**35.**
36. adding machine tape number in		**36.**

UNIT D — Analyzing Sales and Cash Receipts

DIRECTIONS: Place a check mark (✓) in the proper Answers column to show whether each of the following statements is true or false.

	Answers: True	Answers: False	For Scoring
0. Sales tax rates are usually stated as a percentage of sales	✓		**0.** ✓
37. A sale decreases the revenue of a business			**37.**
38. Accounts Receivable is an asset account with a credit balance			**38.**
39. The account Sales has a credit balance			**39.**
40. A sale on account is also known as a charge sale			**40.**
41. The total price of goods sold plus the sales tax collected is recorded as a credit to Sales			**41.**
42. A sales invoice is also known as a sales ticket			**42.**
43. The amount of sales tax collected is a liability			**43.**
44. A business that issues its own credit cards usually records credit card sales as regular charge sales			**44.**

Analyzing transactions into debit and credit parts

The solution to Drill 12-D1 is needed to complete Drill 12-D3.

1.

Cash	
1,680.00	

Sales	
	1,600.00

Sales Tax Payable	
	80.00

2.

3.

4.

5.

6.

7.

8.

Drills 12-D2 and 12-D3 begin on page 129. Use this page with page 130.

[1–4]

COMBINATION JOURNAL

PAGE

1	2					3	4
CASH		DATE	ACCOUNT TITLE	DOC. NO.	POST. REF.	GENERAL	
DEBIT	CREDIT					DEBIT	CREDIT

Name ______________________ Date ____________ Class ____________

DRILL 12-D 2, p. 223
[1, 2]

Analyzing the effect of sales transactions on accounts

Cash	
(1) 2,100.00	

Sales	
	(1) 2,000.00

Accounts Receivable	

Sales Tax Payable	
	(1) 100.00

Recording transactions using a combination journal

DRILL 12-D 3, p. 223

The solution to Drill12-D1 is needed to complete Drill 12-D3.

Transaction	Cash		Accounts Receivable		Sales Credit	Sales Tax Pay. Credit
	Debit	Credit	Debit	Credit		
1. Debit amount	√					
Credit amount					√	
Credit amount						√
2. Debit amount						
Credit amount						
Credit amount						
3. Debit amount						
Credit amount						
Credit amount						
4. Debit amount						
Credit amount						
5. Debit amount						
Credit amount						
6. Debit amount						
Credit amount						
Credit amount						
7. Debit amount						
Credit amount						
Credit amount						
8. Debit amount						
Credit amount						
Credit amount						

[1–4]

FOR MONTH OF 19 PAGE

5	6	7	8	9	10	11
ACCOUNTS RECEIVABLE		SALES CREDIT	SALES TAX PAYABLE CREDIT	ACCOUNTS PAYABLE		PURCHASES DEBIT
DEBIT	CREDIT			DEBIT	CREDIT	

Name ______________________ Date __________ Class __________ *MASTERY PROBLEM 12-M, concluded*

Begin this problem on pages 132 and 133. Use this page with page 134. **[4–8]**

FOR MONTH OF 19 PAGE

	5	6	7	8	9	10	11	
	ACCOUNTS RECEIVABLE		SALES CREDIT	SALES TAX PAYABLE CREDIT	ACCOUNTS PAYABLE		PURCHASES DEBIT	
	DEBIT	CREDIT			DEBIT	CREDIT		
1								1
2								2
3								3
4								4
5								5
6								6
7								7
8								8
9								9
10								10
11								11
12								12
13								13
14								14
15								15
16								16
17								17
18								18
19								19
20								20
21								21
22								22
23								23
24								24
25								25
26								26
27								27
28								28
29								29
30								30
31								31
32								32

Begin Mastery Problem 12-M on this page.

[1–3]

COMBINATION JOURNAL

PAGE

1	2					3	4
CASH						GENERAL	
DEBIT	CREDIT	DATE	ACCOUNT TITLE	DOC. NO.	POST. REF.	DEBIT	CREDIT

Use this page with page 132.

[1–3]

FOR MONTH OF 19 PAGE

	5	6	7	8	9	10	11	
	ACCOUNTS RECEIVABLE		SALES CREDIT	SALES TAX PAYABLE CREDIT	ACCOUNTS PAYABLE		PURCHASES DEBIT	
	DEBIT	CREDIT			DEBIT	CREDIT		
1								1
2								2
3								3
4								4
5								5
6								6
7								7
8								8
9								9
10								10
11								11
12								12
13								13
14								14
15								15
16								16
17								17
18								18
19								19
20								20
21								21
22								22
23								23
24								24
25								25
26								26
27								27
28								28
29								29
30								30
31								31
32								32

Use this page with page 131. Mastery Problem 12-M is needed to complete Mastery Problem 13-M. Your teacher will return Mastery Problem 12-M before it is needed in Mastery Problem 13-M.

[4–8]

PAGE

COMBINATION JOURNAL

1	2					3	4
CASH		DATE	ACCOUNT TITLE	DOC. NO.	POST. REF.	GENERAL	
DEBIT	CREDIT					DEBIT	CREDIT

Name ______________ Date __________ Class ________ *CHALLENGE PROBLEM 12-C, concluded*

[1, 2]

Begin this problem on pages 136 and 137. Use this page with page 138.

FOR MONTH OF 19 PAGE

	5	6	7	8	9	10	11	
	ACCOUNTS PAYABLE		ACCOUNTS RECEIVABLE		PURCHASES DEBIT	SALES CREDIT	SALES TAX PAYABLE CREDIT	
	DEBIT	CREDIT	DEBIT	CREDIT				
1								1
2								2
3								3
4								4
5								5
6								6
7								7
8								8
9								9
10								10
11								11
12								12
13								13
14								14
15								15
16								16
17								17
18								18
19								19
20								20
21								21
22								22
23								23
24								24
25								25
26								26
27								27
28								28
29								29
30								30
31								31
32								32

Journalizing transactions in a combination journal

Begin Challenge Problem 12-C on this page.

CHALLENGE PROBLEM 12-C, p. 226

[1, 2]

PAGE

COMBINATION JOURNAL

DATE	ACCOUNT TITLE	DOC. NO.	POST. REF.	1 GENERAL DEBIT	2 GENERAL CREDIT	3 CASH DEBIT	4 CASH CREDIT

Use this page with page 136.

[1, 2]

FOR MONTH OF 19 PAGE

	5	6	7	8	9	10	11	
	ACCOUNTS PAYABLE		ACCOUNTS RECEIVABLE		PURCHASES DEBIT	SALES CREDIT	SALES TAX PAYABLE CREDIT	
	DEBIT	CREDIT	DEBIT	CREDIT				
1								1
2								2
3								3
4								4
5								5
6								6
7								7
8								8
9								9
10								10
11								11
12								12
13								13
14								14
15								15
16								16
17								17
18								18
19								19
20								20
21								21
22								22
23								23
24								24
25								25
26								26
27								27
28								28
29								29
30								30
31								31
32								32

Use this page with page 135. Challenge Problem 12-C is needed to complete Challenge Problem 13-C. Your teacher will return Challenge Problem 12-C before it is needed in Challenge Problem 13-C.

CHALLENGE PROBLEM 12-C, concluded

[1, 2]

PAGE

COMBINATION JOURNAL

	DATE		ACCOUNT TITLE	DOC. NO.	POST. REF.	1 GENERAL DEBIT	2 GENERAL CREDIT	3 CASH DEBIT	4 CASH CREDIT	
1										1
2										2
3										3
4										4
5										5
6										6
7										7
8										8
9										9
10										10
11										11
12										12
13										13
14										14
15										15
16										16
17										17
18										18
19										19
20										20
21										21
22										22
23										23
24										24
25										25
26										26
27										27
28										28
29										29
30										30
31										31
32										32

Perfect Score. 31 Name ____________

Deduct.......... ___ Date ____________ Class ____________

Your Score .... ___ Checked by ____________

STUDY GUIDE 13

UNIT A — Accounting Terms

DIRECTIONS: Select the one term in Column I that best fits each definition in Column II. Print the letter identifying your choice in the Answers column.

Column I	*Column II*	Answers	For Scoring
A. accounts payable ledger	**0.** A ledger that is summarized in a single account in a general ledger	*G*	**0.** √
B. accounts receivable ledger	**1.** A listing of creditors' accounts, account balances, and total amount due all creditors		**1.**
C. controlling account	**2.** A ledger that contains all accounts needed to prepare an income statement and a balance sheet		**2.**
D. general ledger	**3.** A subsidiary ledger that contains only accounts with creditors		**3.**
E. schedule of accounts payable	**4.** An account in a general ledger that summarizes all the accounts in a subsidiary ledger		**4.**
F. schedule of accounts receivable	**5.** A listing of customers' accounts, account balances, and total amount due from all customers		**5.**
G. subsidiary ledger	**6.** A subsidiary ledger that contains only accounts with charge customers		**6.**

UNIT B — Analyzing a Combination Journal and Ledgers

DIRECTIONS: Place a check mark (√) in the proper Answers column to show whether each of the following statements is true or false.

	Answers: True	Answers: False	For Scoring
0. Transferring information from a journal to ledger accounts is known as journalizing		√	**0.** √
7. The total amount owed to all creditors is summarized in a single general ledger account			**7.**
8. A change in the balance of a customer's account also changes the balance of the controlling account, Accounts Receivable			**8.**
9. The heading of the balance column of an account in the accounts payable ledger is titled *Debit Balance*			**9.**
10. Each amount in the General Debit column of the combination journal is posted separately to an account in the general ledger			**10.**
11. The sum of the totals of all credit columns of a combination journal should equal the Cash Debit column total			**11.**
12. The cash on hand should be proved after the cash columns of the combination journal have been totaled at the end of the month			**12.**
13. Each cash payment to a creditor is posted as a credit to an account in the accounts payable ledger			**13.**
14. The sales account is the controlling account in the general ledger for the accounts receivable ledger			**14.**
15. Each amount in the combination journal Accounts Receivable columns is posted individually to an account in the accounts receivable ledger			**15.**

DIRECTIONS: For each item below, select the choice that best completes the sentence. Print the letter identifying your choice in the Answers column.

Question	Answers	For Scoring
0. The accounts receivable ledger contains an account for each **(A)** cash customer **(B)** charge customer **(C)** creditor	*B*	**0.** ✓
16. Each account in the subsidiary ledgers of Denim Threads has **(A)** two columns **(B)** three columns **(C)** four columns		**16.**
17. The total of the Accounts Payable Debit column of the combination journal is **(A)** posted each day **(B)** posted at the end of the month **(C)** not posted		**17.**
18. The individual amounts in the General Debit column of the combination journal are **(A)** posted separately **(B)** posted only as part of the column total **(C)** not posted		**18.**
19. Each account in the general ledger of Denim Threads has **(A)** two amount columns **(B)** three amount columns **(C)** four amount columns		**19.**
20. The total of the Cash Credit column of the combination journal is **(A)** posted daily **(B)** posted at the end of the month **(C)** not posted		**20.**
21. The accounts payable ledger contains an account for each **(A)** creditor **(B)** charge customer **(C)** cash customer		**21.**
22. Denim Threads arranges the accounts in its accounts payable ledger in **(A)** numeric order **(B)** geographic order **(C)** alphabetic order		**22.**
23. The total of the General Debit column of the combination journal is **(A)** posted daily **(B)** posted at the end of the month **(C)** not posted		**23.**
24. The individual amounts from the Accounts Receivable columns of the combination journal should be posted **(A)** monthly **(B)** weekly **(C)** daily		**24.**
25. The individual amounts in the Sales Credit column of the combination journal are **(A)** posted separately each week **(B)** posted separately each day **(C)** posted only as a part of the column total		**25.**
26. Denim Threads arranges the accounts in its accounts receivable ledger in **(A)** numeric order **(B)** geographic order **(C)** alphabetic order		**26.**
27. Each entry in the Accounts Payable Debit column of the combination journal is an amount that **(A)** is to be collected from a charge customer **(B)** has been paid to a creditor **(C)** has been collected from a charge customer		**27.**
28. The individual amounts in the Accounts Receivable Debit column of the combination journal are **(A)** posted separately to the general ledger **(B)** posted to the general ledger only as part of the column total **(C)** not posted to the general ledger		**28.**
29. The accounts payable ledger form with balance-column ruling is desirable because it shows **(A)** the account number of each creditor **(B)** the name and address of each new creditor **(C)** how much is owed to a creditor at any time		**29.**
30. Each entry in the Accounts Receivable Debit column of the combination journal is an amount that **(A)** is to be collected from a charge customer **(B)** has been paid to a creditor **(C)** has been collected from a charge customer		**30.**
31. The individual amounts from the Accounts Payable columns of the combination journal should be posted **(A)** monthly **(B)** weekly **(C)** daily		**31.**

Analyzing transactions of a merchandising business

The solution to Drill 13-D1 is needed to complete Drill 13-D2.

1.

Accounts Receivable	
84.00	

Sales	
	80.00

Sales Tax Payable	
	4.00

2.

Sales	
	2,000

tax	
	4.00

Cash	
2,100	

3.

Purchase	
350.00	

Accts. Pay.	
	350.00

4.

Purchase	
250.00	

Cash	
	250.00

5.

Cash	
	750.00

RENT EXPENSES	
750.00	

6.

Cash	
	40.00

Supplies	
40.00	

7.

Cash	
62.25	

Accts. Recievable	
	62.25

8.

Manson Drawing	
38.00	

Purchase Merchandise	
	38.00

9.

Accts. Payable	
200.00	

Cash	
	200.00

10.

Salary Expense	
900.00	

Rent Expense	
	900.00

11.

Accts. Payable	
	85.00

Supplies	
85.00	

12.

Benson Drawing	
300	

Cash	
	300

Recording and posting transactions of a merchandising business

DRILL 13-D 2, p. 253
[1]

The solution to Drill 13-D1 is needed to complete Drill 13-D2.

Transaction	Amount columns in the combination journal										
	Cash		General		Accts. Receivable		Sales Credit	Sales Tax Pay. Credit	Accts. Payable		Purch. Debit
	Debit	Credit	Debit	Credit	Debit	Credit			Debit	Credit	
1. Debit amount					√						
Credit amount							√				
Credit amount								√			
2. Debit amount											
Credit amount											
Credit amount											
3. Debit amount											
Credit amount											
4. Debit amount											
Credit amount											
5. Debit amount											
Credit amount											
6. Debit amount											
Credit amount											
7. Debit amount											
Credit amount											
8. Debit amount											
Credit amount											
9. Debit amount											
Credit amount											
10. Debit amount											
Credit amount											
11. Debit amount											
Credit amount											
12. Debit amount											
Credit amount											

[2]

Transaction	Posted separately to			Not Posted Separately to any ledger
	General Ledger	Accts. Rec. Ledger	Accts. Pay. Ledger	
1. Debit amount		√		
Credit amount				√
Credit amount				√
2. Debit amount				
Credit amount				
Credit amount				
3. Debit amount				
Credit amount				
4. Debit amount				
Credit amount				
5. Debit amount				
Credit amount				
6. Debit amount				
Credit amount				
7. Debit amount				
Credit amount				
8. Debit amount				
Credit amount				
9. Debit amount				
Credit amount				
10. Debit amount				
Credit amount				
11. Debit amount				
Credit amount				
12. Debit amount				
Credit amount				

PAGE 9

COMBINATION JOURNAL

Cash Debit (1)	Cash Credit (2)	Date	Account Title	Doc. No.	Post. Ref.	General Debit (3)	General Credit (4)
		19-- Nov. 1	Balance on hand, $4,600.00		✓		
	70000	1	Rent Expense	C120		70000	
	120000	1	Salary Expense	C121		120000	
26250		3	Adrian Leon	R160			
		3	Miranda Specialties	P70			
		4	Marsha Harris	S83			
189000		6	✓	T6	✓		
57750		6	✓	CT6	✓		
	66000	8	✓	C122	✓		
	43000	9	Smith Supply	C123			
		10	Helen Fields	S84			
21000		10	Carlos Mendez	R161			
		11	Supplies	M41		18000	
			Harrison Supplies				
220500		13	✓	T13	✓		
48300		13	✓	CT13	✓		
15750		15	Helen Fields	R162			
		17	Smith Supply	P71			
		18	Adrian Leon	S85			
204750		20	✓	T20	✓		
53550		20	✓	CT20	✓		
	56000	22	Miranda Specialties	C124			
	4500	23	Miscellaneous Expense	C125		4500	
		24	Supplies	M42		12000	
			Purchases				12000
236250		27	✓	T27	✓		
64050		27	✓	CT27	✓		
	3600	28	Credit Card Fee Expense	M43		3600	
		28	Mission Supply	P72			
69300		30	✓	T30	✓		
13650		30	✓	CT30	✓		
1220100	363100	30	Totals			228100	12000

FOR MONTH OF *November* 19-- PAGE *9*

	5	6	7	8	9	10	11	
	ACCOUNTS RECEIVABLE		SALES CREDIT	SALES TAX PAYABLE CREDIT	ACCOUNTS PAYABLE		PURCHASES DEBIT	
	DEBIT	CREDIT			DEBIT	CREDIT		
1								1
2								2
3								3
4		26250						4
5						36000	36000	5
6	5250		5000	250				6
7			180000	9000				7
8			55000	2750				8
9							66000	9
10					43000			10
11	8610		8200	410				11
12		21000						12
13								13
14						18000		14
15			210000	10500				15
16			46000	2300				16
17		15750						17
18						48000	48000	18
19	14700		14000	700				19
20			195000	9750				20
21			51000	2550				21
22					56000			22
23								23
24								24
25								25
26			225000	11250				26
27			61000	3050				27
28								28
29						28000	28000	29
30			66000	3300				30
31			13000	650				31
32	28560	63000	1129200	56460	99000	130000	178000	32
33								33

GENERAL LEDGER

ACCOUNT ACCOUNT NO. 11

DATE		ITEM	POST. REF.	DEBIT	CREDIT	BALANCE DEBIT	BALANCE CREDIT
1991 NOV	1	BALANCE	✓	4600 –		4600 –	

ACCOUNT ACCOUNTS RECEIVABLE ACCOUNT NO. 12

DATE		ITEM	POST. REF.	DEBIT	CREDIT	BALANCE DEBIT	BALANCE CREDIT
NOV	1	ACCOUNTS RECIEVABLE	✓			630 –	

ACCOUNT ACCOUNT NO. 13

DATE		ITEM	POST. REF.	DEBIT	CREDIT	BALANCE DEBIT	BALANCE CREDIT
NOV	1	MERCHANDISE INVENTORY	✓			83211 –	

ACCOUNT ACCOUNT NO. 14

DATE		ITEM	POST. REF.	DEBIT	CREDIT	BALANCE DEBIT	BALANCE CREDIT
NOV	1	SUPPLIES	✓			360 –	

ACCOUNT ACCOUNT NO. 15

DATE		ITEM	POST. REF.	DEBIT	CREDIT	BALANCE DEBIT	BALANCE CREDIT
NOV	1	PREPAID INSURANCE	✓			900 –	

Name ______________ Date ________ Class ________

GENERAL LEDGER

ACCOUNT ACCOUNT NO. 21

DATE		ITEM	POST. REF.	DEBIT	CREDIT	BALANCE DEBIT	BALANCE CREDIT
NOV	1	ACCOUNTS PAYABLE	✓				1 100 —

ACCOUNT ACCOUNT NO. 22

DATE		ITEM	POST. REF.	DEBIT	CREDIT	BALANCE DEBIT	BALANCE CREDIT
NOV	1	SALES TAX PAYABLE	✓				526 40

ACCOUNT ACCOUNT NO. 31

DATE		ITEM	POST. REF.	DEBIT	CREDIT	BALANCE DEBIT	BALANCE CREDIT
NOV	1	SHERRY MARSHALLS, CAPITAL					44 037 30

ACCOUNT ACCOUNT NO. 32

DATE		ITEM	POST. REF.	DEBIT	CREDIT	BALANCE DEBIT	BALANCE CREDIT
NOV	1	SHERRY MARSHALL, DRAWING	✓				

ACCOUNT ACCOUNT NO.

DATE		ITEM	POST. REF.	DEBIT	CREDIT	BALANCE DEBIT	BALANCE CREDIT
NOV	1	HAROLD STARK, CAPITAL	✓				40 037 30

GENERAL LEDGER

ACCOUNT　　　　　　　　　　　　　　　　　　ACCOUNT NO.

DATE	ITEM	POST. REF.	DEBIT	CREDIT	BALANCE	
					DEBIT	CREDIT

ACCOUNT　　　　　　　　　　　　　　　　　　ACCOUNT NO.

DATE	ITEM	POST. REF.	DEBIT	CREDIT	BALANCE	
					DEBIT	CREDIT

ACCOUNT　　　　　　　　　　　　　　　　　　ACCOUNT NO.

DATE	ITEM	POST. REF.	DEBIT	CREDIT	BALANCE	
					DEBIT	CREDIT

ACCOUNT　　　　　　　　　　　　　　　　　　ACCOUNT NO.

DATE	ITEM	POST. REF.	DEBIT	CREDIT	BALANCE	
					DEBIT	CREDIT

ACCOUNT　　　　　　　　　　　　　　　　　　ACCOUNT NO.

DATE	ITEM	POST. REF.	DEBIT	CREDIT	BALANCE	
					DEBIT	CREDIT

GENERAL LEDGER

ACCOUNT ACCOUNT NO.

DATE		ITEM	POST. REF.	DEBIT	CREDIT	BALANCE	
						DEBIT	CREDIT

ACCOUNT ACCOUNT NO.

DATE		ITEM	POST. REF.	DEBIT	CREDIT	BALANCE	
						DEBIT	CREDIT

ACCOUNT ACCOUNT NO.

DATE		ITEM	POST. REF.	DEBIT	CREDIT	BALANCE	
						DEBIT	CREDIT

ACCOUNT ACCOUNT NO.

DATE		ITEM	POST. REF.	DEBIT	CREDIT	BALANCE	
						DEBIT	CREDIT

ACCOUNT ACCOUNT NO.

DATE		ITEM	POST. REF.	DEBIT	CREDIT	BALANCE	
						DEBIT	CREDIT

ACCOUNTS PAYABLE LEDGER

NAME

ADDRESS

DATE		ITEM	POST. REF.	DEBIT	CREDIT	CREDIT BALANCE

NAME

ADDRESS

DATE		ITEM	POST. REF.	DEBIT	CREDIT	CREDIT BALANCE

NAME

ADDRESS

DATE		ITEM	POST. REF.	DEBIT	CREDIT	CREDIT BALANCE

NAME

ADDRESS

DATE		ITEM	POST. REF.	DEBIT	CREDIT	CREDIT BALANCE

ACCOUNTS RECEIVABLE LEDGER

NAME

ADDRESS

DATE		ITEM	POST. REF.	DEBIT	CREDIT	DEBIT BALANCE

NAME

ADDRESS

DATE		ITEM	POST. REF.	DEBIT	CREDIT	DEBIT BALANCE

NAME

ADDRESS

DATE		ITEM	POST. REF.	DEBIT	CREDIT	DEBIT BALANCE

NAME

ADDRESS

DATE		ITEM	POST. REF.	DEBIT	CREDIT	DEBIT BALANCE

[7]

[8]

Name ______________________ Date __________ Class __________

MASTERY PROBLEM 13-M, p. 255
[1, 2, 4, 5]

Posting to ledgers from a combination journal

The combination journal prepared in Mastery Problem 12-M is needed to complete Mastery Problem 13-M.

GENERAL LEDGER

ACCOUNT Cash — ACCOUNT NO. 11

DATE		ITEM	POST. REF.	DEBIT	CREDIT	BALANCE DEBIT	BALANCE CREDIT
19-- Dec.	1	Balance	✓			530000	

ACCOUNT Accounts Receivable — ACCOUNT NO. 12

DATE		ITEM	POST. REF.	DEBIT	CREDIT	BALANCE DEBIT	BALANCE CREDIT
19-- Dec.	1	Balance	✓			45365	

ACCOUNT Merchandise Inventory — ACCOUNT NO. 13

DATE		ITEM	POST. REF.	DEBIT	CREDIT	BALANCE DEBIT	BALANCE CREDIT
19-- Dec.	1	Balance	✓			11000000	

ACCOUNT Supplies — ACCOUNT NO. 14

DATE		ITEM	POST. REF.	DEBIT	CREDIT	BALANCE DEBIT	BALANCE CREDIT
19-- Dec.	1	Balance	✓			85000	

ACCOUNT Prepaid Insurance — ACCOUNT NO. 15

DATE		ITEM	POST. REF.	DEBIT	CREDIT	BALANCE DEBIT	BALANCE CREDIT
19-- Dec.	1	Balance	✓			140000	

ACCOUNT Accounts Payable — ACCOUNT NO. 21

DATE		ITEM	POST. REF.	DEBIT	CREDIT	BALANCE DEBIT	BALANCE CREDIT
19-- Dec.	1	Balance	✓				274500

GENERAL LEDGER

ACCOUNT Sales Tax Payable — ACCOUNT NO. 22

DATE		ITEM	POST. REF.	DEBIT	CREDIT	BALANCE DEBIT	BALANCE CREDIT
19-- Dec.	1	Balance	✓				1092 95

ACCOUNT Gloria Jackson, Capital — ACCOUNT NO. 31

DATE		ITEM	POST. REF.	DEBIT	CREDIT	BALANCE DEBIT	BALANCE CREDIT
19-- Dec.	1	Balance	✓				57082 85

ACCOUNT Gloria Jackson, Drawing — ACCOUNT NO. 32

DATE		ITEM	POST. REF.	DEBIT	CREDIT	BALANCE DEBIT	BALANCE CREDIT

ACCOUNT John Lyons, Capital — ACCOUNT NO. 33

DATE		ITEM	POST. REF.	DEBIT	CREDIT	BALANCE DEBIT	BALANCE CREDIT
19-- Dec.	1	Balance	✓				57082 85

ACCOUNT John Lyons, Drawing — ACCOUNT NO. 34

DATE		ITEM	POST. REF.	DEBIT	CREDIT	BALANCE DEBIT	BALANCE CREDIT

ACCOUNT Income Summary — ACCOUNT NO. 35

DATE		ITEM	POST. REF.	DEBIT	CREDIT	BALANCE DEBIT	BALANCE CREDIT

ACCOUNT Sales — ACCOUNT NO. 41

DATE		ITEM	POST. REF.	DEBIT	CREDIT	BALANCE DEBIT	BALANCE CREDIT

[1, 2, 4, 5]

GENERAL LEDGER

ACCOUNT Purchases ACCOUNT NO. 51

DATE		ITEM	POST. REF.	DEBIT	CREDIT	BALANCE DEBIT	BALANCE CREDIT

ACCOUNT Credit Card Fee Expense ACCOUNT NO. 61

DATE		ITEM	POST. REF.	DEBIT	CREDIT	BALANCE DEBIT	BALANCE CREDIT

ACCOUNT Insurance Expense ACCOUNT NO. 62

DATE		ITEM	POST. REF.	DEBIT	CREDIT	BALANCE DEBIT	BALANCE CREDIT

ACCOUNT Miscellaneous Expense ACCOUNT NO. 63

DATE		ITEM	POST. REF.	DEBIT	CREDIT	BALANCE DEBIT	BALANCE CREDIT

ACCOUNT Rent Expense ACCOUNT NO. 64

DATE		ITEM	POST. REF.	DEBIT	CREDIT	BALANCE DEBIT	BALANCE CREDIT

ACCOUNT Salary Expense ACCOUNT NO. 65

DATE		ITEM	POST. REF.	DEBIT	CREDIT	BALANCE DEBIT	BALANCE CREDIT

ACCOUNT Supplies Expense ACCOUNT NO. 66

DATE		ITEM	POST. REF.	DEBIT	CREDIT	BALANCE DEBIT	BALANCE CREDIT

[1, 4]

ACCOUNTS PAYABLE LEDGER

NAME Dannon, Inc.
ADDRESS 2640 Parker Avenue, Huron, SD 57350-1340

DATE		ITEM	POST. REF.	DEBIT	CREDIT	CREDIT BALANCE
19-- Dec.	1	Balance	✓			930 00

NAME Higgins Hardware
ADDRESS 2210 Harper Avenue, Yankton, SD 57078-6776

DATE		ITEM	POST. REF.	DEBIT	CREDIT	CREDIT BALANCE

NAME Jefferson Hardware
ADDRESS 940 Cherry Drive, Bismarck, ND 58501-4442

DATE		ITEM	POST. REF.	DEBIT	CREDIT	CREDIT BALANCE
19-- Dec.	1	Balance	✓			835 00

NAME Mason, Inc.
ADDRESS 640 High Street, Yankton, SD 57078-2977

DATE		ITEM	POST. REF.	DEBIT	CREDIT	CREDIT BALANCE

NAME Navarro Supply
ADDRESS 1160 West Bradley, Aberdeen, SD 57401-1425

DATE		ITEM	POST. REF.	DEBIT	CREDIT	CREDIT BALANCE

NAME Silva Company
ADDRESS 1460 Capital Street, Bismarck, ND 58501-4380

DATE		ITEM	POST. REF.	DEBIT	CREDIT	CREDIT BALANCE
19-- Dec.	1	Balance	✓			980 00

[1, 4]

ACCOUNTS RECEIVABLE LEDGER

NAME Lois Arnold

ADDRESS 840 Chester, Aberdeen, SD 57401-5330

DATE		ITEM	POST. REF.	DEBIT	CREDIT	DEBIT BALANCE
19-- Dec.	1	Balance	✓			26 25

NAME Donald Pearson

ADDRESS 627 Park Place, Aberdeen, SD 57401-4110

DATE		ITEM	POST. REF.	DEBIT	CREDIT	DEBIT BALANCE
19-- Dec.	1	Balance	✓			131 30

NAME Benjamin Preston

ADDRESS 1260 Harper Lane, Aberdeen, SD 57401-5840

DATE		ITEM	POST. REF.	DEBIT	CREDIT	DEBIT BALANCE
19-- Dec.	1	Balance	✓			84 00

NAME Marsha Rankin

ADDRESS 1120 Arnold Street, Aberdeen, SD 57401-5722

DATE		ITEM	POST. REF.	DEBIT	CREDIT	DEBIT BALANCE
19-- Dec.	1	Balance	✓			212 10

NAME Charles Tyler

ADDRESS 1340 University Avenue, Aberdeen, SD 57401-4958

DATE		ITEM	POST. REF.	DEBIT	CREDIT	DEBIT BALANCE

[4]

[4]

Name ______________________ Date __________ Class __________

CHALLENGE PROBLEM 13-C, p. 255
[1, 2, 4, 5]

Posting to ledgers from a combination journal

The combination journal prepared in Challenge Problem 12-C is needed to complete Challenge Problem 13-C.

GENERAL LEDGER

ACCOUNT Cash — ACCOUNT NO. 11

DATE		ITEM	POST. REF.	DEBIT	CREDIT	BALANCE DEBIT	BALANCE CREDIT
19-- Dec.	1	Balance	✓			530000	

ACCOUNT Accounts Receivable — ACCOUNT NO. 12

DATE		ITEM	POST. REF.	DEBIT	CREDIT	BALANCE DEBIT	BALANCE CREDIT
19-- Dec.	1	Balance	✓			45365	

ACCOUNT Merchandise Inventory — ACCOUNT NO. 13

DATE		ITEM	POST. REF.	DEBIT	CREDIT	BALANCE DEBIT	BALANCE CREDIT
19-- Dec.	1	Balance	✓			11000000	

ACCOUNT Supplies — ACCOUNT NO. 14

DATE		ITEM	POST. REF.	DEBIT	CREDIT	BALANCE DEBIT	BALANCE CREDIT
19-- Dec.	1	Balance	✓			85000	

ACCOUNT Prepaid Insurance — ACCOUNT NO. 15

DATE		ITEM	POST. REF.	DEBIT	CREDIT	BALANCE DEBIT	BALANCE CREDIT
19-- Dec.	1	Balance	✓			140000	

ACCOUNT Accounts Payable — ACCOUNT NO. 21

DATE		ITEM	POST. REF.	DEBIT	CREDIT	BALANCE DEBIT	BALANCE CREDIT
19-- Dec.	1	Balance	✓				274500

GENERAL LEDGER

ACCOUNT Sales Tax Payable — ACCOUNT NO. 22

DATE		ITEM	POST. REF.	DEBIT	CREDIT	BALANCE DEBIT	BALANCE CREDIT
19-- Dec.	1	Balance	✓				1092 95

ACCOUNT Gloria Jackson, Capital — ACCOUNT NO. 31

DATE		ITEM	POST. REF.	DEBIT	CREDIT	BALANCE DEBIT	BALANCE CREDIT
19-- Dec.	1	Balance	✓				57082 85

ACCOUNT Gloria Jackson, Drawing — ACCOUNT NO. 32

DATE		ITEM	POST. REF.	DEBIT	CREDIT	BALANCE DEBIT	BALANCE CREDIT

ACCOUNT John Lyons, Capital — ACCOUNT NO. 33

DATE		ITEM	POST. REF.	DEBIT	CREDIT	BALANCE DEBIT	BALANCE CREDIT
19-- Dec.	1	Balance	✓				57082 85

ACCOUNT John Lyons, Drawing — ACCOUNT NO. 34

DATE		ITEM	POST. REF.	DEBIT	CREDIT	BALANCE DEBIT	BALANCE CREDIT

ACCOUNT Income Summary — ACCOUNT NO. 35

DATE		ITEM	POST. REF.	DEBIT	CREDIT	BALANCE DEBIT	BALANCE CREDIT

ACCOUNT Sales — ACCOUNT NO. 41

DATE		ITEM	POST. REF.	DEBIT	CREDIT	BALANCE DEBIT	BALANCE CREDIT

GENERAL LEDGER

ACCOUNT *Purchases* ACCOUNT NO. *51*

DATE		ITEM	POST. REF.	DEBIT	CREDIT	BALANCE DEBIT	BALANCE CREDIT

ACCOUNT *Credit Card Fee Expense* ACCOUNT NO. *61*

DATE		ITEM	POST. REF.	DEBIT	CREDIT	BALANCE DEBIT	BALANCE CREDIT

ACCOUNT *Insurance Expense* ACCOUNT NO. *62*

DATE		ITEM	POST. REF.	DEBIT	CREDIT	BALANCE DEBIT	BALANCE CREDIT

ACCOUNT *Miscellaneous Expense* ACCOUNT NO. *63*

DATE		ITEM	POST. REF.	DEBIT	CREDIT	BALANCE DEBIT	BALANCE CREDIT

ACCOUNT *Rent Expense* ACCOUNT NO. *64*

DATE		ITEM	POST. REF.	DEBIT	CREDIT	BALANCE DEBIT	BALANCE CREDIT

ACCOUNT *Salary Expense* ACCOUNT NO. *65*

DATE		ITEM	POST. REF.	DEBIT	CREDIT	BALANCE DEBIT	BALANCE CREDIT

ACCOUNT *Supplies Expense* ACCOUNT NO. *66*

DATE		ITEM	POST. REF.	DEBIT	CREDIT	BALANCE DEBIT	BALANCE CREDIT

[1, 4]

ACCOUNTS PAYABLE LEDGER

NAME Dannon, Inc.
ADDRESS 2640 Parker Avenue, Huron, SD 57350-1340

DATE		ITEM	POST. REF.	DEBIT	CREDIT	CREDIT BALANCE
19-- Dec.	1	Balance	✓			93000

NAME Higgins Hardware
ADDRESS 2210 Harper Avenue, Yankton, SD 57078-6776

DATE		ITEM	POST. REF.	DEBIT	CREDIT	CREDIT BALANCE

NAME Jefferson Hardware
ADDRESS 940 Cherry Drive, Bismarck, ND 58501-4442

DATE		ITEM	POST. REF.	DEBIT	CREDIT	CREDIT BALANCE
19-- Dec.	1	Balance	✓			83500

NAME Mason, Inc.
ADDRESS 640 High Street, Yankton, SD 57078-2977

DATE		ITEM	POST. REF.	DEBIT	CREDIT	CREDIT BALANCE

NAME Navarro Supply
ADDRESS 1160 West Bradley, Aberdeen, SD 574[illegible]1-1425

DATE		ITEM	POST. REF.	DEBIT	CREDIT	CREDIT BALANCE

NAME Silva Company
ADDRESS 1460 Capital Street, Bismarck, ND 58501-4380

DATE		ITEM	POST. REF.	DEBIT	CREDIT	CREDIT BALANCE
19-- Dec.	1	Balance	✓			98000

[1, 4]

ACCOUNTS RECEIVABLE LEDGER

NAME Lois Arnold

ADDRESS 840 Chester, Aberdeen, SD 57401-5330

DATE		ITEM	POST. REF.	DEBIT	CREDIT	DEBIT BALANCE
19-- Dec.	1	Balance	✓			2625

NAME Donald Pearson

ADDRESS 627 Park Place, Aberdeen, SD 57401-4110

DATE		ITEM	POST. REF.	DEBIT	CREDIT	DEBIT BALANCE
19-- Dec.	1	Balance	✓			13130

NAME Benjamin Preston

ADDRESS 1260 Harper Lane, Aberdeen, SD 57401-5840

DATE		ITEM	POST. REF.	DEBIT	CREDIT	DEBIT BALANCE
19-- Dec.	1	Balance	✓			8400

NAME Marsha Rankin

ADDRESS 1120 Arnold Street, Aberdeen, SD 57401-5722

DATE		ITEM	POST. REF.	DEBIT	CREDIT	DEBIT BALANCE
19-- Dec.	1	Balance	✓			21210

NAME Charles Tyler

ADDRESS 1340 University Avenue, Aberdeen, SD 57401-4958

DATE		ITEM	POST. REF.	DEBIT	CREDIT	DEBIT BALANCE

[4]

[4]

Name ______________________ Date __________ Class __________

Begin this activity on pages 166 and 167. Use this page with page 168.

[1, 6–10]

FOR MONTH OF 19 PAGE

	5	6	7	8	9	10	11	
	ACCOUNTS RECEIVABLE		SALES CREDIT	SALES TAX PAYABLE CREDIT	ACCOUNTS PAYABLE		PURCHASES DEBIT	
	DEBIT	CREDIT			DEBIT	CREDIT		
1								1
2								2
3								3
4								4
5								5
6								6
7								7
8								8
9								9
10								10
11								11
12								12
13								13
14								14
15								15
16								16
17								17
18								18
19								19
20								20
21								21
22								22
23								23
24								24
25								25
26								26
27								27
28								28
29								29
30								30
31								31
32								32
33								33

Begin Reinforcement Activity 2 on this page.

REINFORCEMENT ACTIVITY 2
PART A – p. 256
[1, 5, 6, 8]

AN ACCOUNTING CYCLE FOR A PARTNERSHIP USING A COMBINATION JOURNAL

COMBINATION JOURNAL

PAGE

1	2					3	4
CASH		DATE	ACCOUNT TITLE	DOC. NO.	POST. REF.	GENERAL	
DEBIT	CREDIT					DEBIT	CREDIT

Name ______________________ Date __________ Class __________

Use this page with page 166.

REINFORCEMENT ACTIVITY 2
PART A – p. 256
[1, 5, 6, 8]

FOR MONTH OF 19 PAGE

	5	6	7	8	9	10	11	
	ACCOUNTS RECEIVABLE		SALES CREDIT	SALES TAX PAYABLE CREDIT	ACCOUNTS PAYABLE		PURCHASES DEBIT	
	DEBIT	CREDIT			DEBIT	CREDIT		
1								1
2								2
3								3
4								4
5								5
6								6
7								7
8								8
9								9
10								10
11								11
12								12
13								13
14								14
15								15
16								16
17								17
18								18
19								19
20								20
21								21
22								22
23								23
24								24
25								25
26								26
27								27
28								28
29								29
30								30
31								31
32								32

Use this page with page 165.

[1, 6–10]

PAGE

COMBINATION JOURNAL

1	2					3	4
CASH		DATE	ACCOUNT TITLE	DOC. NO.	POST. REF.	GENERAL	
DEBIT	CREDIT					DEBIT	CREDIT

Name ______________________ Date __________ Class __________

The ledgers used in Reinforcement Activity 2, Part A, will be needed to complete Part B.

GENERAL LEDGER

ACCOUNT ACCOUNT NO.

DATE		ITEM	POST. REF.	DEBIT	CREDIT	BALANCE	
						DEBIT	CREDIT

ACCOUNT ACCOUNT NO.

DATE		ITEM	POST. REF.	DEBIT	CREDIT	BALANCE	
						DEBIT	CREDIT

ACCOUNT ACCOUNT NO.

DATE		ITEM	POST. REF.	DEBIT	CREDIT	BALANCE	
						DEBIT	CREDIT

ACCOUNT ACCOUNT NO.

DATE		ITEM	POST. REF.	DEBIT	CREDIT	BALANCE	
						DEBIT	CREDIT

GENERAL LEDGER

ACCOUNT ACCOUNT NO.

DATE		ITEM	POST. REF.	DEBIT	CREDIT	BALANCE DEBIT	BALANCE CREDIT

ACCOUNT ACCOUNT NO.

DATE		ITEM	POST. REF.	DEBIT	CREDIT	BALANCE DEBIT	BALANCE CREDIT

ACCOUNT ACCOUNT NO.

DATE		ITEM	POST. REF.	DEBIT	CREDIT	BALANCE DEBIT	BALANCE CREDIT

ACCOUNT ACCOUNT NO.

DATE		ITEM	POST. REF.	DEBIT	CREDIT	BALANCE DEBIT	BALANCE CREDIT

GENERAL LEDGER

ACCOUNT ACCOUNT NO.

DATE		ITEM	POST. REF.	DEBIT	CREDIT	BALANCE	
						DEBIT	CREDIT

ACCOUNT ACCOUNT NO.

DATE		ITEM	POST. REF.	DEBIT	CREDIT	BALANCE	
						DEBIT	CREDIT

ACCOUNT ACCOUNT NO.

DATE		ITEM	POST. REF.	DEBIT	CREDIT	BALANCE	
						DEBIT	CREDIT

ACCOUNT ACCOUNT NO.

DATE		ITEM	POST. REF.	DEBIT	CREDIT	BALANCE	
						DEBIT	CREDIT

GENERAL LEDGER

ACCOUNT ACCOUNT NO.

DATE		ITEM	POST. REF.	DEBIT	CREDIT	BALANCE	
						DEBIT	CREDIT

ACCOUNT ACCOUNT NO.

DATE		ITEM	POST. REF.	DEBIT	CREDIT	BALANCE	
						DEBIT	CREDIT

ACCOUNT ACCOUNT NO.

DATE		ITEM	POST. REF.	DEBIT	CREDIT	BALANCE	
						DEBIT	CREDIT

ACCOUNT ACCOUNT NO.

DATE		ITEM	POST. REF.	DEBIT	CREDIT	BALANCE	
						DEBIT	CREDIT

GENERAL LEDGER

ACCOUNT ACCOUNT NO.

DATE		ITEM	POST. REF.	DEBIT	CREDIT	BALANCE DEBIT	BALANCE CREDIT

ACCOUNT ACCOUNT NO.

DATE		ITEM	POST. REF.	DEBIT	CREDIT	BALANCE DEBIT	BALANCE CREDIT

ACCOUNT ACCOUNT NO.

DATE		ITEM	POST. REF.	DEBIT	CREDIT	BALANCE DEBIT	BALANCE CREDIT

ACCOUNT ACCOUNT NO.

DATE		ITEM	POST. REF.	DEBIT	CREDIT	BALANCE DEBIT	BALANCE CREDIT

ACCOUNTS RECEIVABLE LEDGER

NAME

ADDRESS

DATE		ITEM	POST. REF.	DEBIT	CREDIT	DEBIT BALANCE

NAME

ADDRESS

DATE		ITEM	POST. REF.	DEBIT	CREDIT	DEBIT BALANCE

NAME

ADDRESS

DATE		ITEM	POST. REF.	DEBIT	CREDIT	DEBIT BALANCE

NAME

ADDRESS

DATE		ITEM	POST. REF.	DEBIT	CREDIT	DEBIT BALANCE

[3, 6, 10]

ACCOUNTS RECEIVABLE LEDGER

NAME

ADDRESS

DATE		ITEM	POST. REF.	DEBIT	CREDIT	DEBIT BALANCE

NAME

ADDRESS

DATE		ITEM	POST. REF.	DEBIT	CREDIT	DEBIT BALANCE

ACCOUNTS PAYABLE LEDGER

[4, 6, 10]

NAME

ADDRESS

DATE		ITEM	POST. REF.	DEBIT	CREDIT	CREDIT BALANCE

NAME

ADDRESS

DATE		ITEM	POST. REF.	DEBIT	CREDIT	CREDIT BALANCE

ACCOUNTS PAYABLE LEDGER

NAME
ADDRESS

DATE		ITEM	POST. REF.	DEBIT	CREDIT	CREDIT BALANCE

NAME
ADDRESS

DATE		ITEM	POST. REF.	DEBIT	CREDIT	CREDIT BALANCE

NAME
ADDRESS

DATE		ITEM	POST. REF.	DEBIT	CREDIT	CREDIT BALANCE

NAME
ADDRESS

DATE		ITEM	POST. REF.	DEBIT	CREDIT	CREDIT BALANCE

[6]

[12]

Perfect Score. 40 Name ______________________

Deduct......... ___ Date ______________ Class ______________

Your Score.... ___ Checked by ______________________

STUDY GUIDE 14

UNIT A — Accounting Terms

DIRECTIONS: Select the one term in Column I that best fits each definition in Column II. Print the letter identifying your choice in the Answers column.

Column I

- **A.** adjusting entries
- **B.** adjustments
- **C.** cost of merchandise sold
- **D.** inventory
- **E.** merchandise inventory
- **F.** prepaid expenses
- **G.** work sheet

Column II	Answers	For Scoring
0. Analysis paper on which the financial condition of a business is summarized..	*G*	**0.** ✓
1. Journal entries made to bring general ledger accounts up to date...		**1.**
2. An itemized list showing the value of goods on hand.........		**2.**
3. Changes recorded to update ledger account balances at the end of a fiscal period..		**3.**
4. An itemized list showing the value of goods on hand for sale to customers		**4.**
5. The total original purchase price of all merchandise sold during a fiscal period..		**5.**
6. Amounts paid in advance for supplies to be used later and for services to be received		**6.**

UNIT B — Format of Eight-Column Work Sheet

DIRECTIONS: Each part and column of the eight-column work sheet form below is identified by a capital letter. Answer each question below the illustration by printing the identifying capital letter in the Answers column.

	A B C								
	D	E		F		G		H	
		DEBIT	CREDIT	DEBIT	CREDIT	DEBIT	CREDIT	DEBIT	CREDIT
1									
2									

Which capital letter on the work sheet represents the position for writing the column heading for:

	Answers	For Scoring
0. Adjustments?..................	*F*	**0.** ✓
7. Balance Sheet?................		**7.**
8. Account Title?		**8.**
9. Trial Balance?..................		**9.**
10. Income Statement?		**10.**

Which capital letter on the work sheet represents the position for writing the:

	Answers	For Scoring
11. Name of the business?.......		**11.**
12. Date for which the work sheet is prepared?............		**12.**
13. Words *Work Sheet*?..........		**13.**
14. Length of the fiscal period?.		**14.**

UNIT C — Eight-Column Work Sheet Extensions

DIRECTIONS: For each account listed below, place a check mark (√) in the column(s) to which amounts are extended on a work sheet.

	Income Statement		Balance Sheet		For Scoring
	Debit	Credit	Debit	Credit	
0. Cash			√		**0.** √
15. Accounts Receivable					**15.**
16. Merchandise Inventory					**16.**
17. Supplies					**17.**
18. Prepaid Insurance					**18.**
19. Accounts Payable					**19.**
20. Sales Tax Payable					**20.**
21. Ada Blanco, Capital					**21.**
22. Ada Blanco, Drawing					**22.**
23. Luis Cruz, Capital					**23.**
24. Luis Cruz, Drawing					**24.**
25. Income Summary					**25.**
26. Sales					**26.**
27. Purchases					**27.**
28. Credit Card Fee Expense					**28.**
29. Delivery Expense					**29.**
30. Insurance Expense					**30.**
31. Miscellaneous Expense					**31.**
32. Rent Expense					**32.**
33. Salary Expense					**33.**
34. Supplies Expense					**34.**

UNIT D — Analyzing Adjustments on a Work Sheet

DIRECTIONS: For each item below, select the choice that best completes the sentence. Print the letter identifying your choice in the Answers column.

	Answers	For Scoring
0. The Merchandise Inventory amount in a work sheet's Trial Balance Debit column represents the value of merchandise (A) at the end of a fiscal period (B) sold during a fiscal period (C) at the beginning of a fiscal period (D) purchased during a fiscal period	*C*	**0.** √
35. The Supplies amount in a work sheet's Trial Balance Debit column represents the cost of supplies (A) available during a fiscal period (B) used during a fiscal period (C) bought during a fiscal period (D) at the beginning of a fiscal period		**35.**
36. The two accounts used in adjusting supplies are (A) Supplies and Supplies Expense (B) Income Summary and Supplies (C) Income Summary and Supplies Expense (D) Merchandise Inventory and Supplies		**36.**
37. Supplies used during a fiscal period are classified as (A) capital (B) an expense (C) a liability (D) an asset		**37.**
38. The portion of the insurance premiums that has expired during a fiscal period is classified as (A) capital (B) a liability (C) an expense (D) an asset		**38.**
39. The Merchandise Inventory amount extended to a work sheet's Balance Sheet Debit column represents the value of merchandise (A) on hand at the end of a fiscal period (B) sold during a fiscal period (C) purchased during a fiscal period (D) on hand at the beginning of a fiscal period		**39.**
40. The Supplies Expense amount extended to a work sheet's Income Statement Debit column represents the value of supplies (A) at the end of a fiscal period (B) used during a fiscal period (C) available during a fiscal period (D) bought during a fiscal period		**40.**

Name ______________________ Date __________ Class __________

Adjusting the merchandise inventory, supplies, and prepaid insurance accounts

1	2	3	4	5
Business	Adjustment Number	Accounts Affected	Adjustment Column	
			Debit	Credit
A	1	*Income Summary*	*$48,500.00*	
		Merchandise Inventory		*$48,500.00*
	2			
	3			
	4			
B	1			
	2			
	3			
	4			
C	1			
	2			
	3			
	4			

Extending balance sheet and income statement items [1–3]

Jacobs & Nelson Company
Work Sheet
For Month Ended November 30, 19--

	ACCOUNT TITLE	1 TRIAL BALANCE DEBIT	2 TRIAL BALANCE CREDIT	3 ADJUSTMENTS DEBIT	4 ADJUSTMENTS CREDIT	5 INCOME STATEMENT DEBIT	6 INCOME STATEMENT CREDIT	7 BALANCE SHEET DEBIT	8 BALANCE SHEET CREDIT	
1	Cash	964000								1
2	Accounts Receivable	82000								2
3	Merchandise Inventory	8200000		(b) 8000000	(a) 8200000					3
4	Supplies	61000			(c) 18000					4
5	Prepaid Insurance	98000			(d) 8500					5
6	Accounts Payable		312000							6
7	Sales Tax Payable		72000							7
8	J.B. Jacobs, Capital		4169000							8
9	J.B. Jacobs, Drawing	50000								9
10	S.K. Nelson, Capital		4169000							10
11	S.K. Nelson, Drawing	50000								11
12	Income Summary			(a) 8200000	(b) 8000000					12
13	Sales		1420000							13
14	Purchases	410000								14
15	Credit Card Fee Expense	16000								15
16	Insurance Expense			(d) 8500						16
17	Miscellaneous Expense	11000								17
18	Rent Expense	70000								18
19	Salary Expense	130000								19
20	Supplies Expense			(c) 18000						20
21		10142000	10142000	16226500	16226500					21
22										22
23										23
24										24
25										25

Preparing a work sheet [1–7]

The solution to problem 14-1 is needed to complete Problems 15-1 and 16-1.

Downtown Sporting Goods
Work Sheet
For Month Ended December 31, 19--

	ACCOUNT TITLE	1 TRIAL BALANCE DEBIT	2 TRIAL BALANCE CREDIT	3 ADJUSTMENTS DEBIT	4 ADJUSTMENTS CREDIT	5 INCOME STATEMENT DEBIT	6 INCOME STATEMENT CREDIT	7 BALANCE SHEET DEBIT	8 BALANCE SHEET CREDIT	
1	Cash									1
2	Accounts Receivable									2
3	Merchandise Inventory									3
4	Supplies									4
5	Prepaid Insurance									5
6	Accounts Payable									6
7	Sales Tax Payable									7
8	Eileen Brandon, Capital									8
9	Eileen Brandon, Drawing									9
10	Diane Baxter, Capital									10
11	Diane Baxter, Drawing									11
12	Income Summary									12
13	Sales									13
14	Purchases									14
15	Credit Card Fee Expense									15
16	Insurance Expense									16
17	Miscellaneous Expense									17
18	Rent Expense									18
19	Salary Expense									19
20	Supplies Expense									20
21										21
22										22
23										23
24										24
25										25

Preparing a work sheet

Quality Office Supply
Work Sheet
For Month Ended December 31, 19--

	ACCOUNT TITLE	TRIAL BALANCE DEBIT (1)	TRIAL BALANCE CREDIT (2)	ADJUSTMENTS DEBIT (3)	ADJUSTMENTS CREDIT (4)	INCOME STATEMENT DEBIT (5)	INCOME STATEMENT CREDIT (6)	BALANCE SHEET DEBIT (7)	BALANCE SHEET CREDIT (8)	
1	Cash	935000								1
2	Accounts Receivable	96000								2
3	Merchandise Inventory	8630000								3
4	Supplies	67000								4
5	Prepaid Insurance	84000								5
6	Accounts Payable		640000							6
7	Sales Tax Payable		86500							7
8	Alice Brown, Capital		4302500							8
9	Alice Brown, Drawing	75000								9
10	Harold Brown, Capital		3960000							10
11	Harold Brown, Drawing	70000								11
12	Income Summary									12
13	Sales		1730000							13
14	Purchases	432000								14
15	Credit Card Fee Expense	38000								15
16	Insurance Expense									16
17	Miscellaneous Expense	13000								17
18	Rent Expense	125000								18
19	Salary Expense	154000								19
20	Supplies Expense									20
21		10719000	10719000							21
22										22
23										23
24										24
25										25

Preparing a work sheet

Value Appliances
Work Sheet
For Month Ended October 31, 19--

	ACCOUNT TITLE	1 TRIAL BALANCE DEBIT	2 TRIAL BALANCE CREDIT	3 ADJUSTMENTS DEBIT	4 ADJUSTMENTS CREDIT	5 INCOME STATEMENT DEBIT	6 INCOME STATEMENT CREDIT	7 BALANCE SHEET DEBIT	8 BALANCE SHEET CREDIT	
1	Cash	1040000								1
2	Accounts Receivable	192000								2
3	Merchandise Inventory	12000000								3
4	Supplies	86000								4
5	Prepaid Insurance	52000								5
6	Accounts Payable		623000							6
7	Sales Tax Payable		91500							7
8	C.K. Fields, Capital		6380000							8
9	C.K. Fields, Drawing	100000								9
10	John Miller, Capital		6565000							10
11	John Miller, Drawing	90000								11
12	Income Summary									12
13	Sales		1830000							13
14	Purchases	1620000								14
15	Credit Card Fee Expense	34000								15
16	Delivery Expense	19000								16
17	Insurance Expense									17
18	Miscellaneous Expense	6500								18
19	Rent Expense	100000								19
20	Salary Expense	150000								20
21	Supplies Expense									21
22		154 89500	154 89500							22
23										23
24										24
25										25

C & B Hardware
Work Sheet
For Month Ended January 31, 19--

	ACCOUNT TITLE	TRIAL BALANCE (1) DEBIT	TRIAL BALANCE (2) CREDIT	ADJUSTMENTS (3) DEBIT	ADJUSTMENTS (4) CREDIT	INCOME STATEMENT (5) DEBIT	INCOME STATEMENT (6) CREDIT	BALANCE SHEET (7) DEBIT	BALANCE SHEET (8) CREDIT	
1	Cash	8830 00								1
2	Accounts Receivable	960 00								2
3	Merchandise Inventory	93500 00								3
4	Supplies	480 00								4
5	Prepaid Insurance	930 00								5
6	Accounts Payable		4120 00							6
7	Sales Tax Payable		560 00							7
8	Carmen Lopez, Capital		49700 00							8
9	Carmen Lopez, Drawing	800 00								9
10	Janet Carter, Capital		48610 00							10
11	Janet Carter, Drawing	850 00								11
12	Income Summary									12
13	Sales		10200 00							13
14	Purchases	2800 00								14
15	Credit Card Fee Expense	230 00								15
16	Insurance Expense									16
17	Miscellaneous Expense	60 00								17
18	Rent Expense	950 00								18
19	Salary Expense	2800 00								19
20	Supplies Expense									20
21		113190 00	113190 00							21
22										22
23										23
24										24
25										25

Perfect Score. 54 Name ____________________

Deduct........ ___ Date ____________ Class ____________

Your Score.... ___ Checked by ____________________

UNIT A — Accounting Terms

DIRECTIONS: Select the one term in Column I that best fits each definition in Column II. Print the letter identifying your choice in the Answers column.

Column I

A. account form of balance sheet
B. capital statement
C. cycle billing
D. distribution of net income statement
E. gross profit on sales
F. report form of balance sheet
G. statement of account
H. supporting schedule

Column II	Answers	For Scoring
0. A financial statement that summarizes the changes in capital during a fiscal period	*B*	**0.** ✓
1. A business form showing the charges, receipts, and balance of a customer's account		**1.**
2. The revenue remaining after cost of merchandise sold has been deducted		**2.**
3. Preparing and mailing statements of account to customers on different days of each month		**3.**
4. A partnership financial statement showing net income or loss distribution to partners		**4.**
5. A balance sheet listing the assets, liabilities, and capital vertically		**5.**
6. A report prepared to give details about an item on a principal financial statement		**6.**
7. A balance sheet listing assets on the left and equities on the right		**7.**

UNIT B — Classifying Accounts

DIRECTIONS: Decide the classification for each item below. Print the letter(s) identifying your choice in the Answers columns.

Account Classifications

A — Assets
C — Capital
L — Liabilities
E — Expense
R — Revenue
CM — Cost of Merchandise
N — Not an account

	Answers	For Scoring
0. Accounts Payable	*L*	**0.** ✓
8. Cash		**8.**
9. Credit Card Fee Expense		**9.**
10. Accounts Receivable		**10.**
11. Gross Profit		**11.**
12. Purchases		**12.**
13. Sales		**13.**
14. Supplies		**14.**
15. Eva Burgos, Capital		**15.**
16. Eva Burgos, Drawing		**16.**
17. Delivery Expense		**17.**
18. Revenue		**18.**
19. Supplies Expense		**19.**

	Answers	For Scoring
20. Salary Expense		**20.**
21. Merchandise Inventory		**21.**
22. Miscellaneous Expense		**22.**
23. Net Income		**23.**
24. Income Summary		**24.**
25. Rent Expense		**25.**
26. Luis Perez, Capital		**26.**
27. Luis Perez, Drawing		**27.**
28. Insurance Expense		**28.**
29. Cost of Merchandise Sold		**29.**
30. Sales Tax Payable		**30.**
31. Prepaid Insurance		**31.**
32. Share of Net Income		**32.**

DIRECTIONS: Place a check mark (√) in the proper Answers column to show whether each of the following statements is true or false.

	Answers True	Answers False	For Scoring
0. The share of net income for each partner may not necessarily be the same	√		**0.** √
33. An income statement for a merchandising business has three main sections......			**33.**
34. The primary purpose for keeping financial records is to report the financial progress and condition of a business			**34.**
35. A separate statement may be prepared to show the distribution of net income to the partners			**35.**
36. A financial statement that reports changes in capital is sometimes known as a supporting schedule........			**36.**
37. The data for the revenue section of the income statement are obtained from a work sheet's Income Statement Debit column........			**37.**
38. Partners' salaries are listed in the Operating Expenses section of an income statement........			**38.**
39. Data for the cost of merchandise sold section of an income statement are obtained from a work sheet's Trial Balance columns			**39.**
40. Net income is shown on the bottom line of a balance sheet........			**40.**
41. Each partner's withdrawals are shown on an income statement........			**41.**
42. The distribution of net income statement indicates the present capital of each partner........			**42.**
43. If the total amount of assets, revenue, and capital on a balance sheet are the same, the balance sheet is assumed to be correct........			**43.**
44. The cost of merchandise sold is determined by adding the value of the ending merchandise inventory to the amount of the purchases for the fiscal period			**44.**
45. Data needed to prepare the liabilities section of a balance sheet are obtained from a work sheet's Balance Sheet Credit column			**45.**
46. Data needed to prepare the assets section of a balance sheet are obtained from a work sheet's Balance Sheet Credit column........			**46.**
47. Total expenses on an income statement are deducted from the cost of merchandise sold to find the net income			**47.**
48. A net decrease in capital occurs when net income for the fiscal period is greater than withdrawals of cash and merchandise by owners			**48.**
49. If gross profit on sales is greater than total expenses, the difference is net income			**49.**
50. The capital of a business is affected when a business earns an income or incurs a loss from its operation			**50.**
51. Revenue less cost of merchandise sold equals net income			**51.**
52. Changes in the amount of capital occur when a business uses cash to purchase new equipment			**52.**
53. If the debit side of the Income Statement columns on a work sheet is greater than the credit side, a net loss has been incurred			**53.**
54. The information on a capital statement may be included as part of a balance sheet........			**54.**

Figuring the cost of merchandise sold

WORK SHEET DATA	Income Statement		Cost of Merchandise Sold
	Debit	Credit	
Business 1:			
Purchases	$ 4,600.00		
Income Summary	62,000.00	$64,000.00	________
Business 2:			
Purchases	$ 3,980.00		
Income Summary	74,000.00	$72,000.00	________
Business 3:			
Purchases	$ 4,350.00		
Income Summary	68,000.00	$66,350.00	________

Figuring the net income or loss — DRILL 15-D 2, p. 296

Business	Account Title	Income Statement		Net Income (+) or Net Loss (−)
		Debit	Credit	
1	Income Summary	$54,000.00	$52,500.00	
	Sales		14,100.00	
	Purchases	3,600.00		
	Total Expenses	1,800.00		________
2	Income Summary	$36,200.00	$33,900.00	
	Sales		10,200.00	
	Purchases	9,850.00		
	Total Expenses	4,730.00		________
3	Income Summary	$44,200.00	$46,400.00	
	Sales		12,400.00	
	Purchases	3,200.00		
	Total Expenses	1,400.00		________

Figuring the distribution of net income or loss

DRILL 15-D 3, p. 297
[1, 2]

Business	Partner	Agreement on sharing of net income or loss	[1] $15,000.00 net income	[2] $8,000.00 net loss
1	A	50% of income or loss		
	B	50% of income or loss		
2	A	60% of income or loss		
	B	40% of income or loss		
3	A	40% of income or loss		
	B	30% of income or loss		
	C	30% of income or loss		

Extra form

Name ____________________ Date __________ Class __________

[1]

Preparing financial statements

The work sheet completed in Problem 14-1 is needed to complete Problem 15-1.

[2]

[3]

[4]

The solution to Problem 15-1 is needed to complete Problem 16-1.

Name ______________________ Date __________ Class __________

PROBLEM 15-2, p. 297

Preparing a distribution of net income statement and capital statement

[1]

[2]

[3]

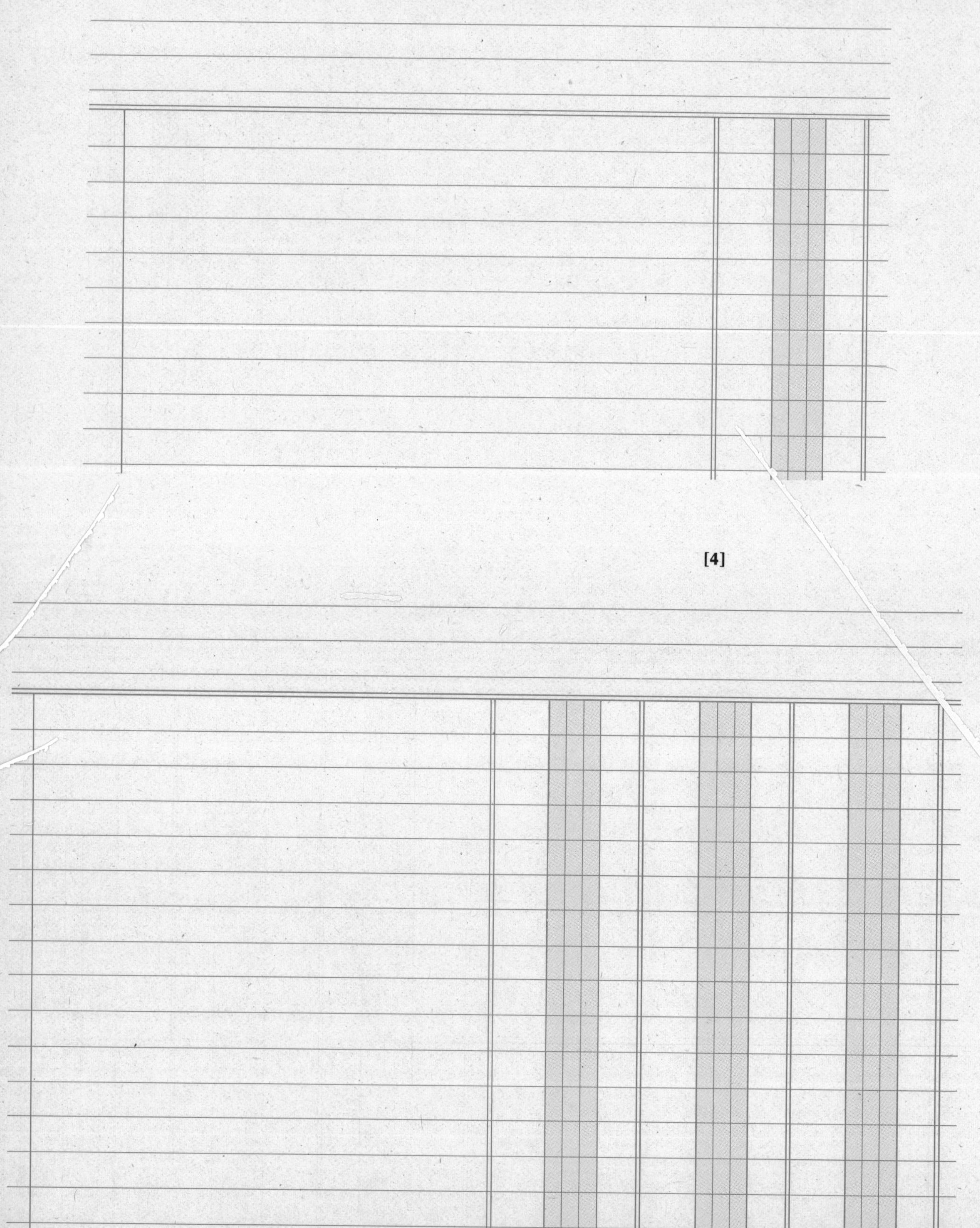

[4]

Preparing a work sheet and financial statements

[1]

Household Furniture
Work Sheet
For Month Ended December 31, 19--

	ACCOUNT TITLE	TRIAL BALANCE DEBIT (1)	TRIAL BALANCE CREDIT (2)	ADJUSTMENTS DEBIT (3)	ADJUSTMENTS CREDIT (4)	INCOME STATEMENT DEBIT (5)	INCOME STATEMENT CREDIT (6)	BALANCE SHEET DEBIT (7)	BALANCE SHEET CREDIT (8)	
1	Cash	9800 00								1
2	Accounts Receivable	1100 00								2
3	Merchandise Inventory	115000 00								3
4	Supplies	460 00								4
5	Prepaid Insurance	730 00								5
6	Accounts Payable		6120 00							6
7	Sales Tax Payable		748 00							7
8	Frank Garcia, Capital		56800 00							8
9	Frank Garcia, Drawing	950 00								9
10	James Allen, Capital		57403 00							10
11	James Allen, Drawing	875 00								11
12	Income Summary									12
13	Sales		18700 00							13
14	Purchases	7200 00								14
15	Credit Card Fee Expense	420 00								15
16	Delivery Expense	250 00								16
17	Insurance Expense									17
18	Miscellaneous Expense	86 00								18
19	Rent Expense	1100 00								19
20	Salary Expense	1800 00								20
21	Supplies Expense									21
22		139771 00	139771 00							22
23										23
24										24
25										25

The work sheet prepared for Mastery Problem 15-M is needed to complete Challenge Problem 15-C.

[2]

[3]

[4]

[5]

Preparing financial statements (unequal distribution of net income; additional investment)

CHALLENGE PROBLEM 15-C, p. 298

The work sheet completed for Mastery Problem 15-M is needed to complete Challenge Problem 15-C.

[1]

[2]

Perfect Score. 47 Name ____________

Deduct.......... ___ Date ____________ Class ____________

Your Score.... ___ Checked by ____________

UNIT A — Analyzing Adjusting Entries and Closing Entries

DIRECTIONS: For each transaction below, print in the proper Answers column the identifying capital letters of the accounts to be debited and credited. Select the capital letters from the list at the left.

A. Eva Burgos, Capital
B. Eva Burgos, Drawing
C. Income Summary
D. Insurance Expense
E. Merchandise Inventory
F. Luis Perez, Capital
G. Luis Perez, Drawing
H. Prepaid Insurance
I. Purchases
J. Sales
K. Supplies
L. Supplies Expense

	Answers Debit	Answers Credit	For Scoring Debit	For Scoring Credit
0–0. Make the adjustment for beginning merchandise inventory..................	*C*	*E*	**0.** ✓	**0.** ✓
1–2. Record ending merchandise inventory			**1.**	**2.**
3–4. Adjust the supplies account............			**3.**	**4.**
5–6. Adjust the prepaid insurance account.			**5.**	**6.**
7–8. Close the sales account			**7.**	**8.**
9–10. Close the purchases account			**9.**	**10.**
11–12. Close the insurance expense account .			**11.**	**12.**
13–14. Close the supplies expense account ...			**13.**	**14.**
15–16. Close the income summary account (net income balance).....................			**15.**	**16.**
17–18. Close the income summary account (net loss balance)			**17.**	**18.**
19–20. Close the partners' drawing accounts.			**19.**	**20.**

UNIT B — Analyzing Adjusting Entries and Closing Entries

DIRECTIONS: Place a check mark (√) in the proper Answers column to show whether each of the following statements is true or false.

	Answers True	Answers False	For Scoring
0. When a four-column general ledger account is closed, a line is drawn in both the Debit and Credit Balance columns	√		**0.** ✓
21. Transfers of amounts from one ledger account to another should be made only by posting journal entries..................			**21.**
22. In figuring cost of merchandise sold, the ending merchandise inventory is deducted from the merchandise available for sale			**22.**
23. After all adjusting entries are posted, the beginning merchandise inventory amount appears on the income summary account's credit side			**23.**
24. A work sheet's income statement columns contain the data for journalizing the adjusting entries..................			**24.**
25. After posting the beginning merchandise inventory adjusting entry, the merchandise inventory account has a zero balance..................			**25.**
26. Revenue accounts are closed to the debit side of the income summary account .			**26.**
27. After all closing entries are posted, the income statement accounts are the only general ledger accounts that have balances..................			**27.**
28. The income summary account is closed to the drawing accounts			**28.**
29. The purpose of the post-closing trial balance is to prove the general ledger equality of debits and credits			**29.**
30. One reason for recording closing entries is to bring the partners' capital accounts in the general ledger up to date..................			**30.**
31. A closing entry is made to close the drawing accounts to Income Summary			**31.**
32. After all closing entries are posted, the total of the partners' capital accounts is the end of the fiscal period capital..................			**32.**

UNIT C — Examining Adjusting Entries and Closing Entries

DIRECTIONS: For each item below, select the choice that best completes the sentence. Print the letter identifying your choice in the Answers column.

	Answers	For Scoring
0. The adjusting entry for the beginning merchandise inventory includes a credit to **(A)** Income Summary **(B)** Merchandise Inventory **(C)** Purchases **(D)** Sales ..	*B*	**0.** ✓
33. After the adjusting entry for beginning merchandise inventory has been posted, the merchandise inventory account has a **(A)** debit balance **(B)** credit balance **(C)** zero balance		**33.**
34. After the adjusting entry for beginning merchandise inventory has been posted, the income summary account has a **(A)** debit balance **(B)** credit balance **(C)** zero balance		**34.**
35. After the adjusting entry for ending merchandise inventory has been posted, the merchandise inventory account has a **(A)** debit balance **(B)** credit balance **(C)** zero balance		**35.**
36. After the supplies adjusting entry has been posted, the supplies account balance represents the value of supplies **(A)** inventory at the beginning of the fiscal period **(B)** bought during the fiscal period **(C)** used during the fiscal period **(D)** inventory at the end of the fiscal period		**36.**
37. After the supplies adjusting entry has been posted, the supplies expense account balance represents the value of supplies **(A)** inventory at the beginning of the fiscal period **(B)** bought during the fiscal period **(C)** used during the fiscal period **(D)** inventory at the end of the fiscal period		**37.**
38. After the prepaid insurance adjusting entry has been posted, the prepaid insurance account balance represents the value of insurance premiums **(A)** prepaid at the beginning of the fiscal period **(B)** prepaid during the fiscal period **(C)** expired during the fiscal period **(D)** prepaid at the end of the fiscal period		**38.**
39. After the prepaid insurance adjusting entry has been posted, the insurance expense account balance represents the value of insurance premiums **(A)** prepaid at the beginning of the fiscal period **(B)** prepaid during the fiscal period **(C)** expired during the fiscal period **(D)** prepaid at the end of the fiscal period		**39.**
40. The work sheet columns from which information is obtained for the first two closing entries at the end of the fiscal period are the **(A)** Trial Balance columns **(B)** Adjustments columns **(C)** Income Statement columns **(D)** Balance Sheet columns..............................		**40.**
41. After the journal entry to close the cost and expense accounts has been posted, the purchases account has a **(A)** debit balance **(B)** credit balance **(C)** zero balance		**41.**
42. After the journal entry to close the cost and expense accounts has been posted, each expense account has a **(A)** debit balance **(B)** credit balance **(C)** zero balance		**42.**
43. After the journal entry to close the revenue account has been posted, the sales account has a **(A)** debit balance **(B)** credit balance **(C)** zero balance.......................		**43.**
44. After the journal entry to close the income summary account has been posted, the income summary account has a **(A)** debit balance **(B)** credit balance **(C)** zero balance		**44.**
45. After the journal entry to close the partners' drawing accounts has been posted, the drawing accounts have **(A)** debit balances **(B)** credit balances **(C)** zero balances		**45.**
46. After all closing entries have been posted, the accounts that remain open are the **(A)** asset, liability, and partners' capital accounts **(B)** partners' capital, revenue, and cost accounts **(C)** revenue, cost, and expense accounts **(D)** none of the above........................		**46.**
47. In preparing a post-closing trial balance, an accountant lists **(A)** the accounts in alphabetic order **(B)** only those accounts that have balances **(C)** all the general ledger accounts **(D)** none of the above		**47.**

Drill 16-D 1 is on page 202

Recording adjusting entries [1, 2]

Business 1

Business 2

Business 3

Recording adjusting entries

DRILL 16-D 1, p. 316
[1, 2]

Drill 16-D2 is on page 201

Recording closing entries

DRILL 16-D 3, p. 317
[1, 2]

Name ______________________ Date __________ Class __________

PROBLEM 16-1, p. 318
[1–3]

Completing the work at the end of a fiscal period

The solutions to Problems 14-1 and 15-1 are needed to complete Problem 16-1.

COMBINATION JOURNAL

PAGE

	1	2					3	4	
	CASH		DATE	ACCOUNT TITLE	DOC. NO.	POST. REF.	GENERAL		
	DEBIT	CREDIT					DEBIT	CREDIT	
1									1
2									2
3									3
4									4
5									5
6									6
7									7
8									8
9									9
10									10
11									11
12									12
13									13
14									14
15									15
16									16
17									17
18									18
19									19
20									20
21									21
22									22
23									23
24									24
25									25
26									26
27									27
28									28
29									29
30									30

[3]

GENERAL LEDGER

ACCOUNT Cash — ACCOUNT NO. 11

DATE		ITEM	POST. REF.	DEBIT	CREDIT	BALANCE DEBIT	BALANCE CREDIT
19-- Dec.	1	Balance	✓			106800	
	31		2	1510200		1617000	
	31		2		735000	882000	

ACCOUNT Accounts Receivable — ACCOUNT NO. 12

DATE		ITEM	POST. REF.	DEBIT	CREDIT	BALANCE DEBIT	BALANCE CREDIT
19-- Dec.	1	Balance	✓			64000	
	31		2	96000		160000	
	31		2		86000	74000	

ACCOUNT Merchandise Inventory — ACCOUNT NO. 13

DATE		ITEM	POST. REF.	DEBIT	CREDIT	BALANCE DEBIT	BALANCE CREDIT
19-- Dec.	1	Balance	✓			9260000	

ACCOUNT Supplies — ACCOUNT NO. 14

DATE		ITEM	POST. REF.	DEBIT	CREDIT	BALANCE DEBIT	BALANCE CREDIT
19-- Dec.	1	Balance	✓			31500	
	16		1	21500		53000	

ACCOUNT Prepaid Insurance — ACCOUNT NO. 15

DATE		ITEM	POST. REF.	DEBIT	CREDIT	BALANCE DEBIT	BALANCE CREDIT
19-- Dec.	1	Balance	✓			76000	

ACCOUNT Accounts Payable — ACCOUNT NO. 21

DATE		ITEM	POST. REF.	DEBIT	CREDIT	BALANCE DEBIT	BALANCE CREDIT
19-- Dec.	1	Balance	✓				439000
	31		2	491000		52000	
	31		2		513000		461000

[3]

GENERAL LEDGER

ACCOUNT Sales Tax Payable ACCOUNT NO. 22

DATE		ITEM	POST. REF.	DEBIT	CREDIT	BALANCE DEBIT	BALANCE CREDIT
19-- Dec.	1	Balance	✓				59300
	17		2	59300			—
	31		3		62200		62200

ACCOUNT Eileen Brandon, Capital ACCOUNT NO. 31

DATE		ITEM	POST. REF.	DEBIT	CREDIT	BALANCE DEBIT	BALANCE CREDIT
19-- Dec.	1	Balance	✓				4560000

ACCOUNT Eileen Brandon, Drawing ACCOUNT NO. 32

DATE		ITEM	POST. REF.	DEBIT	CREDIT	BALANCE DEBIT	BALANCE CREDIT
19-- Dec.	1		1	70000		70000	

ACCOUNT Diane Baxter, Capital ACCOUNT NO. 33

DATE		ITEM	POST. REF.	DEBIT	CREDIT	BALANCE DEBIT	BALANCE CREDIT
19-- Dec.	1	Balance	✓				4480000

ACCOUNT Diane Baxter, Drawing ACCOUNT NO. 34

DATE		ITEM	POST. REF.	DEBIT	CREDIT	BALANCE DEBIT	BALANCE CREDIT
19-- Dec.	1		1	65000		65000	

ACCOUNT Income Summary ACCOUNT NO. 35

DATE		ITEM	POST. REF.	DEBIT	CREDIT	BALANCE DEBIT	BALANCE CREDIT

[3]

GENERAL LEDGER

ACCOUNT *Sales* ACCOUNT NO. 41

DATE		ITEM	POST. REF.	DEBIT	CREDIT	BALANCE DEBIT	BALANCE CREDIT
19-- Dec.	31		2		1556000		1556000

ACCOUNT *Purchases* ACCOUNT NO. 51

DATE		ITEM	POST. REF.	DEBIT	CREDIT	BALANCE DEBIT	BALANCE CREDIT
19-- Dec.	31		2	382000		382000	

ACCOUNT *Credit Card Fee Expense* ACCOUNT NO. 61

DATE		ITEM	POST. REF.	DEBIT	CREDIT	BALANCE DEBIT	BALANCE CREDIT
19-- Dec.	29		2	28000		28000	

ACCOUNT *Insurance Expense* ACCOUNT NO. 62

DATE		ITEM	POST. REF.	DEBIT	CREDIT	BALANCE DEBIT	BALANCE CREDIT

ACCOUNT *Miscellaneous Expense* ACCOUNT NO. 63

DATE		ITEM	POST. REF.	DEBIT	CREDIT	BALANCE DEBIT	BALANCE CREDIT
19-- Dec.	7		1	4300		4300	
	17		2	4900		9200	

ACCOUNT *Rent Expense* ACCOUNT NO. 64

DATE		ITEM	POST. REF.	DEBIT	CREDIT	BALANCE DEBIT	BALANCE CREDIT
19-- Dec.	1		1	95000		95000	

[3]

GENERAL LEDGER

ACCOUNT Salary Expense ACCOUNT NO. 65

DATE		ITEM	POST. REF.	DEBIT	CREDIT	BALANCE DEBIT	BALANCE CREDIT
19-- Dec.	1		1	625 00		625 00	
	15		1	625 00		1250 00	

ACCOUNT Supplies Expense ACCOUNT NO. 66

DATE		ITEM	POST. REF.	DEBIT	CREDIT	BALANCE DEBIT	BALANCE CREDIT

[4]

ACCOUNT TITLE	DEBIT	CREDIT

Completing a work sheet; recording adjusting and closing entries [1, 2]

Melbourne Supply
Work Sheet
For Month Ended November 30, 19--

	ACCOUNT TITLE	TRIAL BALANCE 1 DEBIT	2 CREDIT	ADJUSTMENTS 3 DEBIT	4 CREDIT	INCOME STATEMENT 5 DEBIT	6 CREDIT	BALANCE SHEET 7 DEBIT	8 CREDIT	
1	Cash									1
2	Accounts Receivable									2
3	Merchandise Inventory									3
4	Supplies									4
5	Prepaid Insurance									5
6	Accounts Payable									6
7	Sales Tax Payable									7
8	Ralph Bedo, Capital									8
9	Ralph Bedo, Drawing									9
10	Steve Falk, Capital									10
11	Steve Falk, Drawing									11
12	Income Summary									12
13	Sales									13
14	Purchases									14
15	Credit Card Fee Expense									15
16	Insurance Expense									16
17	Miscellaneous Expense									17
18	Rent Expense									18
19	Salary Expense									19
20	Supplies Expense									20
21										21
22										22
23										23
24										24
25										25

[9]

GENERAL LEDGER

ACCOUNT *Cash* ACCOUNT NO. 11

DATE		ITEM	POST. REF.	DEBIT	CREDIT	BALANCE DEBIT	BALANCE CREDIT
19-- Nov.	1	Balance	✓			631000	
	30		5	1244000		1875000	
	30		5		962000	913000	

ACCOUNT *Accounts Receivable* ACCOUNT NO. 12

DATE		ITEM	POST. REF.	DEBIT	CREDIT	BALANCE DEBIT	BALANCE CREDIT
19-- Nov.	1	Balance	✓			73000	
	30		5	67000		140000	
	30		5		78500	61500	

ACCOUNT *Merchandise Inventory* ACCOUNT NO. 13

DATE		ITEM	POST. REF.	DEBIT	CREDIT	BALANCE DEBIT	BALANCE CREDIT
19-- Nov.	1	Balance	✓			4950000	

ACCOUNT *Supplies* ACCOUNT NO. 14

DATE		ITEM	POST. REF.	DEBIT	CREDIT	BALANCE DEBIT	BALANCE CREDIT
19-- Nov.	1	Balance	✓			34000	
	12		2	17000		51000	

ACCOUNT *Prepaid Insurance* ACCOUNT NO. 15

DATE		ITEM	POST. REF.	DEBIT	CREDIT	BALANCE DEBIT	BALANCE CREDIT
19-- Nov.	1	Balance	✓			64000	

ACCOUNT *Accounts Payable* ACCOUNT NO. 21

DATE		ITEM	POST. REF.	DEBIT	CREDIT	BALANCE DEBIT	BALANCE CREDIT
19-- Nov.	1	Balance	✓				296000
	30		5	284000			12000
	30		5		208000		220000

GENERAL LEDGER

ACCOUNT Sales Tax Payable — ACCOUNT NO. 22

DATE		ITEM	POST. REF.	DEBIT	CREDIT	BALANCE DEBIT	BALANCE CREDIT
19-- Nov.	1	Balance	✓				63000
	18		3	63000		—	—
	30		5		67000		67000

ACCOUNT Ralph Bedo, Capital — ACCOUNT NO. 31

DATE		ITEM	POST. REF.	DEBIT	CREDIT	BALANCE DEBIT	BALANCE CREDIT
19-- Nov.	1	Balance	✓				2696500

ACCOUNT Ralph Bedo, Drawing — ACCOUNT NO. 32

DATE		ITEM	POST. REF.	DEBIT	CREDIT	BALANCE DEBIT	BALANCE CREDIT
19-- Nov.	15		2	80000		80000	

ACCOUNT Steve Falk, Capital — ACCOUNT NO. 33

DATE		ITEM	POST. REF.	DEBIT	CREDIT	BALANCE DEBIT	BALANCE CREDIT
19-- Nov.	1	Balance	✓				2696500

ACCOUNT Steve Falk, Drawing — ACCOUNT NO. 34

DATE		ITEM	POST. REF.	DEBIT	CREDIT	BALANCE DEBIT	BALANCE CREDIT
19-- Nov.	15		2	80000		80000	

ACCOUNT Income Summary — ACCOUNT NO. 35

DATE		ITEM	POST. REF.	DEBIT	CREDIT	BALANCE DEBIT	BALANCE CREDIT

GENERAL LEDGER

ACCOUNT *Sales* ACCOUNT NO. *41*

DATE		ITEM	POST. REF.	DEBIT	CREDIT	BALANCE DEBIT	BALANCE CREDIT
19-- Nov.	30		5		1240000		1240000

ACCOUNT *Purchases* ACCOUNT NO. *51*

DATE		ITEM	POST. REF.	DEBIT	CREDIT	BALANCE DEBIT	BALANCE CREDIT
19-- Nov.	30		5	420000		420000	

ACCOUNT *Credit Card Fee Expense* ACCOUNT NO. *61*

DATE		ITEM	POST. REF.	DEBIT	CREDIT	BALANCE DEBIT	BALANCE CREDIT
19-- Nov.	29		5	32000		32000	

ACCOUNT *Insurance Expense* ACCOUNT NO. *62*

DATE		ITEM	POST. REF.	DEBIT	CREDIT	BALANCE DEBIT	BALANCE CREDIT

ACCOUNT *Miscellaneous Expense* ACCOUNT NO. *63*

DATE		ITEM	POST. REF.	DEBIT	CREDIT	BALANCE DEBIT	BALANCE CREDIT
19-- Nov.	9		2	3600		3600	
	23		4	4900		8500	

ACCOUNT *Rent Expense* ACCOUNT NO. *64*

DATE		ITEM	POST. REF.	DEBIT	CREDIT	BALANCE DEBIT	BALANCE CREDIT
19-- Nov.	1		1	80000		80000	

[9]

GENERAL LEDGER

ACCOUNT Salary Expense ACCOUNT NO. 65

DATE		ITEM	POST. REF.	DEBIT	CREDIT	BALANCE	
						DEBIT	CREDIT
19-- Nov.	1		1	90000		90000	
	15		3	90000		180000	

ACCOUNT Supplies Expense ACCOUNT NO. 66

DATE		ITEM	POST. REF.	DEBIT	CREDIT	BALANCE	
						DEBIT	CREDIT

Begin income statement on page 213.

[10]

ACCOUNT TITLE	DEBIT	CREDIT

[3]

[4]

[5]

[6]

Name ____________ Date ________ Class ________

PROBLEM 16-2, concluded
[7–9]

COMBINATION JOURNAL

PAGE

1	2					3	4
CASH		DATE	ACCOUNT TITLE	DOC. NO.	POST. REF.	GENERAL	
DEBIT	CREDIT					DEBIT	CREDIT

Completing the work at the end of a fiscal period **[1, 2]**

Dubolt Associates
Work Sheet
For Month Ended October 31, 19--

	ACCOUNT TITLE	TRIAL BALANCE (1) DEBIT	TRIAL BALANCE (2) CREDIT	ADJUSTMENTS (3) DEBIT	ADJUSTMENTS (4) CREDIT	INCOME STATEMENT (5) DEBIT	INCOME STATEMENT (6) CREDIT	BALANCE SHEET (7) DEBIT	BALANCE SHEET (8) CREDIT	
1	Cash									1
2	Accounts Receivable									2
3	Merchandise Inventory									3
4	Supplies									4
5	Prepaid Insurance									5
6	Accounts Payable									6
7	Sales Tax Payable									7
8	Susan Kramer, Capital									8
9	Susan Kramer, Drawing									9
10	Benny Long, Capital									10
11	Benny Long, Drawing									11
12	Income Summary									12
13	Sales									13
14	Purchases									14
15	Credit Card Fee Expense									15
16	Insurance Expense									16
17	Miscellaneous Expense									17
18	Rent Expense									18
19	Salary Expense									19
20	Supplies Expense									20
21										21
22										22
23										23
24										24
25										25

[9]

GENERAL LEDGER

ACCOUNT Cash — ACCOUNT NO. 11

DATE		ITEM	POST. REF.	DEBIT	CREDIT	BALANCE DEBIT	BALANCE CREDIT
19-- Oct.	1	Balance	✓			409800	
	31		3	1317200		1727000	
	31		3		864000	863000	

ACCOUNT Accounts Receivable — ACCOUNT NO. 12

DATE		ITEM	POST. REF.	DEBIT	CREDIT	BALANCE DEBIT	BALANCE CREDIT
19-- Oct.	1	Balance	✓			68000	
	31		3	72000		140000	
	31		3		82000	58000	

ACCOUNT Merchandise Inventory — ACCOUNT NO. 13

DATE		ITEM	POST. REF.	DEBIT	CREDIT	BALANCE DEBIT	BALANCE CREDIT
19-- Oct.	1	Balance	✓			5580000	

ACCOUNT Supplies — ACCOUNT NO. 14

DATE		ITEM	POST. REF.	DEBIT	CREDIT	BALANCE DEBIT	BALANCE CREDIT
19-- Oct.	1	Balance	✓			42000	
	7		1	14000		56000	

ACCOUNT Prepaid Insurance — ACCOUNT NO. 15

DATE		ITEM	POST. REF.	DEBIT	CREDIT	BALANCE DEBIT	BALANCE CREDIT
19-- Oct.	1	Balance	✓			74000	

ACCOUNT Accounts Payable — ACCOUNT NO. 21

DATE		ITEM	POST. REF.	DEBIT	CREDIT	BALANCE DEBIT	BALANCE CREDIT
19-- Oct.	1	Balance	✓				330000
	31		3	298000			32000
	31		3		288000		320000

[9]

GENERAL LEDGER

ACCOUNT Sales Tax Payable — ACCOUNT NO. 22

DATE		ITEM	POST. REF.	DEBIT	CREDIT	BALANCE DEBIT	BALANCE CREDIT
19-- Oct.	1	Balance	✓				64800
	19		2	64800		—	—
	30		3		67300		67300

ACCOUNT Susan Kramer, Capital — ACCOUNT NO. 31

DATE		ITEM	POST. REF.	DEBIT	CREDIT	BALANCE DEBIT	BALANCE CREDIT
19-- Oct.	1	Balance	✓				2915000

ACCOUNT Susan Kramer, Drawing — ACCOUNT NO. 32

DATE		ITEM	POST. REF.	DEBIT	CREDIT	BALANCE DEBIT	BALANCE CREDIT
19-- Oct.	1		1	75000		75000	

ACCOUNT Benny Long, Capital — ACCOUNT NO. 33

DATE		ITEM	POST. REF.	DEBIT	CREDIT	BALANCE DEBIT	BALANCE CREDIT
19-- Oct.	1	Balance	✓				2864000

ACCOUNT Benny Long, Drawing — ACCOUNT NO. 34

DATE		ITEM	POST. REF.	DEBIT	CREDIT	BALANCE DEBIT	BALANCE CREDIT
19-- Oct.	1		1	75000		75000	

ACCOUNT Income Summary — ACCOUNT NO. 35

DATE		ITEM	POST. REF.	DEBIT	CREDIT	BALANCE DEBIT	BALANCE CREDIT

[9]

GENERAL LEDGER

ACCOUNT *Sales* ACCOUNT NO. *41*

DATE		ITEM	POST. REF.	DEBIT	CREDIT	BALANCE DEBIT	BALANCE CREDIT
19-- Oct.	31		3		1346000		1346000

ACCOUNT *Purchases* ACCOUNT NO. *51*

DATE		ITEM	POST. REF.	DEBIT	CREDIT	BALANCE DEBIT	BALANCE CREDIT
19-- Oct.	31		3	470000		470000	

ACCOUNT *Credit Card Fee Expense* ACCOUNT NO. *61*

DATE		ITEM	POST. REF.	DEBIT	CREDIT	BALANCE DEBIT	BALANCE CREDIT
19-- Oct.	28		✓	36000		36000	

ACCOUNT *Insurance Expense* ACCOUNT NO. *62*

DATE		ITEM	POST. REF.	DEBIT	CREDIT	BALANCE DEBIT	BALANCE CREDIT

ACCOUNT *Miscellaneous Expense* ACCOUNT NO. *63*

DATE		ITEM	POST. REF.	DEBIT	CREDIT	BALANCE DEBIT	BALANCE CREDIT
19-- Oct.	6		1	5200		5200	
	20		2	3100		8300	
	27		3	2000		10300	

ACCOUNT *Rent Expense* ACCOUNT NO. *64*

DATE		ITEM	POST. REF.	DEBIT	CREDIT	BALANCE DEBIT	BALANCE CREDIT
19-- Oct.	1		1	90000		90000	

[9]

GENERAL LEDGER

ACCOUNT *Salary Expense* ACCOUNT NO. *65*

DATE		ITEM	POST. REF.	DEBIT	CREDIT	BALANCE DEBIT	BALANCE CREDIT
19-- Oct.	1		1	625 00		625 00	
	15		2	625 00		1250 00	

ACCOUNT *Supplies Expense* ACCOUNT NO. *66*

DATE		ITEM	POST. REF.	DEBIT	CREDIT	BALANCE DEBIT	BALANCE CREDIT

Begin income statement on page 221.

[10]

ACCOUNT TITLE	DEBIT	CREDIT

[3]

[4]

[5]

[6]

Name ________________ Date ________ Class ________

MASTERY PROBLEM 16-M, concluded

[7–9]

PAGE

COMBINATION JOURNAL

1	2					3	4
CASH		DATE	ACCOUNT TITLE	DOC. NO.	POST. REF.	GENERAL	
DEBIT	CREDIT					DEBIT	CREDIT

Locating and correcting errors on a completed work sheet

Mayberry Electronics
Work Sheet
For Month Ended January 31, 19--

	ACCOUNT TITLE	TRIAL BALANCE DEBIT (1)	TRIAL BALANCE CREDIT (2)	ADJUSTMENTS DEBIT (3)	ADJUSTMENTS CREDIT (4)	INCOME STATEMENT DEBIT (5)	INCOME STATEMENT CREDIT (6)	BALANCE SHEET DEBIT (7)	BALANCE SHEET CREDIT (8)	
1	Cash	732000						732000		1
2	Accounts Receivable	41500						45100		2
3	Merchandise Inventory	3734000		(b) 3520000	(a) 3734000			3520000		3
4	Supplies	29000			(c) 17000			12000		4
5	Prepaid Insurance	41500			(d) 32500			9000		5
6	Accounts Payable		194000					194000		6
7	Sales Tax Payable		46100						46100	7
8	Helen Mayberry, Capital		1955550						1955550	8
9	Helen Mayberry, Drawing	70000						70000		9
10	Steve Mayberry, Capital		1955550						1955550	10
11	Steve Mayberry, Drawing	70000						70000		11
12	Income Summary			(a) 3734000	(b) 3520000	3734000	3520000			12
13	Sales		962000				962000			13
14	Purchases	236000				236000				14
15	Credit Card Fee Expense	18000								15
16	Insurance Expense			(d) 32500			32500			16
17	Miscellaneous Expense	6200				6200				17
18	Rent Expense	60000				60000				18
19	Salary Expense	75000				75000				19
20	Supplies Expense			(c) 17000			17000			20
21		5113200	5113200	7303500	7303500	4111200	4531500	4652100	3957200	21
22						420300			420300	22
23	Net Income					4531500	4531500	4652100	4377500	23
24										24
25										25

Mayberry Electronics
Work Sheet
For Month Ended January 31, 19--

	ACCOUNT TITLE	1 TRIAL BALANCE DEBIT	2 TRIAL BALANCE CREDIT	3 ADJUSTMENTS DEBIT	4 ADJUSTMENTS CREDIT	5 INCOME STATEMENT DEBIT	6 INCOME STATEMENT CREDIT	7 BALANCE SHEET DEBIT	8 BALANCE SHEET CREDIT	
1	Cash	732000								1
2	Accounts Receivable	41500								2
3	Merchandise Inventory	3734000								3
4	Supplies	29000								4
5	Prepaid Insurance	41500								5
6	Accounts Payable		194000							6
7	Sales Tax Payable		46100							7
8	Helen Mayberry, Capital		1955550							8
9	Helen Mayberry, Drawing	70000								9
10	Steve Mayberry, Capital		1955550							10
11	Steve Mayberry, Drawing	70000								11
12	Income Summary									12
13	Sales		962000							13
14	Purchases	236000								14
15	Credit Card Fee Expense	18000								15
16	Insurance Expense									16
17	Miscellaneous Expense	6200								17
18	Rent Expense	60000								18
19	Salary Expense	75000								19
20	Supplies Expense									20
21		5113200	5113200							21
22										22
23										23
24										24
25										25

		1	2	3	4	5	6	7	8
	ACCOUNT TITLE	TRIAL BALANCE		ADJUSTMENTS		INCOME STATEMENT		BALANCE SHEET	
		DEBIT	CREDIT	DEBIT	CREDIT	DEBIT	CREDIT	DEBIT	CREDIT
1									
2									
3									
4									
5									
6									
7									
8									
9									
10									
11									
12									
13									
14									
15									
16									
17									
18									
19									
20									
21									
22									
23									
24									
25									

Extra form

AN ACCOUNTING CYCLE FOR A PARTNERSHIP USING A COMBINATION JOURNAL [1, 2]

The ledgers used in Part A are needed to complete Part B.

Infocus
Work Sheet
For Month Ended December 31, 19--

	ACCOUNT TITLE	1 TRIAL BALANCE DEBIT	2 TRIAL BALANCE CREDIT	3 ADJUSTMENTS DEBIT	4 ADJUSTMENTS CREDIT	5 INCOME STATEMENT DEBIT	6 INCOME STATEMENT CREDIT	7 BALANCE SHEET DEBIT	8 BALANCE SHEET CREDIT	
1	Cash									1
2	Accounts Receivable									2
3	Merchandise Inventory									3
4	Supplies									4
5	Prepaid Insurance									5
6	Accounts Payable									6
7	Sales Tax Payable									7
8	Ruth Dunn, Capital									8
9	Ruth Dunn, Drawing									9
10	Frank Gallagher, Capital									10
11	Frank Gallagher, Drawing									11
12	Income Summary									12
13	Sales									13
14	Purchases									14
15	Credit Card Fee Expense									15
16	Insurance Expense									16
17	Miscellaneous Expense									17
18	Rent Expense									18
19	Salary Expense									19
20	Supplies Expense									20
21										21
22										22
23										23
24										24
25										25

[3]

[4]

[5]

[6]

COMBINATION JOURNAL

PAGE

1	2					3	4
CASH		DATE	ACCOUNT TITLE	DOC. NO.	POST. REF.	GENERAL	
DEBIT	CREDIT					DEBIT	CREDIT

[10]

ACCOUNT TITLE	DEBIT	CREDIT

Perfect Score. 41 Name ____________

Deduct.......... ___ Date ____________ Class ____________

Your Score .... ___ Checked by ____________

STUDY GUIDE 17

UNIT A — Accounting Terms

DIRECTIONS: Select the one term in Column I that best fits each definition in Column II. Print the letter identifying your choice in the Answers column.

Column I

- **A.** automated data processing (ADP)
- **B.** automation
- **C.** central processing unit (CPU)
- **D.** chart of accounts setup form
- **E.** computer
- **F.** computer program
- **G.** computer programmer
- **H.** computer service center
- **I.** data
- **J.** data processing
- **K.** data processing system
- **L.** electronic data processing (EDP)
- **M.** financial statement setup form
- **N.** input
- **O.** manual data processing
- **P.** output
- **Q.** processing
- **R.** storage

Column II	Answers	For Scoring
0. A person who prepares a computer program	*G*	**0.** ✓
1. A series of operations performed upon data		**1.**
2. Information produced by a data processing system		**2.**
3. An EDP form used to describe output format of financial statements..		**3.**
4. A combination of procedures, forms, and machines converting data into useful information..............................		**4.**
5. A business established to sell computer services............		**5.**
6. A system using automated machines to process data		**6.**
7. A computer unit that processes data and controls other computer units...		**7.**
8. A system in which data are processed mostly by hand		**8.**
9. Filing or holding data until needed		**9.**
10. An EDP form used to describe chart of accounts data......		**10.**
11. A process by which work is done mostly by machines		**11.**
12. A set of instructions followed by a computer to process data		**12.**
13. A group of interconnected machines that process data according to stored instructions....................................		**13.**
14. Data put into a system...		**14.**
15. Automated data processing using a computer................		**15.**
16. Working with data according to precise instructions		**16.**
17. Detailed or factual information..................................		**17.**

UNIT B — Assigning Account Numbers to New Accounts

DIRECTIONS: Select the three-digit number in Column I required to complete each new account number for the accounts shown in capital letters in Column II. Print the identifying letter of the three-digit number in the Answers column. Use the unused middle number method.

Column I

- **A.** 000
- **B.** 100
- **C.** 125
- **D.** 250
- **E.** 500
- **F.** 501
- **G.** 750
- **H.** 875

Column II	Answers	For Scoring
12000 Merchandise Inventory		
0. 12 ? OFFICE SUPPLIES..	*D*	**0.** ✓
12500 Store Supplies		
18. 13 ? OFFICE EQUIPMENT.................................		**18.**
19. 13 ? STORE EQUIPMENT		**19.**
62000 Delivery Expense		
20. 62 ? INSURANCE EXPENSE..............................		**20.**
62250 Miscellaneous Expense		
64000 Salary Expense		
21. 64 ? STORE SUPPLIES EXPENSE		**21.**
65000 Utilities Expense		

DIRECTIONS: Place a check mark (√) in the proper Answers column to show whether each of the following statements is true or false.

	Answers True	Answers False	For Scoring
0. When the amount of data increases a business generally needs faster recording and reporting procedures	√		**0.** √
22. One way to classify data processing systems is according to the procedures and equipment used			**22.**
23. Automated data processing eliminates any manual work to be done			**23.**
24. Accuracy is more important in a manual data processing system than in an automated data processing system			**24.**
25. A total data processing system consists of three phases — input, processing, and storage			**25.**
26. Electronic data processing is the most common automated data processing system			**26.**
27. Basic accounting principles change when an automated data processing system is used			**27.**
28. Automated machines are designed to work more efficiently with alphabetic names than with account numbers			**28.**
29. Businesses using EDP normally need at least a five-digit account number in their chart of accounts			**29.**
30. In a five-digit account coding system, the first digit identifies the ledger division			**30.**
31. Writing *EX* in the account classification column of a chart of accounts setup form indicates that an expense account is being described			**31.**
32. New accounts to be added to a chart of accounts are described on a form titled New Accounts Setup Form			**32.**
33. Headings on financial statements (business name, statement name, and date) print as a result of computer program instructions			**33.**
34. An account number must appear on each line of a financial statement setup form			**34.**
35. Writing a *3* in the statement code column of a financial statement setup form indicates that the statement being described is a capital statement			**35.**
36. Writing a *1* in the statement code column of a financial statement setup form indicates that the statement being described is an income statement			**36.**
37. Writing a *2* in the statement code column of a financial statement setup form indicates that the statement being described is a balance sheet			**37.**
38. Writing a *0* in the column code column of a financial statement setup form indicates that only the amount is to print			**38.**
39. Writing a *1* in the column code column of a financial statement setup form indicates that only the description is to print			**39.**
40. On all financial statement setup forms, the description is aligned at the left in the description column			**40.**
41. Each description written in the description column of a financial statement setup form will always print on output			**41.**

Name ____________________ Date __________ Class __________

DRILL 17-D 1, p. 341

Adding new general ledger accounts

Account Number	Account Title
12000	Merchandise Inventory
_____	Office Supplies
12500	Store Supplies
13000	Delivery Equipment
_____	Office Equipment
13250	Store Equipment
61000	Advertising Expense
_____	Credit Card Fee Expense
61250	Delivery Expense
_____	Insurance Expense
61500	Miscellaneous Expense
_____	Office Supplies Expense
62000	Rent Expense
62500	Salary Expense
_____	Store Supplies Expense

DRILL 17-D 2, p. 342

Analyzing a chart of accounts setup form

1. ____________________
2. ____________________
3. ____________________
4. ____________________
5. ____________________
6. ____________________
7. ____________________
8. ____________________
9. ____________________
10. ____________________

DRILL 17-D 3, p. 342

Analyzing a financial statement setup form

1. ____________________
2. ____________________
3. ____________________
4. ____________________
5. ____________________
6. ____________________
7. ____________________
8. ____________________
9. ____________________
10. ____________________

CHART OF ACCOUNTS SETUP

CLIENT NO.__________ NAME OF BUSINESS____________________

	ACCOUNT NUMBER	ACCT. CLASS.	ACCOUNT TITLE	NORM. BAL.	
1					1
2					2
3					3
4					4
5					5
6					6
7					7
8					8
9					9
10					10
11					11
12					12
13					13
14					14
15					15
16					16
17					17
18					18
19					19
20					20
21					21
22					22
23					23
24					24
25					25
26					26
27					27

ACCOUNT CLASSIFICATION:

AS = ASSET CA = CAPITAL CO = COST

LI = LIABILITY EX = EXPENSE RE = REVENUE

PREPARED BY__________

DATE__________

The chart of accounts prepared in Problem 17-1 is needed to complete Problems 18-1, 19-1, and 19-2.

Name ____________________ Date __________ Class __________ *PROBLEM 17-2, p. 343*

Preparing financial statement setup forms

FINANCIAL STATEMENT SETUP

CLIENT NO. __________

	ACCOUNT NUMBER	STMT. CODE	COL. CODE	DESCRIPTION	
1					1
2					2
3					3
4					4
5					5
6					6
7					7
8					8
9					9
10					10
11					11
12					12
13					13
14					14
15					15
16					16
17					17
18					18
19					19
20					20
21					21
22					22
23					23
24					24
25					25
26					26
27					27

STATEMENT CODE:
1 = INCOME STATEMENT
2 = DISTRIBUTION OF NET INCOME STATEMENT
3 = CAPITAL STATEMENT
4 = BALANCE SHEET

COLUMN CODE:
0 = ONLY DESCRIPTION PRINTS
1 = DESCRIPTION AND AMOUNT PRINT
2 = DESCRIPTION AND TOTAL AMOUNT PRINT

PREPARED BY ____________________

DATE ____________________

FINANCIAL STATEMENT SETUP

CLIENT NO.______________

	ACCOUNT NUMBER	STMT. CODE	COL. CODE	DESCRIPTION	
1					1
2					2
3					3
4					4
5					5
6					6
7					7
8					8
9					9
10					10
11					11
12					12
13					13
14					14
15					15
16					16
17					17
18					18
19					19
20					20
21					21
22					22
23					23
24					24
25					25
26					26
27					27

STATEMENT CODE:
1 = INCOME STATEMENT
2 = DISTRIBUTION OF NET INCOME STATEMENT
3 = CAPITAL STATEMENT
4 = BALANCE SHEET

COLUMN CODE:
0 = ONLY DESCRIPTION PRINTS
1 = DESCRIPTION AND AMOUNT PRINT
2 = DESCRIPTION AND TOTAL AMOUNT PRINT

PREPARED BY______________

DATE______________

FINANCIAL STATEMENT SETUP

CLIENT NO. ____________

	ACCOUNT NUMBER	STMT. CODE	COL. CODE	DESCRIPTION	
1					1
2					2
3					3
4					4
5					5
6					6
7					7
8					8
9					9
10					10
11					11
12					12
13					13
14					14
15					15
16					16
17					17
18					18
19					19
20					20
21					21
22					22
23					23
24					24
25					25
26					26
27					27

STATEMENT CODE:
1 = INCOME STATEMENT
2 = DISTRIBUTION OF NET INCOME STATEMENT
3 = CAPITAL STATEMENT
4 = BALANCE SHEET

COLUMN CODE:
0 = ONLY DESCRIPTION PRINTS
1 = DESCRIPTION AND AMOUNT PRINT
2 = DESCRIPTION AND TOTAL AMOUNT PRINT

PREPARED BY ____________________

DATE ____________________

FINANCIAL STATEMENT SETUP

CLIENT NO.______________

	ACCOUNT NUMBER	STMT. CODE	COL. CODE	DESCRIPTION	
1					1
2					2
3					3
4					4
5					5
6					6
7					7
8					8
9					9
10					10
11					11
12					12
13					13
14					14
15					15
16					16
17					17
18					18
19					19
20					20
21					21
22					22
23					23
24					24
25					25
26					26
27					27

STATEMENT CODE:
1 = INCOME STATEMENT
2 = DISTRIBUTION OF NET INCOME STATEMENT
3 = CAPITAL STATEMENT
4 = BALANCE SHEET

COLUMN CODE:
0 = ONLY DESCRIPTION PRINTS
1 = DESCRIPTION AND AMOUNT PRINT
2 = DESCRIPTION AND TOTAL AMOUNT PRINT

PREPARED BY______________

DATE______________

Name ______________________ Date __________ Class __________

MASTERY PROBLEM 17-M, p. 344

[1]

Adding new accounts to general ledger chart of accounts

Account Number	ASSETS	Account Number	REVENUE
11000	Cash	41000	Sales
11500	Accounts Receivable		
12000	Merchandise Inventory		**COST OF MERCHANDISE SOLD**
_____	Office Supplies (New Account)	51000	Purchases
_____	Store Supplies (New Account)		**EXPENSES**
12500	Prepaid Insurance	61000	Advertising Expense
13000	Delivery Equipment	_____	Credit Card Fee Expense (New Account)
_____	Office Equipment (New Account)	61500	Delivery Expense
_____	Store Equipment (New Account)	62000	Insurance Expense
	LIABILITIES	62500	Miscellaneous Expense
21000	Accounts Payable	_____	Office Supplies Expense (New Account)
	CAPITAL	63000	Rent Expense
		63500	Salary Expense
31000	Carol Bennett, Capital	_____	Store Supplies Expense (New Account)
31500	Carol Bennett, Drawing		
32000	Steve Franklin, Capital		
32500	Steve Franklin, Drawing		
33000	Income Summary		

[2]

CHART OF ACCOUNTS SETUP

CLIENT NO. __________ NAME OF BUSINESS ______________________

	ACCOUNT NUMBER	ACCT. CLASS.	ACCOUNT TITLE	NORM. BAL.	
1					1
2					2
3					3
4					4
5					5
6					6
7					7
8					8
9					9

ACCOUNT CLASSIFICATION:

AS = ASSET CA = CAPITAL CO = COST

LI = LIABILITY EX = EXPENSE RE = REVENUE

PREPARED BY ______________________

DATE ______________________

The chart of accounts prepared in Mastery Problem 17-M is needed to complete Mastery Problems 18-M and 19-M.

CHART OF ACCOUNTS SETUP

CLIENT NO.____________ NAME OF BUSINESS________________________

	ACCOUNT NUMBER	ACCT. CLASS.	ACCOUNT TITLE	NORM. BAL.	
1					1
2					2
3					3
4					4
5					5
6					6
7					7
8					8
9					9
10					10
11					11
12					12
13					13
14					14
15					15
16					16
17					17
18					18
19					19
20					20
21					21
22					22
23					23
24					24
25					25
26					26
27					27

ACCOUNT CLASSIFICATION:

AS = ASSET CA = CAPITAL CO = COST

LI = LIABILITY EX = EXPENSE RE = REVENUE

PREPARED BY____________________

DATE____________________

Name ______________________ Date __________ Class __________

CHALLENGE PROBLEM 17-C, p. 344

[1]

Adding new accounts to general ledger chart of accounts

Account Number	ASSETS	Account Number	REVENUE
11000	Cash	41000	Sales
11500	Accounts Receivable		
12000	Merchandise Inventory		**COST OF MERCHANDISE SOLD**
12500	Office Supplies	51000	Purchases
____	Store Supplies (New Account)		
13000	Prepaid Insurance		**EXPENSES**
____	Office Equipment (New Account)	61000	Advertising Expense
13500	Store Equipment	61500	Credit Card Fee Expense
	LIABILITIES	62000	Insurance Expense
21000	Accounts Payable	62500	Miscellaneous Expense
	CAPITAL	63000	Office Supplies Expense
31000	Susan Adkins, Capital	63500	Rent Expense
31500	Susan Adkins, Drawing	64000	Salary Expense
____	Marsha Gilbert, Capital (New Account)	____	Store Supplies Expense (New Account)
____	Marsha Gilbert, Drawing (New Account)		
____	Patricia Mason, Capital (New Account)		
____	Patricia Mason, Drawing (New Account) (New Partners)		
32000	Income Summary		

[2]

CHART OF ACCOUNTS SETUP

CLIENT NO. __________ NAME OF BUSINESS ______________________

	ACCOUNT NUMBER	ACCT. CLASS.	ACCOUNT TITLE	NORM. BAL.	
1					1
2					2
3					3
4					4
5					5
6					6
7					7
8					8
9					9

ACCOUNT CLASSIFICATION:

AS = ASSET CA = CAPITAL CO = COST

LI = LIABILITY EX = EXPENSE RE = REVENUE

PREPARED BY ______________________

DATE ______________________

The chart of accounts prepared in Challenge Problem 17-C is needed to complete Challenge Problems 18-C and 19-C.

[3]

FINANCIAL STATEMENT SETUP

CLIENT NO.____________

	ACCOUNT NUMBER	STMT. CODE	COL. CODE	DESCRIPTION	
1					1
2					2
3					3
4					4
5					5
6					6
7					7
8					8
9					9
10					10
11					11
12					12
13					13
14					14
15					15
16					16
17					17
18					18
19					19
20					20
21					21
22					22
23					23
24					24
25					25
26					26
27					27

STATEMENT CODE:
1 = INCOME STATEMENT
2 = DISTRIBUTION OF NET INCOME STATEMENT
3 = CAPITAL STATEMENT
4 = BALANCE SHEET

COLUMN CODE:
0 = ONLY DESCRIPTION PRINTS
1 = DESCRIPTION AND AMOUNT PRINT
2 = DESCRIPTION AND TOTAL AMOUNT PRINT

PREPARED BY____________

DATE____________

Perfect Score. 36	Name ________________
Deduct......... ___	Date ____________ Class ____________
Your Score.... ___	Checked by ________________

UNIT A — Accounting Terms

DIRECTIONS: Select the one term in Column I that best fits each definition in Column II. Print the letter identifying your choice in the Answers column.

Column I

A. entry register
B. input unit
C. journal entry transmittal (JET)
D. output
E. output unit
F. printout
G. systems flowchart

Column II	Answers	For Scoring
0. Information produced by a data processing system	*D*	**0.** ✓
1. A special EDP form used for recording accounting transactions		**1.**
2. A computer unit that converts data from human-readable to machine-readable form		**2.**
3. A chart made of symbols showing steps required in EDP ...		**3.**
4. A computer printout of transaction data entered into a computer		**4.**
5. A computer unit that converts data from machine-readable to human-readable form		**5.**
6. Computer output in printed, human-readable form		**6.**

UNIT B — Identifying Flowchart Symbols

DIRECTIONS: Match each item in Column II with its flowchart symbol in Column I. Print the letter identifying the symbol in the Answers column.

Column I

A –
B –
C –
D –
E –
F –
G –
H –
I –
J –

Column II	Answers	For Scoring
0. File	*E*	**0.** ✓
7. Magnetic disk..........		**7.**
8. Manual flow lines ...		**8.**
9. Processing		**9.**
10. Manual operation ...		**10.**
11. Keying operation ...		**11.**
12. Document..........		**12.**
13. Automatic flow lines		**13.**
14. Input/output		**14.**
15. Data		**15.**

DIRECTIONS: Place a check mark (√) in the proper Answers column to indicate whether each of the following statements is true or false.

	Answers: True	Answers: False	For Scoring
0. In EDP a minimum of human effort is required to process data	√		**0.** √
16. A different computer unit is used in each EDP phase			**16.**
17. Although all EDP units combine to form a computer, a central processing unit is often referred to as the "computer"			**17.**
18. A direct-entry terminal is a common input unit			**18.**
19. Data entered on a direct-entry terminal are sent to an external storage unit based on instructions in a computer program			**19.**
20. A card punch machine is linked to a CPU by electrical cables			**20.**
21. A printer is the most common output unit of computers handling accounting data			**21.**
22. Magnetic disks are often used to store ledger data in an automated accounting system			**22.**
23. Storage units attached to and under the control of a CPU are known as auxiliary storage			**23.**
24. Disk packs are all the same size			**24.**
25. A disk pack cannot be removed from a disk drive			**25.**
26. Each of the disks in a disk pack looks something like a record for a stereo system			**26.**
27. A magnetic disk drive is not linked to a CPU			**27.**
28. Computer programs are stored in the input unit of a computer			**28.**
29. One computer program is needed for a complete automated general ledger accounting system			**29.**
30. An entry register is also known as a transaction register			**30.**
31. A journal entry transmittal is also known as a transaction transmittal			**31.**
32. Data are recorded on a journal entry transmittal in the same order as data are entered on direct-entry terminals			**32.**
33. One disadvantage of using a journal entry transmittal is all source documents are kept in the accounting department			**33.**
34. One advantage of using a journal entry transmittal is that data are more rapidly entered on direct-entry terminals			**34.**
35. A batch number is assigned to an opening entry recorded on a journal entry transmittal			**35.**
36. Account titles for an opening entry are not entered on a journal entry transmittal			**36.**

Name ____________________ Date __________ Class __________

Analyzing a systems flowchart

1. ____________________

2. ____________________

3. ____________________

4. ____________________

5. ____________________

6. ____________________

7. ____________________

8. ____________________

9. ____________________

10. ____________________

Recording an opening entry in an EDP general ledger accounting system

PROBLEM 18-1, p. 358

The chart of accounts prepared in Problem 17-1 is needed to complete Problem 18-1.

JOURNAL ENTRY TRANSMITTAL

CLIENT NO. ________ DATE ____________ PAGE ____ OF ____ PAGES

	BCH. NO.	REF. NUMBER	ACCOUNT NUMBER	EXPLANATION	DEBIT	CREDIT	
1							1
2							2
3							3
4							4
5							5
6							6
7							7
8							8
9							9
10							10
11							11
12							12

PREPARED BY ____________ PAGE TOTALS

Recording an opening entry in an EDP general ledger accounting system

MASTERY PROBLEM 18-M, p. 359

The chart of accounts prepared in Mastery Problem 17-M is needed to complete Mastery Problem 18-M.

JOURNAL ENTRY TRANSMITTAL

CLIENT NO.________ DATE________________ PAGE _____ OF _____ PAGES

	BCH. NO.	REF. NUMBER	ACCOUNT NUMBER	EXPLANATION	DEBIT	CREDIT	
1							1
2							2
3							3
4							4
5							5
6							6
7							7
8							8
9							9
10							10
11							11
12							12

PREPARED BY________________ PAGE TOTALS

Recording an opening entry in an EDP general ledger accounting system

CHALLENGE PROBLEM 18-C, p. 359

The chart of accounts prepared in Challenge Problem 17-C is needed to complete Challenge Problem 18-C.

JOURNAL ENTRY TRANSMITTAL

CLIENT NO.________ DATE________________ PAGE _____ OF _____ PAGES

	BCH. NO.	REF. NUMBER	ACCOUNT NUMBER	EXPLANATION	DEBIT	CREDIT	
1							1
2							2
3							3
4							4
5							5
6							6
7							7
8							8
9							9
10							10
11							11
12							12

PREPARED BY________________ PAGE TOTALS

Perfect Score. 42 Name ______________________

Deduct.......... ___ Date ______________ Class ______________

Your Score.... ___ Checked by ______________________

UNIT A — Batching Business Transactions

DIRECTIONS: For each transaction in Column II, select from Column I the batch in which the transaction would be recorded. Print the letter identifying the batch in the Answers column.

Column I

A. Accounts Payable
B. Accounts Receivable
C. Cash Payments
D. Cash Receipts
E. General

Column II	Answers	For Scoring
0. Bought office supplies on account	*A*	**0.** √
1. Paid salaries		**1.**
2. Cash received from sales		**2.**
3. Purchased merchandise on account		**3.**
4. Purchased merchandise for cash		**4.**
5. Susan Fields, partner, withdrew cash		**5.**
6. Bought office supplies for cash		**6.**
7. Paid for insurance policy		**7.**
8. Paid on account		**8.**
9. Sold merchandise on account		**9.**
10. Cash received on account		**10.**
11. Paid miscellaneous expense		**11.**
12. Jeffrey Nosan, partner, withdrew merchandise		**12.**

UNIT B — Examining Automated General Ledger Accounting Procedures

DIRECTIONS: For a business using a computer service center, determine where the procedures in Column II are completed. Print the letter identifying the location from Column I in the Answers column.

Column I

A. at the business
B. at the computer service center

Column II	Answers	For Scoring
0. Prepares work sheet printout	*B*	**0.** √
13. Processes batched transactions		**13.**
14. Designs numbering system for general ledger chart of accounts		**14.**
15. Prepares post-closing trial balance		**15.**
16. Prepares entry registers		**16.**
17. Completes work sheet		**17.**
18. Prepares chart of accounts and financial statement setup forms		**18.**
19. Plans adjusting entries on work sheet		**19.**
20. Prepares JET form for opening entry		**20.**
21. Inspects financial statements for business decisions		**21.**
22. Prepares JET form for batched transactions		**22.**
23. Processes opening entry		**23.**

DIRECTIONS: Place a check mark (√) in the proper Answers column to show whether each of the following statements is true or false.

	Answers True	Answers False	For Scoring
0. Source documents are not required as objective evidence for transactions processed through EDP procedures		√	**0.** √
24. Methods of arranging transactions for EDP are the same regardless of the nature of the business			**24.**
25. Arranging similar transactions in one group is known as batching			**25.**
26. Batching procedures increase the number of journal entries			**26.**
27. With batching, the total amount of a group of transactions is entered as one combined entry			**27.**
28. A number used to identify a single or a group of source documents is known as a reference number			**28.**
29. An accounts payable batch includes all supplies and equipment bought on account and all purchases of merchandise on account			**29.**
30. A reference number is entered on a JET form for each line that contains transaction information			**30.**
31. Account titles are written in the explanation column of a JET form			**31.**
32. A cash payments batch includes payments of expenses, withdrawals of merchandise, and payments on account			**32.**
33. A general batch includes all transactions that cannot be included in any other batch			**33.**
34. A computer posts transaction data to general ledger accounts stored on magnetic disk			**34.**
35. An entry register is printed by a computer before transaction data are posted to general ledger accounts			**35.**
36. Financial statements are prepared by a computer at the end of each fiscal period			**36.**
37. In an EDP system, a trial balance is prepared manually on a work sheet printout at the end of each fiscal period			**37.**
38. A work sheet printout provides spaces for planning adjusting entries and extending amounts to income statement and balance sheet columns			**38.**
39. Adjustments are processed by computer and posted to general ledger accounts.			**39.**
40. Closing entries to be processed by EDP are recorded on a JET form			**40.**
41. A computer prepares an entry register for adjusting entries but not for closing entries			**41.**
42. A post-closing trial balance is not prepared in an automated general ledger accounting system			**42.**

Name ______________________ Date __________ Class __________ *DRILL 19-D 1, p. 379*

Batching transactions

Trans. No.	Accounts Payable Batch	Cash Payments Batch	Accounts Receivable Batch	Cash Receipts Batch	General Batch
1.	√				
2.					
3.					
4.					
5.					
6.					
7.					
8.					
9.					
10.					

Analyzing a journal entry transmittal *DRILL 19-D 2, p. 379*

1. ______________________
2. ______________________
3. ______________________
4. ______________________
5. ______________________
6. ______________________
7. ______________________
8. ______________________
9. ______________________
10. ______________________

Recording weekly batched transactions for EDP using a journal entry transmittal

The chart of accounts prepared in Problem 17-1 is needed to complete Problem 19-1.

JOURNAL ENTRY TRANSMITTAL

CLIENT NO.__________ DATE____________________ PAGE ______ OF ______ PAGES

	BCH. NO.	REF. NUMBER	ACCOUNT NUMBER	EXPLANATION	DEBIT	CREDIT	
1							1
2							2
3							3
4							4
5							5
6							6
7							7
8							8
9							9
10							10
11							11
12							12
13							13
14							14
15							15
16							16
17							17
18							18
19							19
20							20
21							21
22							22
23							23
24							24
25							25
26							26
27							27

PREPARED BY____________________ PAGE TOTALS

Recording adjusting and closing entries for EDP using a journal entry transmittal [1]

The chart of accounts prepared in Problem 17-1 is needed to complete Problem 19-2.

SOTO AUTO SUPPLY
WORK SHEET
FOR MONTH ENDED MARCH 31, 19--

	TRIAL BALANCE		ADJUSTMENTS		INCOME STATEMENT		BALANCE SHEET	
	DEBIT	CREDIT	DEBIT	CREDIT	DEBIT	CREDIT	DEBIT	CREDIT
CASH....................	$ 14,086.00							
ACCOUNTS RECEIVABLE.....	760.00							
MERCHANDISE INVENTORY...	225,420.00							
OFFICE SUPPLIES.........	811.00							
STORE SUPPLIES..........	520.00							
PREPAID INSURANCE.......	1,250.00							
OFFICE EQUIPMENT........	1,100.00							
STORE EQUIPMENT.........	1,840.00							
ACCOUNTS PAYABLE........		$ 4,330.00						
ALICE SOTO, CAPITAL.....		119,840.00						
ALICE SOTO, DRAWING.....	1,542.00							
FRANK SOTO, CAPITAL.....		116,540.00						
FRANK SOTO, DRAWING.....	1,528.00							
INCOME SUMMARY..........								
SALES...................		15,580.00						
PURCHASES...............	3,820.00							
ADVERTISING EXPENSE.....	68.00							
CREDIT CARD FEE EXPENSE.	215.00							
INSURANCE EXPENSE.......								
MISCELLANEOUS EXPENSE...	80.00							
OFFICE SUPPLIES EXPENSE.								
RENT EXPENSE............	850.00							
SALARY EXPENSE..........	2,400.00							
STORE SUPPLIES EXPENSE..								
	$256,290.00	$256,290.00						

[2]

JOURNAL ENTRY TRANSMITTAL

CLIENT NO.________ DATE________________ PAGE ______ OF ______ PAGES

	BCH. NO.	REF. NUMBER	ACCOUNT NUMBER	EXPLANATION	DEBIT	CREDIT	
1							1
2							2
3							3
4							4
5							5
6							6
7							7
8							8
9							9
10							10
11							11
12							12
13							13
14							14
15							15
16							16
17							17
18							18
19							19
20							20
21							21
22							22
23							23
24							24
25							25
26							26
27							27

PREPARED BY________________ PAGE TOTALS

Name ______________________ Date __________ Class __________

PROBLEM 19-2, concluded

[3]

JOURNAL ENTRY TRANSMITTAL

CLIENT NO. ________ DATE ________________ PAGE _____ OF _____ PAGES

	BCH. NO.	REF. NUMBER	ACCOUNT NUMBER	EXPLANATION	DEBIT	CREDIT	
1							1
2							2
3							3
4							4
5							5
6							6
7							7
8							8
9							9
10							10
11							11
12							12
13							13
14							14
15							15
16							16
17							17
18							18
19							19
20							20
21							21
22							22
23							23
24							24
25							25
26							26
27							27

PREPARED BY ________________ PAGE TOTALS

JOURNAL ENTRY TRANSMITTAL

CLIENT NO.________ DATE________________ PAGE ____ OF ____ PAGES

	BCH. NO.	REF. NUMBER	ACCOUNT NUMBER	EXPLANATION	DEBIT	CREDIT	
1							1
2							2
3							3
4							4
5							5
6							6
7							7
8							8
9							9
10							10
11							11
12							12
13							13
14							14
15							15
16							16
17							17
18							18
19							19
20							20
21							21
22							22
23							23
24							24
25							25
26							26
27							27

PREPARED BY________________ PAGE TOTALS

Recording weekly batched transactions for EDP using a journal entry transmittal

The chart of accounts prepared in Mastery Problem 17-M is needed to complete Mastery Problem 19-M.

JOURNAL ENTRY TRANSMITTAL

CLIENT NO. __________ DATE ______________________ PAGE ______ OF ______ PAGES

	BCH. NO.	REF. NUMBER	ACCOUNT NUMBER	EXPLANATION	DEBIT	CREDIT	
1							1
2							2
3							3
4							4
5							5
6							6
7							7
8							8
9							9
10							10
11							11
12							12
13							13
14							14
15							15
16							16
17							17
18							18
19							19
20							20
21							21
22							22
23							23
24							24
25							25
26							26
27							27

PREPARED BY ______________________ PAGE TOTALS

Recording weekly batched transactions for EDP using a journal entry transmittal

The chart of accounts prepared in Challenge Problem 17-C is needed to complete Challenge Problem 19-C.

JOURNAL ENTRY TRANSMITTAL

CLIENT NO.________ DATE______________________ PAGE ______ OF ______ PAGES

	BCH. NO.	REF. NUMBER	ACCOUNT NUMBER	EXPLANATION	DEBIT	CREDIT	
1							1
2							2
3							3
4							4
5							5
6							6
7							7
8							8
9							9
10							10
11							11
12							12
13							13
14							14
15							15
16							16
17							17
18							18
19							19
20							20
21							21
22							22
23							23
24							24
25							25
26							26
27							27

PREPARED BY____________________ PAGE TOTALS

Name ____________________ Date __________ Class __________

REINFORCEMENT ACTIVITY 3, p. 384

[1]

AN ACCOUNTING CYCLE FOR A PARTNERSHIP USING AUTOMATED DATA PROCESSING

CHART OF ACCOUNTS SETUP

CLIENT NO. __________ NAME OF BUSINESS ____________________

	ACCOUNT NUMBER	ACCT. CLASS.	ACCOUNT TITLE	NORM. BAL.	
1					1
2					2
3					3
4					4
5					5
6					6
7					7
8					8
9					9
10					10
11					11
12					12
13					13
14					14
15					15
16					16
17					17
18					18
19					19
20					20
21					21
22					22
23					23
24					24
25					25
26					26

ACCOUNT CLASSIFICATION:

AS = ASSET CA = CAPITAL CO = COST

LI = LIABILITY EX = EXPENSE RE = REVENUE

PREPARED BY ____________________

DATE ____________________

[2]

FINANCIAL STATEMENT SETUP

CLIENT NO.____________

	ACCOUNT NUMBER	STMT. CODE	COL. CODE	DESCRIPTION	
1					1
2					2
3					3
4					4
5					5
6					6
7					7
8					8
9					9
10					10
11					11
12					12
13					13
14					14
15					15
16					16
17					17
18					18
19					19
20					20
21					21
22					22
23					23
24					24
25					25
26					26
27					27

STATEMENT CODE:
1 = INCOME STATEMENT
2 = DISTRIBUTION OF NET INCOME STATEMENT
3 = CAPITAL STATEMENT
4 = BALANCE SHEET

COLUMN CODE:
0 = ONLY DESCRIPTION PRINTS
1 = DESCRIPTION AND AMOUNT PRINT
2 = DESCRIPTION AND TOTAL AMOUNT PRINT

PREPARED BY____________

DATE____________

[2]

FINANCIAL STATEMENT SETUP

CLIENT NO. __________

	ACCOUNT NUMBER	STMT. CODE	COL. CODE	DESCRIPTION	
1					1
2					2
3					3
4					4
5					5
6					6
7					7
8					8
9					9
10					10
11					11
12					12
13					13
14					14
15					15
16					16
17					17
18					18
19					19
20					20
21					21
22					22
23					23
24					24
25					25
26					26
27					27

STATEMENT CODE:
1 = INCOME STATEMENT
2 = DISTRIBUTION OF NET INCOME STATEMENT
3 = CAPITAL STATEMENT
4 = BALANCE SHEET

COLUMN CODE:
0 = ONLY DESCRIPTION PRINTS
1 = DESCRIPTION AND AMOUNT PRINT
2 = DESCRIPTION AND TOTAL AMOUNT PRINT

PREPARED BY ____________________

DATE ____________________

FINANCIAL STATEMENT SETUP

CLIENT NO.____________

	ACCOUNT NUMBER	STMT. CODE	COL. CODE	DESCRIPTION	
1					1
2					2
3					3
4					4
5					5
6					6
7					7
8					8
9					9
10					10
11					11
12					12
13					13
14					14
15					15
16					16
17					17
18					18
19					19
20					20
21					21
22					22
23					23
24					24
25					25
26					26
27					27

STATEMENT CODE:
1 = INCOME STATEMENT
2 = DISTRIBUTION OF NET INCOME STATEMENT
3 = CAPITAL STATEMENT
4 = BALANCE SHEET

COLUMN CODE:
0 = ONLY DESCRIPTION PRINTS
1 = DESCRIPTION AND AMOUNT PRINT
2 = DESCRIPTION AND TOTAL AMOUNT PRINT

PREPARED BY____________

DATE____________

[2]

FINANCIAL STATEMENT SETUP

CLIENT NO. ______________

	ACCOUNT NUMBER	STMT. CODE	COL. CODE	DESCRIPTION	
1					1
2					2
3					3
4					4
5					5
6					6
7					7
8					8
9					9
10					10
11					11
12					12
13					13
14					14
15					15
16					16
17					17
18					18
19					19
20					20
21					21
22					22
23					23
24					24
25					25
26					26
27					27

STATEMENT CODE:
1 = INCOME STATEMENT
2 = DISTRIBUTION OF NET INCOME STATEMENT
3 = CAPITAL STATEMENT
4 = BALANCE SHEET

COLUMN CODE:
0 = ONLY DESCRIPTION PRINTS
1 = DESCRIPTION AND AMOUNT PRINT
2 = DESCRIPTION AND TOTAL AMOUNT PRINT

PREPARED BY ______________________

DATE ______________________

[3]

JOURNAL ENTRY TRANSMITTAL

CLIENT NO.__________ DATE______________________________ PAGE ______ OF ______ PAGES

	BCH. NO.	REF. NUMBER	ACCOUNT NUMBER	EXPLANATION	DEBIT	CREDIT	
1							1
2							2
3							3
4							4
5							5
6							6
7							7
8							8
9							9
10							10
11							11
12							12
13							13
14							14
15							15
16							16
17							17
18							18
19							19
20							20
21							21
22							22
23							23
24							24
25							25
26							26
27							27

PREPARED BY______________________ PAGE TOTALS

[4]

JOURNAL ENTRY TRANSMITTAL

CLIENT NO. ________ DATE ____________ PAGE ____ OF ____ PAGES

	BCH. NO.	REF. NUMBER	ACCOUNT NUMBER	EXPLANATION	DEBIT	CREDIT	
1							1
2							2
3							3
4							4
5							5
6							6
7							7
8							8
9							9
10							10
11							11
12							12
13							13
14							14
15							15
16							16
17							17
18							18
19							19
20							20
21							21
22							22
23							23
24							24
25							25
26							26
27							27

PREPARED BY ____________ PAGE TOTALS

[5]

JOURNAL ENTRY TRANSMITTAL

CLIENT NO.________ DATE________________________ PAGE ______ OF ______ PAGES

	BCH. NO.	REF. NUMBER	ACCOUNT NUMBER	EXPLANATION	DEBIT	CREDIT	
1							1
2							2
3							3
4							4
5							5
6							6
7							7
8							8
9							9
10							10
11							11
12							12
13							13
14							14
15							15
16							16
17							17
18							18
19							19
20							20
21							21
22							22
23							23
24							24
25							25
26							26
27							27

PREPARED BY________________________ PAGE TOTALS

[6]

JOURNAL ENTRY TRANSMITTAL

CLIENT NO. __________ DATE ______________________ PAGE ______ OF ______ PAGES

	BCH. NO.	REF. NUMBER	ACCOUNT NUMBER	EXPLANATION	DEBIT	CREDIT	
1							1
2							2
3							3
4							4
5							5
6							6
7							7
8							8
9							9
10							10
11							11
12							12
13							13
14							14
15							15
16							16
17							17
18							18
19							19
20							20
21							21
22							22
23							23
24							24
25							25
26							26
27							27

PREPARED BY ______________________ PAGE TOTALS

[7]

JOURNAL ENTRY TRANSMITTAL

CLIENT NO.________ DATE________________________ PAGE ______ OF ______ PAGES

	BCH. NO.	REF. NUMBER	ACCOUNT NUMBER	EXPLANATION	DEBIT	CREDIT	
1							1
2							2
3							3
4							4
5							5
6							6
7							7
8							8
9							9
10							10
11							11
12							12
13							13
14							14
15							15
16							16
17							17
18							18
19							19
20							20
21							21
22							22
23							23
24							24
25							25
26							26
27							27

PREPARED BY____________________ PAGE TOTALS

[8]

JOURNAL ENTRY TRANSMITTAL

CLIENT NO. ______ DATE ______ PAGE ______ OF ______ PAGES

	BCH. NO.	REF. NUMBER	ACCOUNT NUMBER	EXPLANATION	DEBIT	CREDIT	
1							1
2							2
3							3
4							4
5							5
6							6
7							7
8							8
9							9
10							10
11							11
12							12
13							13
14							14
15							15
16							16
17							17
18							18
19							19
20							20
21							21
22							22
23							23
24							24
25							25
26							26
27							27

PREPARED BY ______ PAGE TOTALS

[9]

BACKPACKERS
WORK SHEET
FOR MONTH ENDED JUNE 30, 19--

	TRIAL BALANCE		ADJUSTMENTS		INCOME STATEMENT		BALANCE SHEET	
	DEBIT	CREDIT	DEBIT	CREDIT	DEBIT	CREDIT	DEBIT	CREDIT
CASH....................	$ 16,329.00							
ACCOUNTS RECEIVABLE.....	710.00							
MERCHANDISE INVENTORY...	123,500.00							
OFFICE SUPPLIES.........	487.00							
STORE SUPPLIES..........	491.00							
PREPAID INSURANCE.......	720.00							
OFFICE EQUIPMENT........	1,160.00							
STORE EQUIPMENT.........	2,820.00							
ACCOUNTS PAYABLE........		$ 6,286.00						
ANNE PALMER, CAPITAL....		68,600.00						
ANNE PALMER, DRAWING....	929.00							
MARTHA PALMER, CAPITAL..		66,800.00						
MARTHA PALMER, DRAWING..	992.00							
INCOME SUMMARY..........								
SALES...................		16,282.00						
PURCHASES...............	6,240.00							
ADVERTISING EXPENSE.....	225.00							
CREDIT CARD FEE EXPENSE.	240.00							
INSURANCE EXPENSE.......								
MISCELLANEOUS EXPENSE...	125.00							
OFFICE SUPPLIES EXPENSE.								
RENT EXPENSE............	1,200.00							
SALARY EXPENSE..........	1,800.00							
STORE SUPPLIES EXPENSE..								
	$157,968.00	$157,968.00						

[10]

JOURNAL ENTRY TRANSMITTAL

CLIENT NO. ________ DATE ____________________ PAGE _____ OF _____ PAGES

	BCH. NO.	REF. NUMBER	ACCOUNT NUMBER	EXPLANATION	DEBIT	CREDIT	
1							1
2							2
3							3
4							4
5							5
6							6
7							7
8							8
9							9
10							10
11							11
12							12
13							13
14							14
15							15
16							16
17							17
18							18
19							19
20							20
21							21
22							22
23							23
24							24
25							25
26							26
27							27

PREPARED BY ____________________ PAGE TOTALS

JOURNAL ENTRY TRANSMITTAL

CLIENT NO.________ DATE____________________ PAGE _____ OF _____ PAGES

	BCH. NO.	REF. NUMBER	ACCOUNT NUMBER	EXPLANATION	DEBIT	CREDIT	
1							1
2							2
3							3
4							4
5							5
6							6
7							7
8							8
9							9
10							10
11							11
12							12
13							13
14							14
15							15
16							16
17							17
18							18
19							19
20							20
21							21
22							22
23							23
24							24
25							25
26							26
27							27

PREPARED BY____________________ PAGE TOTALS

Perfect Score. 66 Name ____________

Deduct......... ___ Date ____________ Class ____________

Your Score.... ___ Checked by ____________

STUDY GUIDE 20

UNIT A — Accounting Terms

DIRECTIONS: Select the one term in Column I that best fits each definition in Column II. Print the letter identifying your choice in the Answers column.

Column I	Column II	Answers	For Scoring
A. cash discount	**0.** A business' printed or catalog price	*F*	**0.** ✓
B. cash payments journal	**1.** An account that reduces a related account on financial statements		**1.**
C. contra account	**2.** A cash discount on purchases taken by a buyer		**2.**
D. corporation	**3.** A deduction that a seller allows on the amount of an invoice to encourage prompt payment		**3.**
E. debit memorandum	**4.** Merchandise returned by a buyer for credit		**4.**
F. list price	**5.** Credit allowed for part of the price of merchandise that is not returned		**5.**
G. purchases allowance	**6.** A special journal used to record only purchases on account		**6.**
H. purchases discount	**7.** A special journal used to record only cash payments transactions		**7.**
I. purchases journal	**8.** A reduction in the list price granted to customers		**8.**
J. purchases return	**9.** A form prepared by the buyer showing the price deduction taken by the buyer for returns and allowances		**9.**
K. trade discount	**10.** An organization with the legal rights of a "person" and which may be owned by many persons		**10.**

UNIT B — Recording Transactions in Special Journals

DIRECTIONS: In Answers Column 1, print the abbreviation for the journal in which each transaction is to be recorded. In Columns 2 and 3, print the letters identifying the accounts to be debited and credited for each transaction.

P — purchases journal G — general journal CP — cash payments journal

Account Title

A. Accounts Payable
B. Accounts Receivable
C. Alton Company
D. Cash
E. Delivery Expense
F. Kem Company
G. Levy Company
H. Purchases
I. Purchases Discount
J. Purchases Returns and Allowances
K. Rent Expense
L. Royal Supplies
M. Supplies

Transaction	Answers 1 Journal	Answers 2 Debit	Answers 3 Credit	For Scoring 1 Journal	For Scoring 2 Debit	For Scoring 3 Credit
0–0–0. Paid December rent	*CP*	*K*	*D*	**0.** ✓	**0.** ✓	**0.** ✓
11–12–13. Paid on account to Alton Co.; less a purchase discount				**11.**	**12.**	**13.**
14–15–16. Returned merchandise to Kem Company				**14.**	**15.**	**16.**
17–18–19. Paid cash for supplies				**17.**	**18.**	**19.**
20–21–22. Paid cash for delivery expense				**20.**	**21.**	**22.**
23–24–25. Discovered that supplies bought for cash last month had been recorded in error as a debit to purchases				**23.**	**24.**	**25.**
26–27–28. Paid on account to Levy Co.; no discount allowed				**26.**	**27.**	**28.**
29–30–31. Bought supplies on account from Royal Supplies				**29.**	**30.**	**31.**
32–33–34. Purchased merchandise for cash				**32.**	**33.**	**34.**
35–36–37. Purchased merchandise on account from Levy Co.				**35.**	**36.**	**37.**

DIRECTIONS: Place a check mark (√) in the proper Answers column to show whether each of the following statements is true or false.

	Answers True	Answers False	For Scoring
0. The principal difference between the accounting records of sole proprietorships and corporations is in the capital accounts	√		**0.** √
38. Accounting records should be kept with the assumption that the business will continue for only one year			**38.**
39. A corporation can own property but cannot incur liabilities			**39.**
40. The source document for recording a purchase on account is an invoice from the creditor			**40.**
41. A purchase on account can be recorded on one line of a purchases journal			**41.**
42. Purchases are recorded at list price			**42.**
43. All transactions recorded in a purchases journal increase the balance of the purchases account			**43.**
44. All transactions recorded in a purchases journal decrease the balance of the accounts payable account			**44.**
45. All transactions recorded in a purchases journal decrease the balance of a creditor's account			**45.**
46. Each entry in a purchases journal represents an amount owed to the person or business named in the Account Credited column			**46.**
47. Each amount in the amount column of a purchases journal is posted individually as a credit to a creditor's account in the accounts payable ledger			**47.**
48. Each amount in the amount column of a purchases journal is posted as a debit to Accounts Payable			**48.**
49. The monthly total of a purchases journal is posted as a credit to Purchases			**49.**
50. The source document for each cash payment is a check stub			**50.**
51. When a cash payments journal is used, all payments of cash are recorded in it			**51.**
52. Trade discounts are recorded as debits to Purchases Discount			**52.**
53. The terms of sale 2/10, n/30 mean that the buyer may deduct 2% of the invoice amount if payment is made within 30 days from the invoice date			**53.**
54. The terms of sale 1/15, n/30 mean that 1% of the invoice amount may be deducted if paid within 15 days of its date and the total amount is due within 30 days			**54.**
55. The terms of sale EOM mean that full payment is expected not later than the end of the month in which the invoice is dated			**55.**
56. Purchases discounts are added to purchases when net purchases are figured			**56.**
57. Purchases Discount is sometimes called a contra account			**57.**
58. Each amount in the Accounts Payable Debit column of a cash payments journal is posted individually to the account named in the Account Title column			**58.**
59. Each amount in the Accounts Payable Debit column of a cash payments journal is posted individually to Accounts Payable			**59.**
60. The monthly total of the General Debit column of a cash payments journal is posted to the general ledger			**60.**
61. A general journal is used only to record transactions that cannot be recorded in the special journals being used			**61.**
62. The amount on a debit memorandum is a deduction from Accounts Payable in the books of the buyer			**62.**
63. Each amount in the General Debit column of a general journal is posted individually to a customer's account in the accounts receivable ledger			**63.**
64. The amount recorded in the Credit column of a general journal for supplies bought on account must be posted twice			**64.**
65. A purchases return or allowance transaction increases the amount owed to creditors			**65.**
66. A contra purchases account always has a debit balance			**66.**

Name ______________________ Date __________ Class __________

DRILL 20-D 1, p. 410

Analyzing transactions affecting purchases and cash payments

Trans. No.	(a) Account Debited	(b) Account Credited	(c) Journal in Which Recorded	(d) Name of Amount Column Used in Journal	(e)
				For Amount Debited	For Amount Credited
1.	*Purchases*	*Cash*	*Cash Payments*	*General Debit*	*Cash Credit*
2.					
3.					
4.					
5.					
6.					
7.					
8.					
9.					
10.					

DRILL 20-D 2, p. 410

Posting transactions from special journals

Trans. No.	(a) Accounts affected	(b) Amounts posted separately to	(c)	(d) Amounts not posted separately to any ledger
		General Ledger	Accounts Payable Ledger	
1.	*Purchases*	✓		
	Cash			✓
2.				
3.				
4.				
5.				
6.				
7.				
8.				
9.				
10.				

Journalizing and posting transactions affecting purchases

PROBLEM 20-1, p. 411
[1–3]

PURCHASES JOURNAL

PAGE

DATE		ACCOUNT CREDITED	PURCH. NO.	POST. REF.	PURCHASES, DR. ACCTS. PAY. CR.

[2]

ACCOUNTS PAYABLE LEDGER

NAME Brozek Company

ADDRESS 141 Indigo Ave., Tulsa, OK 74101-4983

DATE		ITEM	POST. REF.	DEBIT	CREDIT	CREDIT BALANCE
19-- Feb.	1	Balance	✓			24500

NAME Eagle Company

ADDRESS 233 Adamson Drive, Broken Arrow, OK 74012-4119

DATE		ITEM	POST. REF.	DEBIT	CREDIT	CREDIT BALANCE
19-- Feb.	1	Balance	✓			89600

NAME Franz Supplies

ADDRESS 2047 Fulton Drive, Claremore, OK 74017-2882

DATE		ITEM	POST. REF.	DEBIT	CREDIT	CREDIT BALANCE

NAME Kinlaw Company

ADDRESS 1997 Mapleridge Road, Tulsa, OK 74102-7985

DATE		ITEM	POST. REF.	DEBIT	CREDIT	CREDIT BALANCE
19-- Feb.	1	Balance	✓			121500

NAME Ortiz Company

ADDRESS 431 Hunting Creek, Muskogee, OK 74401-7323

DATE		ITEM	POST. REF.	DEBIT	CREDIT	CREDIT BALANCE
19-- Feb.	1	Balance	✓			8700

[3]

GENERAL LEDGER

ACCOUNT Accounts Payable — ACCOUNT NO. 2102

DATE		ITEM	POST. REF.	DEBIT	CREDIT	BALANCE DEBIT	BALANCE CREDIT
19-- Feb.	1	Balance	✓				244300

ACCOUNT Purchases — ACCOUNT NO. 5101

DATE		ITEM	POST. REF.	DEBIT	CREDIT	BALANCE DEBIT	BALANCE CREDIT

[4]

Journalizing and posting transactions affecting cash payments [1–4]

CASH PAYMENTS JOURNAL

PAGE

	DATE	ACCOUNT TITLE	CHECK NO.	POST. REF.	1 GENERAL DEBIT	2 GENERAL CREDIT	3 ACCOUNTS PAYABLE DEBIT	4 PURCHASES DISCOUNT CREDIT	5 CASH CREDIT	
1										1
2										2
3										3
4										4
5										5
6										6
7										7
8										8
9										9
10										10
11										11
12										12
13										13
14										14
15										15
16										16
17										17
18										18
19										19
20										20
21										21
22										22
23										23

[2]

ACCOUNTS PAYABLE LEDGER

NAME Ayala Company

ADDRESS 731 Riddle Road, Phoenix, AZ 85002-4822

DATE		ITEM	POST. REF.	DEBIT	CREDIT	CREDIT BALANCE
19-- Feb.	1	Balance	✓			125800

NAME Clark's Furnishings

ADDRESS 3401 Brookline Drive, Scottsdale, AZ 85251-1984

DATE		ITEM	POST. REF.	DEBIT	CREDIT	CREDIT BALANCE
19-- Feb.	1	Balance	✓			290300

NAME Irvine Company

ADDRESS 637 Devil's Backbone Drive, Glendale, AZ 85301-3247

DATE		ITEM	POST. REF.	DEBIT	CREDIT	CREDIT BALANCE
19-- Feb.	1	Balance	✓			83000

NAME Ragland Company

ADDRESS 4993 Quail Run Road, Tempe, AZ 85281-5780

DATE		ITEM	POST. REF.	DEBIT	CREDIT	CREDIT BALANCE
19-- Feb.	1	Balance	✓			179300

Name ______________________ Date __________ Class __________

PROBLEM 20-2, concluded
[3, 4]

GENERAL LEDGER

ACCOUNT *Cash* ACCOUNT NO. *1101*

DATE		ITEM	POST. REF.	DEBIT	CREDIT	BALANCE DEBIT	BALANCE CREDIT
19-- Feb.	1	Balance	✓			2237500	

ACCOUNT *Supplies* ACCOUNT NO. *1105*

DATE		ITEM	POST. REF.	DEBIT	CREDIT	BALANCE DEBIT	BALANCE CREDIT
19-- Feb.	1	Balance	✓			74500	

ACCOUNT *Accounts Payable* ACCOUNT NO. *2102*

DATE		ITEM	POST. REF.	DEBIT	CREDIT	BALANCE DEBIT	BALANCE CREDIT
19-- Feb.	1	Balance	✓				678400

ACCOUNT *Purchases* ACCOUNT NO. *5101*

DATE		ITEM	POST. REF.	DEBIT	CREDIT	BALANCE DEBIT	BALANCE CREDIT

ACCOUNT *Purchases Discount* ACCOUNT NO. *5101.2*

DATE		ITEM	POST. REF.	DEBIT	CREDIT	BALANCE DEBIT	BALANCE CREDIT

ACCOUNT *Delivery Expense* ACCOUNT NO. *6103*

DATE		ITEM	POST. REF.	DEBIT	CREDIT	BALANCE DEBIT	BALANCE CREDIT

ACCOUNT *Rent Expense* ACCOUNT NO. *6110*

DATE		ITEM	POST. REF.	DEBIT	CREDIT	BALANCE DEBIT	BALANCE CREDIT

PURCHASES JOURNAL

PAGE

	DATE		ACCOUNT CREDITED	PURCH. NO.	POST. REF.	PURCHASES. DR. ACCTS. PAY. CR.	
1							1
2							2
3							3
4							4
5							5
6							6
7							7
8							8
9							9
10							10
11							11
12							12
13							13
14							14

[1]

GENERAL JOURNAL

PAGE

	DATE		ACCOUNT TITLE	POST. REF.	DEBIT	CREDIT	
1							1
2							2
3							3
4							4
5							5
6							6
7							7
8							8
9							9
10							10
11							11
12							12
13							13
14							14

[1, 3]

CASH PAYMENTS JOURNAL

PAGE

	DATE	ACCOUNT TITLE	CHECK NO.	POST. REF.	GENERAL DEBIT (1)	GENERAL CREDIT (2)	ACCOUNTS PAYABLE DEBIT (3)	PURCHASES DISCOUNT CREDIT (4)	CASH CREDIT (5)	
1										1
2										2
3										3
4										4
5										5
6										6
7										7
8										8
9										9
10										10
11										11
12										12
13										13
14										14
15										15
16										16
17										17
18										18
19										19
20										20
21										21
22										22
23										23

ACCOUNTS PAYABLE LEDGER

NAME Barton Company
ADDRESS 743 Epworth Ave., Davenport, IA 52801-2973

DATE		ITEM	POST. REF.	DEBIT	CREDIT	CREDIT BALANCE
19-- Feb.	1	Balance	✓			348 00

NAME Cycle Enterprises
ADDRESS 3405 Clifton Ave., Davenport, IA 52802-8953

DATE		ITEM	POST. REF.	DEBIT	CREDIT	CREDIT BALANCE

NAME Gear Shop Supplies
ADDRESS 3811 Dogwood Drive, Moline, IL 61265-7986

DATE		ITEM	POST. REF.	DEBIT	CREDIT	CREDIT BALANCE
19-- Feb.	1	Balance	✓			3312 00

NAME Jessup Company
ADDRESS 3779 Westmont Circle, Des Moines, IA 50302-4227

DATE		ITEM	POST. REF.	DEBIT	CREDIT	CREDIT BALANCE
19-- Feb.	1	Balance	✓			1290 00

[1, 4]

ACCOUNTS PAYABLE LEDGER

NAME Sumiyo Motorcycles

ADDRESS 578 Abilene Trail, Des Moines, IA 50302-8443

DATE		ITEM	POST. REF.	DEBIT	CREDIT	CREDIT BALANCE

GENERAL LEDGER

[1–4]

ACCOUNT Cash — ACCOUNT NO. 1101

DATE		ITEM	POST. REF.	DEBIT	CREDIT	BALANCE DEBIT	BALANCE CREDIT
19-- Feb.	1	Balance	✓			26880 00	

ACCOUNT Supplies — ACCOUNT NO. 1105

DATE		ITEM	POST. REF.	DEBIT	CREDIT	BALANCE DEBIT	BALANCE CREDIT
19-- Feb.	1	Balance	✓			1061 30	

ACCOUNT Accounts Payable — ACCOUNT NO. 2102

DATE		ITEM	POST. REF.	DEBIT	CREDIT	BALANCE DEBIT	BALANCE CREDIT
19-- Feb.	1	Balance	✓				4950 00

ACCOUNT Purchases — ACCOUNT NO. 5101

DATE		ITEM	POST. REF.	DEBIT	CREDIT	BALANCE DEBIT	BALANCE CREDIT

GENERAL LEDGER

ACCOUNT *Purchases Returns and Allowances* ACCOUNT NO. *5101.1*

DATE		ITEM	POST. REF.	DEBIT	CREDIT	BALANCE DEBIT	BALANCE CREDIT

ACCOUNT *Purchases Discount* ACCOUNT NO. *5101.2*

DATE		ITEM	POST. REF.	DEBIT	CREDIT	BALANCE DEBIT	BALANCE CREDIT

ACCOUNT *Delivery Expense* ACCOUNT NO. *6103*

DATE		ITEM	POST. REF.	DEBIT	CREDIT	BALANCE DEBIT	BALANCE CREDIT

ACCOUNT *Miscellaneous Expense* ACCOUNT NO. *6108*

DATE		ITEM	POST. REF.	DEBIT	CREDIT	BALANCE DEBIT	BALANCE CREDIT

ACCOUNT *Rent Expense* ACCOUNT NO. *6110*

DATE		ITEM	POST. REF.	DEBIT	CREDIT	BALANCE DEBIT	BALANCE CREDIT

[4]

Journalizing and posting transactions affecting purchases and cash payments

MASTERY PROBLEM 20-M, p. 414

[1, 2]

PURCHASES JOURNAL

PAGE

	DATE		ACCOUNT CREDITED	PURCH. NO.	POST. REF.	PURCHASES, DR. ACCTS. PAY. CR.	
1							1
2							2
3							3
4							4
5							5
6							6
7							7
8							8
9							9

[1]

GENERAL JOURNAL

PAGE

	DATE		ACCOUNT TITLE	POST. REF.	DEBIT	CREDIT	
1							1
2							2
3							3
4							4
5							5
6							6
7							7
8							8
9							9
10							10
11							11
12							12
13							13
14							14
15							15
16							16
17							17
18							18
19							19

[1, 3]

CASH PAYMENTS JOURNAL

PAGE

	DATE	ACCOUNT TITLE	CHECK NO.	POST. REF.	1 GENERAL DEBIT	2 GENERAL CREDIT	3 ACCOUNTS PAYABLE DEBIT	4 PURCHASES DISCOUNT CREDIT	5 CASH CREDIT	
1										1
2										2
3										3
4										4
5										5
6										6
7										7
8										8
9										9
10										10
11										11
12										12
13										13
14										14
15										15
16										16
17										17
18										18
19										19
20										20
21										21
22										22
23										23

ACCOUNTS PAYABLE LEDGER

NAME Ajax Paint Company
ADDRESS 2312 Ravine Street, Santa Rosa, CA 95401-7686

DATE		ITEM	POST. REF.	DEBIT	CREDIT	CREDIT BALANCE
19-- May	1	Balance	✓			317 00

NAME Drake Supply Company
ADDRESS 1771 Northbend Drive, Santa Rosa, CA 95401-6109

DATE		ITEM	POST. REF.	DEBIT	CREDIT	CREDIT BALANCE

NAME Keminiski Company
ADDRESS 100 Terrace Drive, Eureka, CA 95501-7510

DATE		ITEM	POST. REF.	DEBIT	CREDIT	CREDIT BALANCE
19-- May	1	Balance	✓			616 00

NAME Leidy Paint Supply
ADDRESS 1026 West Front Street, Richmond, CA 94801-3813

DATE		ITEM	POST. REF.	DEBIT	CREDIT	CREDIT BALANCE

[1, 4]

ACCOUNTS PAYABLE LEDGER

NAME *Patterson Company*

ADDRESS *209 Betz Road, Eureka, CA 95501-2214*

DATE		ITEM	POST. REF.	DEBIT	CREDIT	CREDIT BALANCE
19-- May	1	Balance	✓			1294 00

GENERAL LEDGER

[1–4]

ACCOUNT *Cash* — ACCOUNT NO. *1101*

DATE		ITEM	POST. REF.	DEBIT	CREDIT	BALANCE DEBIT	BALANCE CREDIT
19-- May	1	Balance	✓			16170 00	

ACCOUNT *Supplies* — ACCOUNT NO. *1105*

DATE		ITEM	POST. REF.	DEBIT	CREDIT	BALANCE DEBIT	BALANCE CREDIT
19-- May	1	Balance	✓			326 30	

ACCOUNT *Accounts Payable* — ACCOUNT NO. *2102*

DATE		ITEM	POST. REF.	DEBIT	CREDIT	BALANCE DEBIT	BALANCE CREDIT
19-- May	1	Balance	✓				2227 00

GENERAL LEDGER

ACCOUNT *Purchases* ACCOUNT NO. *5101*

DATE		ITEM	POST. REF.	DEBIT	CREDIT	BALANCE	
						DEBIT	CREDIT

ACCOUNT *Purchases Returns and Allowances* ACCOUNT NO. *5101.1*

DATE		ITEM	POST. REF.	DEBIT	CREDIT	BALANCE	
						DEBIT	CREDIT

ACCOUNT *Purchases Discount* ACCOUNT NO. *5101.2*

DATE		ITEM	POST. REF.	DEBIT	CREDIT	BALANCE	
						DEBIT	CREDIT

ACCOUNT *Delivery Expense* ACCOUNT NO. *6103*

DATE		ITEM	POST. REF.	DEBIT	CREDIT	BALANCE	
						DEBIT	CREDIT

ACCOUNT *Miscellaneous Expense* ACCOUNT NO. *6108*

DATE		ITEM	POST. REF.	DEBIT	CREDIT	BALANCE	
						DEBIT	CREDIT

ACCOUNT *Rent Expense* ACCOUNT NO. *6110*

DATE		ITEM	POST. REF.	DEBIT	CREDIT	BALANCE	
						DEBIT	CREDIT

[4]

Journalizing transactions in a combined purchases-cash payments journal [1, 2]

PURCHASES — CASH PAYMENTS JOURNAL

PAGE

	DATE	ACCOUNT TITLE	DOC. NO.	POST. REF.	1 GENERAL DEBIT	2 GENERAL CREDIT	3 PURCHASES DEBIT	4 ACCOUNTS PAYABLE DEBIT	5 ACCOUNTS PAYABLE CREDIT	6 PURCHASES DISCOUNT CREDIT	7 CASH CREDIT	
1												1
2												2
3												3
4												4
5												5
6												6
7												7
8												8
9												9
10												10
11												11
12												12
13												13
14												14
15												15
16												16
17												17
18												18
19												19
20												20
21												21
22												22

[1]

GENERAL JOURNAL

PAGE

	DATE		ACCOUNT TITLE	POST. REF.	DEBIT	CREDIT	
1							1
2							2
3							3
4							4
5							5
6							6
7							7
8							8
9							9
10							10
11							11
12							12
13							13
14							14
15							15
16							16
17							17
18							18
19							19
20							20
21							21
22							22
23							23
24							24
25							25
26							26
27							27
28							28
29							29
30							30
31							31
32							32
33							33

[3]

Perfect Score. 52 Name ______

Deduct........ —— Date ______ Class ______

Your Score.... —— Checked by ______

STUDY GUIDE 21

UNIT A — Accounting Terms

DIRECTIONS: Select the one term in Column I that best fits each definition in Column II. Print the letter identifying your choice in the Answers column.

Column I

A. cash receipts journal
B. credit memorandum
C. sales allowance
D. sales journal
E. sales return
F. terms of sale

Column II	Answers	For Scoring
0. An agreement between a buyer and a seller about payment for merchandise........	*F*	**0.** √
1. A special journal used to record only sales on account		**1.**
2. Credit allowed a customer for part of the sales price of merchandise not returned		**2.**
3. A form prepared by the seller showing the amount deducted for returns and allowances		**3.**
4. Merchandise returned from a customer for a credit on account or a cash refund........		**4.**
5. A special journal in which only cash receipts transactions are recorded........		**5.**

UNIT B — Recording Transactions in Special Journals

DIRECTIONS: In Answers Column 1, print the abbreviation for the journal in which each transaction is to be recorded. In Answers Columns 2 and 3, print the letters identifying the accounts to be debited and credited for each transaction.

S — sales journal G — general journal CP — cash payments journal
P — purchases journal CR — cash receipts journal

Account Title

A. Accounts Payable
B. Accounts Receivable
C. Cash
D. David Grant
E. Delivery Expense
F. Jan Newton
G. Purchases
H. Purchases Discount
I. Purchases Returns and Allowances
J. Sales
K. Sales Returns and Allowances
L. Sales Tax Payable

Transaction	Answers 1 Journal	Answers 2 Debit	Answers 3 Credit	For Scoring 1 Journal	For Scoring 2 Debit	For Scoring 3 Credit
0–0–0. Paid cash for delivery expense........	*CP*	*E*	*C*	**0.**√	**0.**√	**0.**√
6– 7– 8. Recorded cash sales plus sales tax........				**6.**	**7.**	**8.**
9–10–11. Received cash on account from Jan Newton........				**9.**	**10.**	**11.**
12–13–14. Recorded credit card sales plus sales tax........				**12.**	**13.**	**14.**
15–16–17. Found that a sale on account to Jan Newton was incorrectly charged to the account of David Grant				**15.**	**16.**	**17.**
18–19–20. Sold merchandise on account to David Grant plus sales tax........				**18.**	**19.**	**20.**
21–22–23. Credited Jan Newton's account for merchandise returned plus sales tax				**21.**	**22.**	**23.**

UNIT C — Analyzing Special Journals

DIRECTIONS: Place a check mark (√) in the proper Answers column to show whether each of the following statements is true or false.

	Answers True	Answers False	For Scoring
0. Revenue should be recorded only when cash is received		√	**0.** √
24. A sale on account can be recorded on one line of a sales journal			**24.**
25. All transactions recorded in a sales journal decrease the balance of the sales account			**25.**
26. All transactions recorded in a sales journal decrease the balance of the accounts receivable account			**26.**
27. All transactions recorded in a sales journal increase the balance of a customer's account			**27.**
28. A return of merchandise sold is recorded in a general journal			**28.**
29. Some sale of merchandise transactions are recorded in a cash receipts journal			**29.**
30. Each sales journal entry represents a decrease in accounts receivable			**30.**
31. Each Accounts Receivable Debit column entry in the sales journal represents an amount owed by the person named in the Account Debited column			**31.**
32. Each Accounts Receivable Debit column entry in the sales journal must be posted to a subsidiary ledger account			**32.**
33. The amount of sales tax charged each customer is revenue			**33.**
34. One of the monthly totals of a sales journal is posted as a credit to Sales			**34.**
35. One of the monthly totals of a sales journal is posted as a debit to Accounts Receivable			**35.**
36. One of the monthly totals of a sales journal is posted as a debit to Sales Tax Payable			**36.**
37. Sales Tax Payable is a contra account to the sales account			**37.**
38. Sales transactions in which cash is received are recorded in a sales journal			**38.**
39. Each amount in the Accounts Receivable Credit column of a cash receipts journal is posted individually to the account of the customer named in the Account Title column			**39.**
40. Each amount in the General Credit column of a cash receipts journal is posted individually to the accounts receivable ledger account named in the Account Title column			**40.**
41. Completion of posting special column monthly totals of the cash receipts journal is indicated by writing the general ledger account number below the column total			**41.**
42. Completion of posting General column monthly totals of the cash receipts journal is indicated by writing the general ledger account number below the column total			**42.**
43. The amount on a credit memorandum is a deduction from the balance of the accounts receivable account			**43.**
44. A charge customer issues a credit memorandum when merchandise is returned to the seller			**44.**
45. Sales allowances decrease the amount of sales			**45.**
46. Better information is provided if sales returns and allowances are recorded in a separate account			**46.**
47. The sales returns and allowances account usually has a credit balance			**47.**
48. Sales Returns and Allowances is a contra account to the sales account			**48.**
49. Posting an amount to the wrong customer's account results in an incorrect balance in the general ledger's accounts receivable account			**49.**
50. Each Debit column amount in the general journal is posted individually to the general ledger account named in the Account Title column			**50.**
51. The best order to post special journals is (1) Purchases, (2) Cash Payments, (3) General, (4) Sales, and (5) Cash Receipts			**51.**
52. A contra sales account always has a credit balance			**52.**

Name ______________________ Date __________ Class __________ DRILL 21-D 1, p. 431

Analyzing transactions affecting sales and cash receipts

Trans. No.	(a) Account Debited	(b) Account Credited	(c) Journal in Which Recorded	(d) Name of Amount Column Used in Journal — For Amount Debited	(e) Name of Amount Column Used in Journal — For Amount Credited
1.	*Cash*	*Sales* *Sales Tax Payable*	*Cash Receipts*	*Cash Debit*	*Sales Credit* *Sales Tax Pay. Credit*
2.					
3.					
4.					
5.					
6.					
7.					

Posting transactions from special journals

DRILL 21-D 2, p. 431
[1, 2]

Trans. No.	(a) Accounts affected	(b) Amounts posted separately to General Ledger	(c) Amounts posted separately to Accounts Receivable Ledger	(d) Amounts not posted separately to any ledger
1.	*Cash*			✓
	Sales			✓
	Sales Tax Payable			✓
2.				
3.				
4.				
5.				
6.				
7.				

Journalizing and posting sales on account transactions

PROBLEM 21-1, p. 432
[1–3]

SALES JOURNAL

PAGE

	DATE		ACCOUNT DEBITED	SALE NO.	POST. REF.	1 ACCOUNTS RECEIVABLE DEBIT	2 SALES CREDIT	3 SALES TAX PAYABLE CREDIT	
1									1
2									2
3									3
4									4
5									5
6									6
7									7
8									8
9									9
10									10
11									11
12									12

ACCOUNTS RECEIVABLE LEDGER

NAME Cara Adamson

ADDRESS 590 Plum Drive, Mesa, AZ 85201-1203

DATE		ITEM	POST. REF.	DEBIT	CREDIT	DEBIT BALANCE
19-- Mar.	1	Balance	✓			42100

NAME Sara Adkinson

ADDRESS 4389 Thompson Road, Phoenix, AZ 85002-1587

DATE		ITEM	POST. REF.	DEBIT	CREDIT	DEBIT BALANCE
19-- Mar.	1	Balance	✓			14400

NAME Martha James

ADDRESS 657 Hampton Street, Gila Bend, AZ 85337-4921

DATE		ITEM	POST. REF.	DEBIT	CREDIT	DEBIT BALANCE
19-- Mar.	1	Balance	✓			36000

NAME Sherman Kook

ADDRESS 435 Yuma Avenue, Holbrook, AZ 86025-3274

DATE		ITEM	POST. REF.	DEBIT	CREDIT	DEBIT BALANCE
19-- Mar.	1	Balance	✓			33450

[2, 4]

ACCOUNTS RECEIVABLE LEDGER

NAME Samual Sammons

ADDRESS 3467 Mohave Avenue, Mesa, AZ 85201-1239

DATE		ITEM	POST. REF.	DEBIT	CREDIT	DEBIT BALANCE
19-- Mar.	1	Balance	✓			24800

NAME Roger Watkins

ADDRESS 6722 Hubbard Street, Phoenix, AZ 85002-1522

DATE		ITEM	POST. REF.	DEBIT	CREDIT	DEBIT BALANCE
19-- Mar.	1	Balance	✓			25500

GENERAL LEDGER

[3, 4]

ACCOUNT Accounts Receivable ACCOUNT NO. 1103

DATE		ITEM	POST. REF.	DEBIT	CREDIT	BALANCE	
						DEBIT	CREDIT
19-- Mar.	1	Balance	✓			176250	

ACCOUNT Sales Tax Payable ACCOUNT NO. 2106

DATE		ITEM	POST. REF.	DEBIT	CREDIT	BALANCE	
						DEBIT	CREDIT

ACCOUNT Sales ACCOUNT NO. 4101

DATE		ITEM	POST. REF.	DEBIT	CREDIT	BALANCE	
						DEBIT	CREDIT

[4]

Journalizing and posting cash receipts transactions [1–5]

CASH RECEIPTS JOURNAL

PAGE 6

	DATE		ACCOUNT TITLE	DOC. NO.	POST. REF.	1 GENERAL DEBIT	2 GENERAL CREDIT	3 ACCOUNTS RECEIVABLE CREDIT	4 SALES CREDIT	5 SALES TAX PAYABLE CREDIT	6 CASH DEBIT	
1												1
2												2
3												3
4												4
5												5
6												6
7												7
8												8
9												9
10												10
11												11
12												12
13												13
14												14
15												15
16												16
17												17
18												18
19												19
20												20
21												21
22												22
23												23

[2]

ACCOUNTS RECEIVABLE LEDGER

NAME Martin Chambers

ADDRESS 145 Ocean Drive, Camden, NJ 08108-2031

DATE		ITEM	POST. REF.	DEBIT	CREDIT	DEBIT BALANCE
19-- Mar.	1	Balance	✓			15000

NAME Nancy Fitzgerald

ADDRESS 3634 Ferris Street, Camden, NJ 08101-1334

DATE		ITEM	POST. REF.	DEBIT	CREDIT	DEBIT BALANCE
19-- Mar.	1	Balance	✓			45000

NAME Paul Gionet

ADDRESS 611 Sailfish Avenue, Elizabeth, NJ 07201-1238

DATE		ITEM	POST. REF.	DEBIT	CREDIT	DEBIT BALANCE
19-- Mar.	1	Balance	✓			18900

NAME Terri Johnston

ADDRESS 4323 Maria Place, Camden, NJ 08110-2576

DATE		ITEM	POST. REF.	DEBIT	CREDIT	DEBIT BALANCE
19-- Mar.	1	Balance	✓			11500

NAME Carrie Sciotto

ADDRESS 7524 Beekman Blvd., Elizabeth, NJ 07202-1133

DATE		ITEM	POST. REF.	DEBIT	CREDIT	DEBIT BALANCE
19-- Mar.	1	Balance	✓			25300

GENERAL LEDGER

ACCOUNT Cash ACCOUNT NO. 1101

DATE		ITEM	POST. REF.	DEBIT	CREDIT	BALANCE DEBIT	BALANCE CREDIT
19-- Mar.	1	Balance	✓			7752 50	

ACCOUNT Accounts Receivable ACCOUNT NO. 1103

DATE		ITEM	POST. REF.	DEBIT	CREDIT	BALANCE DEBIT	BALANCE CREDIT
19-- Mar.	1	Balance	✓			1157 00	

ACCOUNT Sales Tax Payable ACCOUNT NO. 2106

DATE		ITEM	POST. REF.	DEBIT	CREDIT	BALANCE DEBIT	BALANCE CREDIT

ACCOUNT Sales ACCOUNT NO. 4101

DATE		ITEM	POST. REF.	DEBIT	CREDIT	BALANCE DEBIT	BALANCE CREDIT

Name ______________________ Date __________ Class __________

PROBLEM 21-3, p. 434

[1, 2]

Journalizing and posting sales and cash receipts transactions

SALES JOURNAL

PAGE

DATE		ACCOUNT DEBITED	SALE NO.	POST. REF.	1 ACCOUNTS RECEIVABLE DEBIT	2 SALES CREDIT	3 SALES TAX PAYABLE CREDIT

[1]

GENERAL JOURNAL

PAGE

DATE		ACCOUNT TITLE	POST. REF.	DEBIT	CREDIT

[1, 3–5]

CASH RECEIPTS JOURNAL

PAGE

					1	2	3	4	5	6	
	DATE	ACCOUNT TITLE	DOC. NO.	POST. REF.	GENERAL		ACCOUNTS RECEIVABLE CREDIT	SALES CREDIT	SALES TAX PAYABLE CREDIT	CASH DEBIT	
					DEBIT	CREDIT					
1											1
2											2
3											3
4											4
5											5
6											6
7											7
8											8
9											9
10											10
11											11
12											12
13											13
14											14
15											15
16											16
17											17
18											18
19											19
20											20
21											21
22											22
23											23
24											24
25											25

ACCOUNTS RECEIVABLE LEDGER

NAME Kevin Hoffman
ADDRESS 352 Patrick Avenue, Duluth, MN 55802-1342

DATE		ITEM	POST. REF.	DEBIT	CREDIT	DEBIT BALANCE
19-- Feb.	1	Balance	✓			17900

NAME Stephen Norstrand
ADDRESS 8234 Swan River Drive, Duluth, MN 55810-2189

DATE		ITEM	POST. REF.	DEBIT	CREDIT	DEBIT BALANCE
19-- Feb.	1	Balance	✓			49500

NAME Sara Norwood
ADDRESS 642 Pinecreek Drive, Duluth, MN 55803-1567

DATE		ITEM	POST. REF.	DEBIT	CREDIT	DEBIT BALANCE
19-- Feb.	1	Balance	✓			43500

NAME Doris Schultz
ADDRESS 456 Charlton Drive, Duluth, MN 55811-2591

DATE		ITEM	POST. REF.	DEBIT	CREDIT	DEBIT BALANCE
19-- Feb.	1	Balance	✓			33500

ACCOUNTS RECEIVABLE LEDGER

NAME Lucy Stacy
ADDRESS 798 Rosemont Avenue, Duluth, MN 55803-1589

DATE		ITEM	POST. REF.	DEBIT	CREDIT	DEBIT BALANCE
19-- Feb.	1	Balance	✓			58000

NAME Samuel Wilton
ADDRESS 579 South Rushmore, Duluth, MN 55813-2705

DATE		ITEM	POST. REF.	DEBIT	CREDIT	DEBIT BALANCE
19-- Feb.	1	Balance	✓			54900

NAME Karl Zimmerman
ADDRESS 1925 Lytle Drive, Duluth, MN 55810-2330

DATE		ITEM	POST. REF.	DEBIT	CREDIT	DEBIT BALANCE
19-- Feb.	1	Balance	✓			26700

Name ______________________ Date __________ Class __________

PROBLEM 21-3, continued
[1, 2, 4–6]

GENERAL LEDGER

ACCOUNT *Cash* ACCOUNT NO. *1101*

DATE		ITEM	POST. REF.	DEBIT	CREDIT	BALANCE DEBIT	BALANCE CREDIT
19-- *Feb.*	*1*	*Balance*	*✓*			*559340*	

ACCOUNT *Accounts Receivable* ACCOUNT NO. *1103*

DATE		ITEM	POST. REF.	DEBIT	CREDIT	BALANCE DEBIT	BALANCE CREDIT
19-- *Feb.*	*1*	*Balance*	*✓*			*284000*	

ACCOUNT *Sales Tax Payable* ACCOUNT NO. *2106*

DATE		ITEM	POST. REF.	DEBIT	CREDIT	BALANCE DEBIT	BALANCE CREDIT

ACCOUNT *Sales* ACCOUNT NO. *4101*

DATE		ITEM	POST. REF.	DEBIT	CREDIT	BALANCE DEBIT	BALANCE CREDIT

ACCOUNT *Sales Returns and Allowances* ACCOUNT NO. *4101.1*

DATE		ITEM	POST. REF.	DEBIT	CREDIT	BALANCE DEBIT	BALANCE CREDIT

[6]

Name ______________________ Date __________ Class __________

MASTERY PROBLEM, 21-M, p. 436

[1, 2]

Journalizing and posting sales and cash receipts transactions

SALES JOURNAL

PAGE

DATE		ACCOUNT DEBITED	SALE NO.	POST. REF.	1 ACCOUNTS RECEIVABLE DEBIT	2 SALES CREDIT	3 SALES TAX PAYABLE CREDIT

[1]

GENERAL JOURNAL

PAGE

DATE		ACCOUNT TITLE	POST. REF.	DEBIT	CREDIT

[1, 3–5]

CASH RECEIPTS JOURNAL

PAGE

	DATE		ACCOUNT TITLE	DOC. NO.	POST. REF.	1 GENERAL DEBIT	2 GENERAL CREDIT	3 ACCOUNTS RECEIVABLE CREDIT	4 SALES CREDIT	5 SALES TAX PAYABLE CREDIT	6 CASH DEBIT	
1												1
2												2
3												3
4												4
5												5
6												6
7												7
8												8
9												9
10												10
11												11
12												12
13												13
14												14
15												15
16												16
17												17
18												18
19												19
20												20
21												21
22												22
23												23
24												24
25												25

GENERAL LEDGER

ACCOUNT *Cash* ACCOUNT NO. *1101*

DATE		ITEM	POST. REF.	DEBIT	CREDIT	BALANCE DEBIT	BALANCE CREDIT
19-- Apr.	1	Balance	✓			5872 51	

ACCOUNT *Accounts Receivable* ACCOUNT NO. *1103*

DATE		ITEM	POST. REF.	DEBIT	CREDIT	BALANCE DEBIT	BALANCE CREDIT
19-- Apr.	1	Balance	✓			2207 00	

ACCOUNT *Sales Tax Payable* ACCOUNT NO. *2106*

DATE		ITEM	POST. REF.	DEBIT	CREDIT	BALANCE DEBIT	BALANCE CREDIT

ACCOUNT *Sales* ACCOUNT NO. *4101*

DATE		ITEM	POST. REF.	DEBIT	CREDIT	BALANCE DEBIT	BALANCE CREDIT

ACCOUNT *Sales Returns and Allowances* ACCOUNT NO. *4101.1*

DATE		ITEM	POST. REF.	DEBIT	CREDIT	BALANCE DEBIT	BALANCE CREDIT

[1, 6]

ACCOUNTS RECEIVABLE LEDGER

NAME Grady Graham
ADDRESS 755 Random Drive, Jackson, MS 39208-1764

DATE		ITEM	POST. REF.	DEBIT	CREDIT	DEBIT BALANCE
19-- Apr.	1	Balance	✓			27500

NAME Melinda Grant
ADDRESS 563 Glen Allen Drive, Jackson, MS 39212-2347

DATE		ITEM	POST. REF.	DEBIT	CREDIT	DEBIT BALANCE
19-- Apr.	1	Balance	✓			18700

NAME David Hill
ADDRESS 452 Elsinore Avenue, Jackson, MS 39204-1591

DATE		ITEM	POST. REF.	DEBIT	CREDIT	DEBIT BALANCE
19-- Apr.	1	Balance	✓			43500

NAME Preston Miles
ADDRESS 75 Renfro Avenue, Jackson, MS 39201-1043

DATE		ITEM	POST. REF.	DEBIT	CREDIT	DEBIT BALANCE
19-- Apr.	1	Balance	✓			19800

[1, 6]

ACCOUNTS RECEIVABLE LEDGER

NAME Ralph Needham

ADDRESS 7054 West Masonwood, Battlefield, MS 39221-4982

DATE		ITEM	POST. REF.	DEBIT	CREDIT	DEBIT BALANCE
19-- Apr.	1	Balance	✓			342 00

NAME Titus Newton

ADDRESS 179 Ottawa Drive, Jackson, MS 39203-1460

DATE		ITEM	POST. REF.	DEBIT	CREDIT	DEBIT BALANCE
19-- Apr.	1	Balance	✓			245 00

NAME Melvin Peterson

ADDRESS 4891 Poppington Drive, Myrtle, MS 38650-9181

DATE		ITEM	POST. REF.	DEBIT	CREDIT	DEBIT BALANCE
19-- Apr.	1	Balance	✓			525 00

[6]

Journalizing and posting sales, purchases, cash receipts, and cash payments transactions

CHALLENGE PROBLEM 21-C, p. 437

[1, 2]

SALES JOURNAL

PAGE

	DATE		ACCOUNT DEBITED	SALE NO.	POST. REF.	1 ACCOUNTS RECEIVABLE DEBIT	2 SALES CREDIT	3 SALES TAX PAYABLE CREDIT	
1									1
2									2
3									3
4									4
5									5
6									6
7									7
8									8
9									9
10									10
11									11
12									12

[1, 3]

PURCHASES JOURNAL

PAGE

	DATE		ACCOUNT CREDITED	PURCH. NO.	POST. REF.	PURCHASES. DR. ACCTS. PAY. CR.	
1							1
2							2
3							3
4							4
5							5
6							6
7							7
8							8
9							9
10							10
11							11
12							12

[1]

GENERAL JOURNAL

PAGE

DATE		ACCOUNT TITLE	POST. REF.	DEBIT	CREDIT

[1, 4–6]

CASH RECEIPTS JOURNAL

PAGE

	DATE		ACCOUNT TITLE	DOC. NO.	POST. REF.	1 GENERAL DEBIT	2 GENERAL CREDIT	3 ACCOUNTS RECEIVABLE CREDIT	4 SALES CREDIT	5 SALES TAX PAYABLE CREDIT	6 CASH DEBIT	
1												1
2												2
3												3
4												4
5												5
6												6
7												7
8												8
9												9
10												10
11												11
12												12
13												13
14												14
15												15
16												16
17												17
18												18
19												19
20												20
21												21
22												22
23												23

[1, 4, 5, 7]

CASH PAYMENTS JOURNAL

PAGE

	DATE	ACCOUNT TITLE	CHECK NO.	POST. REF.	GENERAL DEBIT (1)	GENERAL CREDIT (2)	ACCOUNTS PAYABLE DEBIT (3)	PURCHASES DISCOUNT CREDIT (4)	CASH CREDIT (5)	
1										1
2										2
3										3
4										4
5										5
6										6
7										7
8										8
9										9
10										10
11										11
12										12
13										13
14										14
15										15
16										16
17										17
18										18
19										19
20										20
21										21
22										22
23										23

[1, 8]

ACCOUNTS PAYABLE LEDGER

NAME Foster Company
ADDRESS 122 Vignette Avenue, Dallas, TX 75236-4583

DATE		ITEM	POST. REF.	DEBIT	CREDIT	CREDIT BALANCE
19-- Mar.	1	Balance	✓			1298 00

NAME Newton Paint Company
ADDRESS 244 Ingram Avenue, Dallas, TX 75221-3817

DATE		ITEM	POST. REF.	DEBIT	CREDIT	CREDIT BALANCE
19-- Mar.	1	Balance	✓			1500 00

NAME Shell Supply Company
ADDRESS 54 Three Mile Road, Dallas, TX 75218-3542

DATE		ITEM	POST. REF.	DEBIT	CREDIT	CREDIT BALANCE
19-- Mar.	1	Balance	✓			153 00

NAME Tomah Company
ADDRESS 760 Wesley Drive, Dallas, TX 75215-3002

DATE		ITEM	POST. REF.	DEBIT	CREDIT	CREDIT BALANCE
19-- Mar.	1	Balance	✓			2345 00

[1, 8]

ACCOUNTS RECEIVABLE LEDGER

NAME Earl Butler
ADDRESS 4230 Casco Street, Dallas, TX 75235-4126

DATE		ITEM	POST. REF.	DEBIT	CREDIT	DEBIT BALANCE
19-- Mar.	1	Balance	✓			36700

NAME Chelsea Eastman
ADDRESS 905 Cato Avenue, Dallas, TX 75220-3705

DATE		ITEM	POST. REF.	DEBIT	CREDIT	DEBIT BALANCE
19-- Mar.	1	Balance	✓			17800

NAME Franklin Fox
ADDRESS 741 Dannon Drive, Dallas, TX 75213-2881

DATE		ITEM	POST. REF.	DEBIT	CREDIT	DEBIT BALANCE
19-- Mar.	1	Balance	✓			29900

NAME Loretta Linwood
ADDRESS 593 West Gilman, Dallas, TX 75222-3940

DATE		ITEM	POST. REF.	DEBIT	CREDIT	DEBIT BALANCE
19-- Mar.	1	Balance	✓			11500

NAME Jennifer Wellman
ADDRESS 5421 Moorman Avenue, Dallas, TX 75208-1960

DATE		ITEM	POST. REF.	DEBIT	CREDIT	DEBIT BALANCE
19-- Mar.	1	Balance	✓			45600

GENERAL LEDGER

ACCOUNT Cash — ACCOUNT NO. 1101

DATE		ITEM	POST. REF.	DEBIT	CREDIT	BALANCE DEBIT	BALANCE CREDIT
19-- Mar.	1	Balance	✓			5700 00	

ACCOUNT Accounts Receivable — ACCOUNT NO. 1103

DATE		ITEM	POST. REF.	DEBIT	CREDIT	BALANCE DEBIT	BALANCE CREDIT
19-- Mar.	1	Balance	✓			1415 00	

ACCOUNT Supplies — ACCOUNT NO. 1105

DATE		ITEM	POST. REF.	DEBIT	CREDIT	BALANCE DEBIT	BALANCE CREDIT
19-- Mar.	1	Balance	✓			267 00	

ACCOUNT Accounts Payable — ACCOUNT NO. 2102

DATE		ITEM	POST. REF.	DEBIT	CREDIT	BALANCE DEBIT	BALANCE CREDIT
19-- Mar.	1	Balance	✓				5296 00

ACCOUNT Sales Tax Payable — ACCOUNT NO. 2106

DATE		ITEM	POST. REF.	DEBIT	CREDIT	BALANCE DEBIT	BALANCE CREDIT

ACCOUNT Sales — ACCOUNT NO. 4101

DATE		ITEM	POST. REF.	DEBIT	CREDIT	BALANCE DEBIT	BALANCE CREDIT

GENERAL LEDGER

ACCOUNT *Sales Returns and Allowances* ACCOUNT NO. *4101.1*

DATE		ITEM	POST. REF.	DEBIT	CREDIT	BALANCE DEBIT	BALANCE CREDIT

ACCOUNT *Purchases* ACCOUNT NO. *5101*

DATE		ITEM	POST. REF.	DEBIT	CREDIT	BALANCE DEBIT	BALANCE CREDIT

ACCOUNT *Purchases Returns and Allowances* ACCOUNT NO. *5101.1*

DATE		ITEM	POST. REF.	DEBIT	CREDIT	BALANCE DEBIT	BALANCE CREDIT

ACCOUNT *Purchases Discount* ACCOUNT NO. *5101.2*

DATE		ITEM	POST. REF.	DEBIT	CREDIT	BALANCE DEBIT	BALANCE CREDIT

ACCOUNT *Delivery Expense* ACCOUNT NO. *6103*

DATE		ITEM	POST. REF.	DEBIT	CREDIT	BALANCE DEBIT	BALANCE CREDIT

ACCOUNT *Miscellaneous Expense* ACCOUNT NO. *6108*

DATE		ITEM	POST. REF.	DEBIT	CREDIT	BALANCE DEBIT	BALANCE CREDIT

ACCOUNT *Rent Expense* ACCOUNT NO. *6110*

DATE		ITEM	POST. REF.	DEBIT	CREDIT	BALANCE DEBIT	BALANCE CREDIT

[8]

[8]

Perfect Score. 39 Name ______________________

Deduct......... ___ Date ______________ Class ____________

Your Score .... ___ Checked by ______________________

STUDY GUIDE 22

UNIT A — Examining Payroll Records

DIRECTIONS: Place a check mark (√) in the proper Answers column to show whether each of the following statements is true or false.

	Answers True	Answers False	For Scoring
0. A pay period for all businesses must be monthly		√	**0.** √
1. A business is required by law to withhold certain payroll taxes from salaries earned by employees			**1.**
2. A married person supporting a spouse usually pays less federal income tax than a single person with the same earnings.			**2.**
3. One withholding allowance can be claimed for each person supported by the employee to a maximum of 6 allowances			**3.**
4. Federal law requires that each employer have on file a properly completed Form W-4, Employee's Withholding Allowance Certificate, for each employee.			**4.**
5. Marital status and number of withholding allowances claimed are indicated on Form W-4			**5.**
6. Federal income tax is withheld from employees' earnings only in states that have state income tax			**6.**
7. Employees' withheld taxes represent a liability to an employer until the taxes are paid to the federal or state government			**7.**
8. Some employees are exempt from having federal income tax withheld from their salaries			**8.**
9. FICA tax is paid entirely by the employer			**9.**
10. The FICA tax rate increases as an employee's salary rate increases			**10.**
11. Federal unemployment tax is paid by both employees and employers			**11.**
12. An employee must have a different social security account number for each employer			**12.**
13. An application for a social security card may be obtained from any Internal Revenue Service office and most post offices			**13.**
14. A social security card is issued to anyone upon request and without charge			**14.**
15. If a social security card is lost, the person may apply for a new social security number			**15.**
16. Social security numbers may not be used as identification numbers by any business or other government agency			**16.**
17. Employers most frequently use time cards as the basic source of data to prepare a payroll			**17.**
18. An individual employee's earnings record is used as the source document to prepare the payroll check			**18.**
19. All information about a single payroll is recorded on a payroll register			**19.**
20. An employee's earnings record always shows accumulated earnings of the employee from date of first employment			**20.**
21. Each business should select a system of preparing the payroll which results in adequate control for the least amount of cost			**21.**
22. Pegboard payroll is so named because all payroll records are filed on pegs			**22.**
23. A separate bank account for payroll checks provides additional protection and control			**23.**

UNIT B — Accounting Terms

DIRECTIONS: Select the one term in Column I that best fits each definition given in Column II. Print the letter identifying your choice in the Answers column.

Column I

A. employee's earnings record
B. federal unemployment tax
C. FICA tax
D. medicare
E. pay period
F. payroll
G. payroll register
H. payroll taxes
I. pegboard
J. state unemployment tax
K. total earnings
L. write-it-once principle

Column II	Answers	For Scoring
0. A list of employees that shows the payments due them for a pay period	*F*	**0.** ✓
24. Taxes based on the payroll of a business		**24.**
25. A federal tax paid by employees and employers for old-age, survivors, disability, and hospitalization insurance		**25.**
26. A state tax used to pay benefits to unemployed workers		**26.**
27. Recording data on several forms with one writing		**27.**
28. A business form showing details of all items affecting payments made to an employee		**28.**
29. A business form on which all payroll information is recorded		**29.**
30. The period covered by a salary payment		**30.**
31. The federal health insurance program, designed for people who have reached age 65		**31.**
32. A federal tax used for state and federal administrative expenses of the unemployment program		**32.**
33. The total pay due for a pay period before deductions		**33.**
34. A special device used to write the same information at one time on several forms		**34.**

UNIT C — Figuring Payroll

DIRECTIONS: For each item below, select the choice that best completes the sentence. Print the letter identifying your choice in the Answers column.

	Answers	For Scoring
0. The hours an employee worked each day most frequently are recorded on (A) an employee's earnings record (B) a time card (C) a payroll register	*B*	**0.** ✓
35. Information needed to determine the amount of an employee's federal income tax withholding is (A) wages, payroll period, marital status, number of withholding allowances (B) wages, marital status, age, number of withholding allowances (C) wages, FICA deductions, number of withholding allowances		**35.**
36. Information needed to determine an employee's FICA tax withholding for a pay period is (A) wages, FICA tax rate (B) wages, year-to-date earnings, FICA tax rate (C) wages, number of withholding allowances, FICA tax rate		**36.**
37. An employee's total earnings are figured by (A) total hours × total rate (B) regular hours × regular rate, plus overtime hours × overtime rate (C) regular hours × regular rate, plus overtime hours × 1.5 × overtime rate		**37.**
38. The accumulated earnings column of an employee's earnings record shows accumulated earnings for the (A) year (B) month (C) employee's total employment with the company		**38.**
39. Total employee's deductions include: (A) FICA tax, income tax (B) FICA tax, unemployment tax (C) Income tax, unemployment tax		**39.**

Name ______________________ Date __________ Class __________

DRILL 22-D 1, p. 455

Figuring employees' earnings

Employee Number	Hours Worked		Pay Rate	Amount of Pay		Total Earnings
	Regular	Overtime		Regular	Overtime	
1	40	1	$4.20	*$168.00*	*$6.30*	*$174.30*
2	40	5	6.00	______	______	______
3	30	0	4.00	______	______	______
4	40	4	5.50	______	______	______
5	40	3	6.20	______	______	______
6	40	2	5.80	______	______	______

Determining payroll income tax withholdings

DRILL 22-D 2, p. 456

1. ______________________ 4. ______________________

2. ______________________ 5. ______________________

3. ______________________ 6. ______________________

Applying for a social security account number

PROBLEM 22-1, p. 456

ID CN DO 234

DO NOT WRITE IN THE ABOVE SPACE

APPLICATION FOR A SOCIAL SECURITY NUMBER

See Instructions on Back. **Print in Black or Dark Blue Ink or Use Typewriter.**

1 *Print* FULL NAME YOU WILL USE IN WORK OR BUSINESS — *(First Name)* *(Middle Name or Initial – if none, draw line ___)* *(Last Name)*

2 *Print* FULL NAME GIVEN YOU AT BIRTH

6 YOUR DATE OF BIRTH *(Month)* *(Day)* *(Year)*

3 PLACE OF BIRTH *(City)* *(County if known)* *(State)*

7 YOUR PRESENT AGE *(Age on last birthday)*

4 MOTHER'S FULL NAME AT HER BIRTH *(Her maiden name)*

8 YOUR SEX — MALE ☐ FEMALE ☐

5 FATHER'S FULL NAME *(Regardless of whether living or dead)*

9 YOUR COLOR OR RACE — WHITE ☐ NEGRO ☐ OTHER ☐

10 HAVE YOU EVER BEFORE APPLIED FOR OR HAD A SOCIAL SECURITY, RAILROAD, OR TAX ACCOUNT NUMBER? NO ☐ DON'T KNOW ☐ YES ☐ *(If "YES" Print STATE in which you applied and DATE you applied and SOCIAL SECURITY NUMBER if known)*

11 YOUR MAILING ADDRESS *(Number and Street, Apt. No., P.O. Box, or Rural Route)* *(City)* *(State)* *(Zip Code)*

12 TODAY'S DATE

13 TELEPHONE NUMBER

14 NOTICE: Whoever, with intent to falsify his or someone else's true identity, willfully furnishes or causes to be furnished false information in applying for a social security number, is subject to a fine of not more than $1,000 or imprisonment for up to 1 year, or both.

Sign YOUR NAME HERE *(Do Not Print)*

☐ RESCREEN ☐ ASSIGN ☐ DUP ISSUED

Return completed application to nearest SOCIAL SECURITY ADMINISTRATION OFFICE

FORM SS-5

[1, 2]

EMPLOYEE NO. 14

NAME Pam Swenson

SOC. SEC. NO. 468-28-4140

PERIOD ENDING May 15, 19--

MORNING IN	MORNING OUT	AFTERNOON IN	AFTERNOON OUT	OVERTIME IN	OVERTIME OUT	HOURS REG	HOURS OT
2 7^{58}	2 12^{03}	2 12^{59}	2 5^{02}				
3 8^{04}	3 12^{01}	3 12^{56}	3 5^{01}				
4 7^{57}	4 12^{00}	4 12^{53}	4 5^{04}	4 7^{00}	4 9^{01}		
5 7^{59}	5 12^{02}	5 12^{58}	5 5^{01}				
6 7^{58}	6 12^{01}	6 1^{00}	6 5^{03}				
9 7^{57}	9 12^{02}	9 12^{55}	9 5^{02}				
10 7^{56}	10 12^{02}	10 12^{59}	10 5^{03}				
11 7^{58}	11 12^{01}	11 12^{56}	11 5^{03}	11 5^{59}	11 8^{02}		
12 7^{55}	12 12^{02}	12 12^{57}	12 5^{02}				
13 7^{59}	13 12^{01}	13 12^{58}	13 5^{03}				

	HOURS	RATE	AMOUNT
REGULAR		6.20	
OVERTIME		9.30	
TOTAL HOURS		TOTAL EARNINGS	

EMPLOYEE NO. 19

NAME Chris Greer

SOC. SEC. NO. 433-31-4820

PERIOD ENDING May 15, 19--

MORNING IN	MORNING OUT	AFTERNOON IN	AFTERNOON OUT	OVERTIME IN	OVERTIME OUT	HOURS REG	HOURS OT
3 7^{57}	3 12^{01}	3 1^{00}	3 5^{02}	3 7^{00}	3 8^{00}		
4 7^{56}	4 12^{00}	4 12^{57}	4 5^{01}				
5 7^{58}	5 12^{03}	5 12^{55}	5 5^{05}	5 6^{00}	5 8^{02}		
6 7^{57}	6 12^{02}	6 12^{55}	6 5^{02}				
7 7^{56}	7 12^{01}	7 12^{58}	7 5^{01}				
10 7^{59}	10 12^{00}	10 12^{59}	10 5^{02}	10 6^{00}	10 8^{03}		
11 7^{58}	11 12^{02}	11 12^{58}	11 5^{05}				
12 7^{59}	12 12^{02}	12 12^{57}	12 5^{01}	12 5^{55}	12 8^{01}		
13 7^{58}	13 12^{02}	13 12^{58}	13 5^{03}				
14 7^{59}	14 12^{03}	14 12^{59}	14 5^{03}				

	HOURS	RATE	AMOUNT
REGULAR		7.00	
OVERTIME		10.50	
TOTAL HOURS		TOTAL EARNINGS	

EMPLOYEE NO. 25

NAME Patrick Gray

SOC. SEC. NO. 423-28-2385

PERIOD ENDING May 15, 19--

MORNING IN	MORNING OUT	AFTERNOON IN	AFTERNOON OUT	OVERTIME IN	OVERTIME OUT	HOURS REG	HOURS OT
2 7^{59}	2 12^{00}						
3 7^{55}	3 12^{01}						
4 7^{56}	4 12^{03}						
5 8^{00}	5 12^{00}						
6 7^{57}	6 12^{02}						
7 8^{00}	7 12^{01}						
9 7^{56}	9 12^{00}						
10 7^{59}	10 12^{01}						
11 7^{58}	11 12^{02}						
12 7^{57}	12 12^{01}						
13 8^{00}	13 12^{02}						
14 8^{01}	14 12^{03}						

	HOURS	RATE	AMOUNT
REGULAR		4.50	
OVERTIME		6.75	
TOTAL HOURS		TOTAL EARNINGS	

Name ______________________________ Date ____________ Class ____________

PROBLEM 22-3, p. 456

[1]

Preparing a semimonthly payroll

PAYROLL REGISTER

SEMIMONTHLY PERIOD ENDED

DATE OF PAYMENT

	EMPL. NO.	EMPLOYEE'S NAME	MARITAL STATUS	NO. OF ALLOWANCES	EARNINGS REGULAR	EARNINGS OVERTIME	EARNINGS TOTAL	DEDUCTIONS FEDERAL INCOME TAX	DEDUCTIONS FICA TAX	DEDUCTIONS HOSP. INS.	DEDUCTIONS OTHER	DEDUCTIONS TOTAL	NET PAY	CK. NO.	
1															1
2															2
3															3
4															4
5															5
6															6
7															7
8															8
9															9
10															10
11															11
12															12
13															13
14															14
15															15
16															16
17															17
18															18
19															19
20															20
21															21
22															22

OTHER DEDUCTIONS: B — U.S. SAVINGS BONDS; UW — UNITED WAY

[2, 3]

No. 201 Date ______ 19___ $______

To ______

For ______

Bal. Bro't For'd

Amt. Deposited

Total

Amt. This Check

Bal. Car'd For'd

GENERAL ACCOUNT

No. 201

23-0875
1020

QUITMAN EQUIPMENT COMPANY

______ 19___

Pay to the order of ______ $ ______

______ Dollars

INDUSTRIALISTS' BANK OF DENVER
Denver, CO 80201-3526

⑆1020087511⑆ 2710080081129⑈

Check No. 411

PERIOD ENDING

EARNINGS $

REG. $

O.T. $

DEDUCTIONS $

INC. TAX $

FICA TAX $

GROUP INS. $

HOSP. INS. $

OTHER $

NET PAY $

PAYROLL ACCOUNT

23-0875
1020

______ 19___

NO. 411

Pay to the order of ______ $ ______

______ Dollars

QUITMAN EQUIPMENT COMPANY

INDUSTRIALISTS' BANK OF DENVER
Denver, CO 80201-3526

⑆102008751⑆ 2710080081130⑈

Check No. 415

PERIOD ENDING

EARNINGS $

REG. $

O.T. $

DEDUCTIONS $

INC. TAX $

FICA TAX $

GROUP INS. $

HOSP. INS. $

OTHER $

NET PAY $

PAYROLL ACCOUNT

23-0875
1020

______ 19___

NO. 415

Pay to the order of ______ $ ______

______ Dollars

QUITMAN EQUIPMENT COMPANY

INDUSTRIALISTS' BANK OF DENVER
Denver, CO 80201-3526

⑆102008751⑆ 2710080081130⑈

Preparing an employee's earnings record [1, 2]

EARNINGS RECORD FOR QUARTER ENDING ______

LAST NAME ______ FIRST ______ MIDDLE INITIAL ______ EMPLOYEE NO. ______ MARITAL STATUS ______ WITHHOLDING ALLOWANCES ______

SOCIAL SECURITY NO. ______

RATE OF PAY ______ PER HR. POSITION ______

PAY PERIOD		EARNINGS			DEDUCTIONS					NET PAY	ACCUMULATED EARNINGS
NO.	ENDED	REGULAR	OVERTIME	TOTAL	FEDERAL INCOME TAX	FICA TAX	HOSP. INS.	OTHER	TOTAL		
1											
2											
3											
4											
5											
6											
QUARTERLY TOTALS											

OTHER DEDUCTIONS: B — U.S. SAVINGS BONDS; UW — UNITED WAY

[1]

PAYROLL REGISTER

SEMIMONTHLY PERIOD ENDED

DATE OF PAYMENT

	EMPL. NO.	EMPLOYEE'S NAME	MARITAL STATUS	NO. OF ALLOW-ANCES	EARNINGS			DEDUCTIONS					NET PAY	CK. NO.	
					REGULAR	OVERTIME	TOTAL	FEDERAL INCOME TAX	FICA TAX	HOSP. INS.	OTHER	TOTAL			
1															1
2															2
3															3
4															4
5															5
6															6
7															7
8															8
9															9
10															10
11															11
12															12
13															13
14															14
15															15
16															16
17															17
18															18
19															19
20															20
21															21
22															22

OTHER DEDUCTIONS: B — U.S. SAVINGS BONDS; UW — UNITED WAY

[2, 3]

No. **117** Date ____ 19__ $______

To ______________________

For ______________________

Bal. Bro't For'd		
Amt. Deposited		
Total		
Amt. This Check		
Bal. Car'd For'd		

GENERAL ACCOUNT

No. **117**

47-227
739

GOWANS COMPANY

______________ 19__

Pay to the order of ______________________ $______

______________________ Dollars

COMMERCE BANK OF CEDAR RAPIDS
Cedar Rapids, IA 52401-6821

⑆073902274⑆ 285⑈0032⑈05⑈

Check No. **345**

PERIOD ENDING	
EARNINGS	$
REG.	$
O.T.	$
DEDUCTIONS	$
INC. TAX	$
FICA TAX	$
GROUP INS.	$
HOSP. INS.	$
OTHER	$
NET PAY	$

PAYROLL ACCOUNT

47-227
739

______________ 19__

NO. **345**

Pay to the order of ______________________ $______

______________________ Dollars

COMMERCE BANK OF CEDAR RAPIDS
Cedar Rapids, IA 52401-6821

GOWANS COMPANY

⑆073902274⑆ 285⑈0032⑈06⑈

Check No. **347**

PERIOD ENDING	
EARNINGS	$
REG.	$
O.T.	$
DEDUCTIONS	$
INC. TAX	$
FICA TAX	$
GROUP INS.	$
HOSP. INS.	$
OTHER	$
NET PAY	$

PAYROLL ACCOUNT

47-227
739

______________ 19__

NO. **347**

Pay to the order of ______________________ $______

______________________ Dollars

COMMERCE BANK OF CEDAR RAPIDS
Cedar Rapids, IA 52401-6821

GOWANS COMPANY

⑆073902274⑆ 285⑈0032⑈06⑈

PAYROLL REGISTER

SEMIMONTHLY PERIOD ENDED

DATE OF PAYMENT

	EMPL. NO.	EMPLOYEE'S NAME	MARITAL STATUS	NO. OF ALLOWANCES	EARNINGS			DEDUCTIONS					NET PAY	CK. NO.	
					GUARANTEED	INCENTIVE	TOTAL	FEDERAL INCOME TAX	FICA TAX	HOSP. INS.	OTHER	TOTAL			
1															1
2															2
3															3
4															4
5															5
6															6
7															7
8															8
9															9
10															10
11															11
12															12
13															13
14															14
15															15
16															16
17															17
18															18
19															19
20															20
21															21
22															22

OTHER DEDUCTIONS: B — U.S. SAVINGS BONDS; UW — UNITED WAY

Perfect Score. 32 Name ____________

Deduct......... ___ Date ________ Class ________

Your Score.... ___ Checked by ____________

STUDY GUIDE 23

UNIT A — Analyzing Payroll Records

DIRECTIONS: For each item below, select the choice that best completes the sentence. Print the letter identifying your choice in the Answers column.

	Answers	For Scoring
0. Taxes such as FICA tax, federal unemployment tax, and state unemployment tax as a group are frequently referred to as (A) city taxes (B) payroll taxes (C) income taxes (D) sales taxes	*B*	**0.** √
1. Payroll information for each employee is recorded in a payroll register (A) at the end of each day (B) at the end of each week (C) at the end of each month (D) at the end of each year (E) at the end of each pay period		**1.**
2. When special journals are used, a payroll entry is recorded in a (A) sales journal (B) purchases journal (C) general journal (D) cash receipts journal (E) cash payments journal		**2.**
3. A business' payroll taxes for a pay period are debited to (A) an asset account (B) a liability account (C) a revenue account (D) an expense account		**3.**
4. The total of the Total Earnings column of a payroll register is debited to (A) an asset account (B) a liability account (C) a revenue account (D) an expense account		**4.**
5. The total of the FICA tax column of a payroll register is credited to (A) an asset account (B) a liability account (C) a revenue account (D) an expense account		**5.**
6. The total of the Federal Income Tax column of a payroll register is credited to (A) an asset account (B) a liability account (C) a revenue account (D) an expense account		**6.**
7. The total of the Net Pay column of the payroll register is credited to (A) an asset account (B) a liability account (C) a revenue account (D) an expense account		**7.**
8. FICA taxes are paid by (A) employers only (B) employees only (C) more by the employer than the employee (D) equally by both the employer and the employee		**8.**
9. Until amounts withheld from employees' earnings for income tax and FICA tax are sent to the Internal Revenue Service, the amounts withheld represent (A) an asset (B) a liability (C) revenue (D) an expense		**9.**
10. FICA taxes withheld from employees' wages and employer's FICA taxes owed should be posted to (A) the same asset account (B) separate asset accounts (C) the same liability account (D) separate liability accounts		**10.**
11. When a semimonthly payroll is paid, the credit to Cash is equal to the (A) total earnings of all employees (B) total deductions for income tax and FICA tax (C) total deductions from earnings (D) net amount to employees		**11.**
12. Data needed to prepare Form 941, Employer's Quarterly Federal Tax Return, are obtained from (A) cash payments journal (B) payroll register (C) employees' earnings records (D) Form W-2 Wage and Tax Statement..............		**12.**
13. Form W-3, Transmittal of Income and Tax Statements is sent to the Internal Revenue Service with attached copies of (A) Form 941, Employer's Quarterly Tax Return (B) Form W-2 Wage and Tax Statement for each employee (C) Form 501, Federal Tax Deposit (D) Payroll register..............		**13.**

UNIT B — Recording Payroll Transactions

DIRECTIONS: For each transaction below, print in the proper Answers column the identifying letters of the accounts to be debited and credited.

Account Title

- **A.** Cash
- **B.** Employees Income Tax Payable
- **C.** FICA Tax Payable
- **D.** Payroll Taxes Expense
- **E.** Salary Expense
- **F.** Unemployment Tax Payable — Federal
- **G.** Unemployment Tax Payable — State
- **H.** U.S. Savings Bonds Payable

Transaction	Answers Debit	Answers Credit	For Scoring Debit	For Scoring Credit
0– 0. Paid liability for first quarter state unemployment tax	*G*	*A*	**0.√**	**0.√**
14–15. Paid semimonthly payroll less deductions for employees' income tax, FICA tax, and U.S. Savings Bonds			**14.**	**15.**
16–17. Record employer's payroll tax liabilities for semimonthly period			**16.**	**17.**
18–19. Paid liability for first quarter federal unemployment tax			**18.**	**19.**
20–21. Paid liability for employees' income tax and for FICA tax			**20.**	**21.**

UNIT C — Examining Form W-2

DIRECTIONS: The statements below are related to Form W-2, Wage and Tax Statement for 1983. Some questions below are based on the form. Other questions are general in nature. Place a check mark (√) in the proper Answers column to show whether each of the following statements is true or false.

1 Control number	222		
2 Employer's name, address, and ZIP code Lin's Music Center 2400 Fargo Lane Garland, TX 75041-2579		3 Employer's identification number 31-0318521	4 Employer's State number
		5 Stat. employee ☐ Deceased ☐ Pension plan ☐ Legal rep. ☐ 942 emp. ☐ Subtotal ☐ Correction ☐ Void ☐	
		6	7 Advance EIC payment
8 Employee's social security number 450-59-8679	9 Federal income tax withheld 1,690.65	10 Wages, tips, other compensation 12,265.00	11 FICA tax withheld 735.90
12 Employee's name, address, and ZIP code Joann D. Boyd 2586 Shady Brook Drive Garland, TX 75041-2787		13 FICA wages 12,265.00	14 FICA tips
		16 Employer's use	

Form **W-2 Wage and Tax Statement** Copy B To be filed with employee's FEDERAL tax return This information is being furnished to the Internal Revenue Service. Department of the Treasury Internal Revenue Service

Statement	Answers True	Answers False	For Scoring
0. This Form W-2 shows the total wages earned during 1983 by Ms. Boyd at Lin's Music Center	√		**0.** √
22. If an employee works for several employers during the year, that employee must receive a Form W-2 report from each employer			**22.**
23. When Joann Boyd files her federal income tax return, she must attach Copy A of her Form W-2 to her return			**23.**
24. Joann Boyd's total wages for 1983 from Lin's Music Center are more than her total FICA wages for 1983			**24.**
25. This Form W-2 indicates whether Joann Boyd had more than one employer during 1983			**25.**
26. This Form W-2 shows Joann Boyd's net pay from Lin's Music Center for the entire year			**26.**
27. This Form W-2 shows how many months during 1983 Ms. Boyd was employed by Lin's Music Center			**27.**
28. The same amount was withheld for income tax from the wages of each employee			**28.**
29. The amount withheld for Ms. Boyd's FICA tax was more than the amount withheld for her federal income tax			**29.**
30. This Form W-2 shows the total amount withheld from Ms. Boyd's earnings by Lin's Music Center for her federal income tax			**30.**
31. This Form W-2 shows the total amount withheld from Ms. Boyd's earnings by Lin's Music Center for her FICA tax			**31.**
32. An employer is required to provide employees with a Form W-2 report no later than January 15 of the year following the one for which the report has been completed			**32.**

Analyzing payroll transactions

Business A

Business C

Business B

Business D

[1, 2]

CASH PAYMENTS JOURNAL

PAGE

	DATE		ACCOUNT TITLE	CHECK NO.	POST. REF.	1 GENERAL DEBIT	2 GENERAL CREDIT	3 ACCOUNTS PAYABLE DEBIT	4 PURCHASES DISCOUNT CREDIT	5 CASH CREDIT	
1											1
2											2
3											3
4											4
5											5
6											6
7											7
8											8
9											9
10											10
11											11
12											12
13											13
14											14
15											15
16											16
17											17
18											18
19											19
20											20
21											21
22											22
23											23

[2]

GENERAL LEDGER

ACCOUNT *Employees Income Tax Payable* ACCOUNT NO. 2103

DATE		ITEM	POST. REF.	DEBIT	CREDIT	BALANCE DEBIT	BALANCE CREDIT

ACCOUNT *FICA Tax Payable* ACCOUNT NO. 2105

DATE		ITEM	POST. REF.	DEBIT	CREDIT	BALANCE DEBIT	BALANCE CREDIT

ACCOUNT *U. S. Savings Bonds Payable* ACCOUNT NO. 2110

DATE		ITEM	POST. REF.	DEBIT	CREDIT	BALANCE DEBIT	BALANCE CREDIT

ACCOUNT *Salary Expense* ACCOUNT NO. 6111

DATE		ITEM	POST. REF.	DEBIT	CREDIT	BALANCE DEBIT	BALANCE CREDIT

The general ledger accounts prepared in Problem 23-1 are needed to complete Problem 23-2.

Figuring, recording, and posting employer's payroll taxes

PROBLEM 23-2, p. 475

The general ledger accounts prepared in Problem 23-1 are needed to complete Problem 23-2.

[2]

GENERAL JOURNAL

PAGE

	DATE		ACCOUNT TITLE	POST. REF.	DEBIT	CREDIT	
1							1
2							2
3							3
4							4
5							5
6							6
7							7
8							8
9							9
10							10
11							11

GENERAL LEDGER

[3]

ACCOUNT Unemployment Tax Payable—Federal ACCOUNT NO. 2107

DATE		ITEM	POST. REF.	DEBIT	CREDIT	BALANCE DEBIT	BALANCE CREDIT

ACCOUNT Unemployment Tax Payable - State ACCOUNT NO. 2108

DATE		ITEM	POST. REF.	DEBIT	CREDIT	BALANCE DEBIT	BALANCE CREDIT

ACCOUNT Payroll Taxes Expense ACCOUNT NO. 6109

DATE		ITEM	POST. REF.	DEBIT	CREDIT	BALANCE DEBIT	BALANCE CREDIT

Name ______________________ Date __________ Class __________

Reporting employer's quarterly withholding and payroll taxes

Form **941**

Department of the Treasury
Internal Revenue Service

Employer's Quarterly Federal Tax Return

Your name, address, employer identification number, and calendar quarter of return. (If not correct, please change)	Name (as distinguished from trade name)	Date quarter ended	T
			FF
			FD
	Trade name, if any	Employer identification number	FP
			I
	Address and ZIP code		T

If address is different from prior return, check here ▶ ☐

1 Number of employees (except household) employed in the pay period that includes March 12th (complete for first quarter only) . . . . .

2 Total wages and tips subject to withholding, plus other compensation . . . . →

3 Total income tax withheld from wages, tips, annuities, gambling, etc. . . .

4 Adjustment of withheld income tax for preceding quarters of calendar year . . .

5 Adjusted total of income tax withheld . . . . →

6 Taxable FICA wages paid . . . . $ ________ multiplied by 12.0% =TAX . .

7 Taxable tips reported . . . . $ ________ multiplied by 6.0% =TAX . .

8 Total FICA taxes (add lines 6 and 7) . . . . →

9 Adjustment of FICA taxes (see instructions) . . . .

10 Adjusted total of FICA taxes . . . . →

11 Total taxes (add lines 5 and 10) . . . .

12 Advance earned income credit (EIC) payments, if any (see instructions) . . . .

13 Net taxes (subtract line 12 from line 11) . . . .

Record of Federal Tax Deposits (See instructions on page 4)

Deposit period ending:		I. Tax liability for period	II. Date of deposit	III. Amount deposited
Overpayment from previous quarter. . . .				
First month of quarter	1st through 7th day			
	8th through 15th day			
	16th through 22d day			
	23d through last day			
A First month total	A			
Second month of quarter	1st through 7th day			
	8th through 15th day			
	16th through 22d day			
	23d through last day			
B Second month total	B			
Third month of quarter	1st through 7th day			
	8th through 15th day			
	16th through 22d day			
	23d through last day			
C Third month total	C			
D Total for quarter (add items A, B, and C) .				
E Final deposit made for quarter. (Enter zero if the final deposit made for the quarter is included in item D)				

14 Total deposits for quarter (including final deposit made for quarter) and overpayment from previous quarter. (See instructions for deposit requirements on page 4.) . . . .

Note: *If undeposited taxes at the end of the quarter are $200 or more, deposit the full amount with an authorized financial institution or a Federal Reserve bank according to the instructions on the back of the Federal Tax Deposit Form 501. Enter this deposit in the Record of Federal Tax Deposits and include it on line 14.*

15 Undeposited taxes due (subtract line 14 from line 13—this should be less than $200). Pay to Internal Revenue Service and enter here . . . . →

16 If line 14 is more than line 13, enter overpayment here ▶ $ ______ and check if to be: ☐ Applied to next return, or ☐ Refunded.

17 Number of Forms W-4 enclosed. Do not send originals. (See General and Specific Instructions.) . . . .

18 If you are not liable for returns in the future, write "FINAL" (see instructions) ▶ Date final wages paid ▶

Under penalties of perjury, I declare that I have examined this return, including accompanying schedules and statements, and to the best of my knowledge and belief it is true, correct, and complete.

Date ▶ Signature ▶ Title ▶

Figuring and recording withholding and payroll taxes [1]

CASH PAYMENTS JOURNAL

PAGE

	DATE		ACCOUNT TITLE	CHECK No.	POST. REF.	1 GENERAL DEBIT	2 GENERAL CREDIT	3 ACCOUNTS PAYABLE DEBIT	4 PURCHASES DISCOUNT CREDIT	5 CASH CREDIT	
1											1
2											2
3											3
4											4
5											5
6											6
7											7
8											8
9											9

[2, 3]

CASH PAYMENTS JOURNAL

PAGE

	DATE		ACCOUNT TITLE	CHECK No.	POST. REF.	1 GENERAL DEBIT	2 GENERAL CREDIT	3 ACCOUNTS PAYABLE DEBIT	4 PURCHASES DISCOUNT CREDIT	5 CASH CREDIT	
1											1
2											2
3											3
4											4
5											5
6											6
7											7
8											8
9											9

Recording and posting payroll transactions
[1–3]

CASH PAYMENTS JOURNAL

PAGE

	DATE	ACCOUNT TITLE	CHECK NO.	POST. REF.	1 GENERAL DEBIT	2 GENERAL CREDIT	3 ACCOUNTS PAYABLE DEBIT	4 PURCHASES DISCOUNT CREDIT	5 CASH CREDIT	
1										1
2										2
3										3
4										4
5										5
6										6
7										7
8										8
9										9
10										10
11										11
12										12
13										13
14										14
15										15
16										16
17										17
18										18
19										19
20										20
21										21
22										22
23										23

[1, 3]

GENERAL JOURNAL

PAGE

DATE		ACCOUNT TITLE	POST. REF.	DEBIT	CREDIT

[3]

GENERAL LEDGER

ACCOUNT Employees Income Tax Payable — ACCOUNT NO. 2103

DATE		ITEM	POST. REF.	DEBIT	CREDIT	BALANCE DEBIT	BALANCE CREDIT
19-- Jan.	1	Balance	✓				779 00

ACCOUNT FICA Tax Payable — ACCOUNT NO. 2105

DATE		ITEM	POST. REF.	DEBIT	CREDIT	BALANCE DEBIT	BALANCE CREDIT
19-- Jan.	1	Balance	✓				671 20

ACCOUNT Unemployment Tax Payable—Federal — ACCOUNT NO. 2107

DATE		ITEM	POST. REF.	DEBIT	CREDIT	BALANCE DEBIT	BALANCE CREDIT
19-- Jan.	1	Balance	✓				117 40

[3]

GENERAL LEDGER

ACCOUNT Unemployment Tax Payable - State ACCOUNT NO. 2108

DATE		ITEM	POST. REF.	DEBIT	CREDIT	BALANCE DEBIT	BALANCE CREDIT
19-- Jan.	1	Balance	✓				452 80

ACCOUNT U. S. Savings Bonds Payable ACCOUNT NO. 2110

DATE		ITEM	POST. REF.	DEBIT	CREDIT	BALANCE DEBIT	BALANCE CREDIT
19-- Jan.	1	Balance	✓				280 00

ACCOUNT Payroll Taxes Expense ACCOUNT NO. 6109

DATE		ITEM	POST. REF.	DEBIT	CREDIT	BALANCE DEBIT	BALANCE CREDIT

ACCOUNT Salary Expense ACCOUNT NO. 6111

DATE		ITEM	POST. REF.	DEBIT	CREDIT	BALANCE DEBIT	BALANCE CREDIT

Recording and posting payroll transactions [1–3]

CASH PAYMENTS JOURNAL

PAGE

	DATE	ACCOUNT TITLE	CHECK NO.	POST. REF.	GENERAL (1) DEBIT	GENERAL (2) CREDIT	ACCOUNTS PAYABLE DEBIT (3)	PURCHASES DISCOUNT CREDIT (4)	CASH CREDIT (5)	
1										1
2										2
3										3
4										4
5										5
6										6
7										7
8										8
9										9
10										10
11										11
12										12
13										13
14										14
15										15
16										16
17										17
18										18
19										19
20										20
21										21
22										22
23										23
24										24

[1–3]

CASH PAYMENTS JOURNAL

PAGE

	DATE		ACCOUNT TITLE	CHECK NO.	POST. REF.	1 GENERAL DEBIT	2 GENERAL CREDIT	3 ACCOUNTS PAYABLE DEBIT	4 PURCHASES DISCOUNT CREDIT	5 CASH CREDIT	
1											1
2											2
3											3
4											4
5											5
6											6
7											7

[1–3]

GENERAL JOURNAL

PAGE

	DATE		ACCOUNT TITLE	POST. REF.	DEBIT	CREDIT	
1							1
2							2
3							3
4							4
5							5
6							6
7							7
8							8
9							9
10							10
11							11
12							12
13							13
14							14
15							15

[1, 3]

GENERAL LEDGER

ACCOUNT *Employees Income Tax Payable* ACCOUNT NO. *2103*

DATE		ITEM	POST. REF.	DEBIT	CREDIT	BALANCE DEBIT	BALANCE CREDIT
19-- Jan.	1	Balance	✓				702 90

ACCOUNT *FICA Tax Payable* ACCOUNT NO. *2105*

DATE		ITEM	POST. REF.	DEBIT	CREDIT	BALANCE DEBIT	BALANCE CREDIT
19-- Jan.	1	Balance	✓				766 80

ACCOUNT *Unemployment Tax Payable—Federal* ACCOUNT NO. *2107*

DATE		ITEM	POST. REF.	DEBIT	CREDIT	BALANCE DEBIT	BALANCE CREDIT
19-- Jan.	1	Balance	✓				134 20

[1, 3]

GENERAL LEDGER

ACCOUNT Unemployment Tax Payable - State ACCOUNT NO. 2108

DATE		ITEM	POST. REF.	DEBIT	CREDIT	BALANCE DEBIT	BALANCE CREDIT
19-- Jan.	1	Balance	✓				51760

ACCOUNT U. S. Savings Bonds Payable ACCOUNT NO. 2110

DATE		ITEM	POST. REF.	DEBIT	CREDIT	BALANCE DEBIT	BALANCE CREDIT
19-- Jan.	1	Balance	✓				37500

ACCOUNT Payroll Taxes Expense ACCOUNT NO. 6109

DATE		ITEM	POST. REF.	DEBIT	CREDIT	BALANCE DEBIT	BALANCE CREDIT

ACCOUNT Salary Expense ACCOUNT NO. 6111

DATE		ITEM	POST. REF.	DEBIT	CREDIT	BALANCE DEBIT	BALANCE CREDIT

AN ACCOUNTING CYCLE FOR A CORPORATION USING SPECIAL JOURNALS

[1, 7, 8]

SALES JOURNAL

PAGE 13

	DATE		ACCOUNT DEBITED	SALE NO.	POST. REF.	1 ACCOUNTS RECEIVABLE DEBIT	2 SALES CREDIT	3 SALES TAX PAYABLE CREDIT	
1									1
2									2
3									3
4									4
5									5
6									6
7									7
8									8
9									9
10									10
11									11
12									12

[1, 7, 9]

PURCHASES JOURNAL

PAGE 12

	DATE		ACCOUNT CREDITED	PURCH. NO.	POST. REF.	PURCHASES. DR. ACCTS. PAY. CR.	
1							1
2							2
3							3
4							4
5							5
6							6
7							7
8							8
9							9
10							10
11							11
12							12
13							13
14							14

The general journal used in Reinforcement Activity 4, Part A, is needed to complete Part B.

GENERAL JOURNAL

PAGE 8

DATE		ACCOUNT TITLE	POST. REF.	DEBIT	CREDIT

Name ______________________ Date __________ Class __________

REINFORCEMENT ACTIVITY 4
PART A – *continued*
[1, 7]

GENERAL JOURNAL

PAGE 9

DATE		ACCOUNT TITLE	POST. REF.	DEBIT	CREDIT

[1, 6, 7, 10, 11, 12]

CASH RECEIPTS JOURNAL

PAGE 15

	DATE		ACCOUNT TITLE	DOC. NO.	POST. REF.	1 GENERAL DEBIT	2 GENERAL CREDIT	3 ACCOUNTS RECEIVABLE CREDIT	4 SALES CREDIT	5 SALES TAX PAYABLE CREDIT	6 CASH DEBIT	
1	19-- Dec.	1	Balance on hand, $25,649.80									1
2												2
3												3
4												4
5												5
6												6
7												7
8												8
9												9
10												10
11												11
12												12
13												13
14												14
15												15
16												16
17												17
18												18
19												19
20												20
21												21
22												22
23												23

[1, 7, 10, 11, 13]

CASH PAYMENTS JOURNAL

PAGE 16

	DATE	ACCOUNT TITLE	CHECK NO.	POST. REF.	1 GENERAL DEBIT	2 GENERAL CREDIT	3 ACCOUNTS PAYABLE DEBIT	4 PURCHASES DISCOUNT CREDIT	5 CASH CREDIT	
1										1
2										2
3										3
4										4
5										5
6										6
7										7
8										8
9										9
10										10
11										11
12										12
13										13
14										14
15										15
16										16
17										17
18										18
19										19
20										20
21										21
22										22
23										23
24										24

[1, 7, 10, 11, 13]

CASH PAYMENTS JOURNAL

PAGE 17

	DATE	ACCOUNT TITLE	CHECK NO.	POST. REF.	1 GENERAL DEBIT	2 GENERAL CREDIT	3 ACCOUNTS PAYABLE DEBIT	4 PURCHASES DISCOUNT CREDIT	5 CASH CREDIT	
1										1
2										2
3										3
4										4
5										5
6										6
7										7
8										8
9										9
10										10
11										11
12										12
13										13
14										14
15										15
16										16
17										17
18										18
19										19
20										20
21										21
22										22
23										23
24										24

Name ______________ Date ________ Class ________

The general ledger used in Reinforcement Activity 4, Part A, is needed to complete Part B.

GENERAL LEDGER

ACCOUNT Cash — ACCOUNT NO. 1101

DATE		ITEM	POST. REF.	DEBIT	CREDIT	BALANCE DEBIT	BALANCE CREDIT
19-- Dec.	1	Balance	✓			25 649 80	

ACCOUNT Notes Receivable — ACCOUNT NO. 1102

DATE		ITEM	POST. REF.	DEBIT	CREDIT	BALANCE DEBIT	BALANCE CREDIT
19-- Dec.	1	Balance	✓			3 300 00	

ACCOUNT Accounts Receivable — ACCOUNT NO. 1103

DATE		ITEM	POST. REF.	DEBIT	CREDIT	BALANCE DEBIT	BALANCE CREDIT
19-- Dec.	1	Balance	✓			15 053 10	

ACCOUNT Allowance for Uncollectible Accounts — ACCOUNT NO. 1103.1

DATE		ITEM	POST. REF.	DEBIT	CREDIT	BALANCE DEBIT	BALANCE CREDIT
19-- Dec.	1	Balance	✓				25 50

ACCOUNT Merchandise Inventory — ACCOUNT NO. 1104

DATE		ITEM	POST. REF.	DEBIT	CREDIT	BALANCE DEBIT	BALANCE CREDIT
19-- Dec.	1	Balance	✓			83 370 20	

ACCOUNT Supplies — ACCOUNT NO. 1105

DATE		ITEM	POST. REF.	DEBIT	CREDIT	BALANCE DEBIT	BALANCE CREDIT
19-- Dec.	1	Balance	✓			1 417 90	

GENERAL LEDGER

ACCOUNT Prepaid Insurance — ACCOUNT NO. 1106

DATE		ITEM	POST. REF.	DEBIT	CREDIT	BALANCE DEBIT	BALANCE CREDIT
19-- Dec.	1	Balance	✓			504000	

ACCOUNT Office Equipment — ACCOUNT NO. 1201

DATE		ITEM	POST. REF.	DEBIT	CREDIT	BALANCE DEBIT	BALANCE CREDIT
19-- Dec.	1	Balance	✓			434000	

ACCOUNT Accumulated Depreciation-Office Equipment — ACCOUNT NO. 1201.1

DATE		ITEM	POST. REF.	DEBIT	CREDIT	BALANCE DEBIT	BALANCE CREDIT
19-- Dec.	1	Balance	✓				152000

ACCOUNT Store Equipment — ACCOUNT NO. 1202

DATE		ITEM	POST. REF.	DEBIT	CREDIT	BALANCE DEBIT	BALANCE CREDIT
19-- Dec.	1	Balance	✓			777500	

ACCOUNT Accumulated Depreciation-Store Equipment — ACCOUNT NO. 1202.1

DATE		ITEM	POST. REF.	DEBIT	CREDIT	BALANCE DEBIT	BALANCE CREDIT
19-- Dec.	1	Balance	✓				295500

ACCOUNT Notes Payable — ACCOUNT NO. 2101

DATE		ITEM	POST. REF.	DEBIT	CREDIT	BALANCE DEBIT	BALANCE CREDIT
19-- Dec.	1	Balance	✓				800000

ACCOUNT Accounts Payable — ACCOUNT NO. 2102

DATE		ITEM	POST. REF.	DEBIT	CREDIT	BALANCE DEBIT	BALANCE CREDIT
19-- Dec.	1	Balance	✓				733890

Name ______________________ Date __________ Class __________

GENERAL LEDGER

ACCOUNT Employees Income Tax Payable — ACCOUNT NO. 2103

DATE		ITEM	POST. REF.	DEBIT	CREDIT	BALANCE DEBIT	BALANCE CREDIT
19-- Dec.	1	Balance	✓				99200

ACCOUNT Federal Income Tax Payable — ACCOUNT NO. 2104

DATE		ITEM	POST. REF.	DEBIT	CREDIT	BALANCE DEBIT	BALANCE CREDIT

ACCOUNT FICA Tax Payable — ACCOUNT NO. 2105

DATE		ITEM	POST. REF.	DEBIT	CREDIT	BALANCE DEBIT	BALANCE CREDIT
19-- Dec.	1	Balance	✓				92320

ACCOUNT Sales Tax Payable — ACCOUNT NO. 2106

DATE		ITEM	POST. REF.	DEBIT	CREDIT	BALANCE DEBIT	BALANCE CREDIT
19-- Dec.	1	Balance	✓				220090

ACCOUNT Unemployment Tax Payable - Federal — ACCOUNT NO. 2107

DATE		ITEM	POST. REF.	DEBIT	CREDIT	BALANCE DEBIT	BALANCE CREDIT
19-- Dec.	1	Balance	✓				2400

GENERAL LEDGER

ACCOUNT Unemployment Tax Payable – State — ACCOUNT NO. 2108

DATE		ITEM	POST. REF.	DEBIT	CREDIT	BALANCE DEBIT	BALANCE CREDIT
19-- Dec.	1	Balance	✓				9260

ACCOUNT Dividends Payable — ACCOUNT NO. 2109

DATE		ITEM	POST. REF.	DEBIT	CREDIT	BALANCE DEBIT	BALANCE CREDIT

ACCOUNT Capital Stock — ACCOUNT NO. 3101

DATE		ITEM	POST. REF.	DEBIT	CREDIT	BALANCE DEBIT	BALANCE CREDIT
19-- Dec.	1	Balance	✓				6000000

ACCOUNT Retained Earnings — ACCOUNT NO. 3201

DATE		ITEM	POST. REF.	DEBIT	CREDIT	BALANCE DEBIT	BALANCE CREDIT
19-- Dec.	1	Balance	✓				1562200

ACCOUNT Income Summary — ACCOUNT NO. 3301

DATE		ITEM	POST. REF.	DEBIT	CREDIT	BALANCE DEBIT	BALANCE CREDIT

ACCOUNT Sales — ACCOUNT NO. 4101

DATE		ITEM	POST. REF.	DEBIT	CREDIT	BALANCE DEBIT	BALANCE CREDIT
19-- Dec.	1	Balance	✓				47523840

Name ____________________ Date __________ Class __________

GENERAL LEDGER

ACCOUNT Sales Returns and Allowances — ACCOUNT NO. 4101.1

DATE		ITEM	POST. REF.	DEBIT	CREDIT	BALANCE DEBIT	BALANCE CREDIT
19-- Dec.	1	Balance	✓			357760	

ACCOUNT Purchases — ACCOUNT NO. 5101

DATE		ITEM	POST. REF.	DEBIT	CREDIT	BALANCE DEBIT	BALANCE CREDIT
19-- Dec.	1	Balance	✓			32131220	

ACCOUNT Purchases Returns and Allowances — ACCOUNT NO. 5101.1

DATE		ITEM	POST. REF.	DEBIT	CREDIT	BALANCE DEBIT	BALANCE CREDIT
19-- Dec.	1	Balance	✓				116450

ACCOUNT Purchases Discount — ACCOUNT NO. 5101.2

DATE		ITEM	POST. REF.	DEBIT	CREDIT	BALANCE DEBIT	BALANCE CREDIT
19-- Dec.	1	Balance	✓				234160

ACCOUNT Advertising Expense — ACCOUNT NO. 6101

DATE		ITEM	POST. REF.	DEBIT	CREDIT	BALANCE DEBIT	BALANCE CREDIT
19-- Dec.	1	Balance	✓			611500	

ACCOUNT Bad Debts Expense — ACCOUNT NO. 6102

DATE		ITEM	POST. REF.	DEBIT	CREDIT	BALANCE DEBIT	BALANCE CREDIT

GENERAL LEDGER

ACCOUNT Credit Card Fee Expense ACCOUNT NO. 6103

DATE		ITEM	POST. REF.	DEBIT	CREDIT	BALANCE DEBIT	BALANCE CREDIT
19-- Dec.	1	Balance	✓			475230	

ACCOUNT Depreciation Expense-Office Equipment ACCOUNT NO. 6104

DATE		ITEM	POST. REF.	DEBIT	CREDIT	BALANCE DEBIT	BALANCE CREDIT

ACCOUNT Depreciation Expense-Store Equipment ACCOUNT NO. 6105

DATE		ITEM	POST. REF.	DEBIT	CREDIT	BALANCE DEBIT	BALANCE CREDIT

ACCOUNT Insurance Expense ACCOUNT NO. 6106

DATE		ITEM	POST. REF.	DEBIT	CREDIT	BALANCE DEBIT	BALANCE CREDIT

ACCOUNT Miscellaneous Expense ACCOUNT NO. 6107

DATE		ITEM	POST. REF.	DEBIT	CREDIT	BALANCE DEBIT	BALANCE CREDIT
19-- Dec.	1	Balance	✓			374950	

ACCOUNT Payroll Taxes Expense ACCOUNT NO. 6108

DATE		ITEM	POST. REF.	DEBIT	CREDIT	BALANCE DEBIT	BALANCE CREDIT
19-- Dec.	1	Balance	✓			476890	

GENERAL LEDGER

ACCOUNT *Rent Expense* ACCOUNT NO. 6109

DATE		ITEM	POST. REF.	DEBIT	CREDIT	BALANCE DEBIT	BALANCE CREDIT
19-- Dec.	1	Balance	✓			13 750 00	

ACCOUNT *Salary Expense* ACCOUNT NO. 6110

DATE		ITEM	POST. REF.	DEBIT	CREDIT	BALANCE DEBIT	BALANCE CREDIT
19-- Dec.	1	Balance	✓			68 127 10	

ACCOUNT *Supplies Expense* ACCOUNT NO. 6111

DATE		ITEM	POST. REF.	DEBIT	CREDIT	BALANCE DEBIT	BALANCE CREDIT

ACCOUNT *Interest Income* ACCOUNT NO. 7101

DATE		ITEM	POST. REF.	DEBIT	CREDIT	BALANCE DEBIT	BALANCE CREDIT
19-- Dec.	1	Balance	✓				1 240 00

ACCOUNT *Interest Expense* ACCOUNT NO. 8101

DATE		ITEM	POST. REF.	DEBIT	CREDIT	BALANCE DEBIT	BALANCE CREDIT
19-- Dec.	1	Balance	✓			1 580 00	

ACCOUNT *Federal Income Tax* ACCOUNT NO. 9101

DATE		ITEM	POST. REF.	DEBIT	CREDIT	BALANCE DEBIT	BALANCE CREDIT
19-- Dec.	1	Balance	✓			6 000 00	

ACCOUNTS RECEIVABLE LEDGER

NAME Arlinghouse, Ltd.
ADDRESS 830 Wymore Road, Austin, TX 78751-8010

DATE		ITEM	POST. REF.	DEBIT	CREDIT	DEBIT BALANCE
19-- Dec.	1	Balance	✓			240850

NAME Hampton's, Inc.
ADDRESS 9216 Lane Boulevard, Austin, TX 78703-1287

DATE		ITEM	POST. REF.	DEBIT	CREDIT	DEBIT BALANCE
19-- Dec.	1	Balance	✓			270960

NAME Kaleidoscape Construction
ADDRESS 3715 Fowler Road, Austin, TX 78703-1436

DATE		ITEM	POST. REF.	DEBIT	CREDIT	DEBIT BALANCE
19-- Dec.	1	Balance	✓			331170

NAME Owatonna's
ADDRESS 5910 Rugged Trail, Austin, TX 78703-1408

DATE		ITEM	POST. REF.	DEBIT	CREDIT	DEBIT BALANCE
19-- Dec.	1	Balance	✓			180630

NAME Strickland Systems
ADDRESS 2434 Pitt Road, Austin, TX 78702-1042

DATE		ITEM	POST. REF.	DEBIT	CREDIT	DEBIT BALANCE
19-- Dec.	1	Balance	✓			391380

ACCOUNTS RECEIVABLE LEDGER

[4, 7–9, 12–14]

NAME E. J. Traver

ADDRESS 8532 West 59th Street, Austin, TX 78711-1803

DATE		ITEM	POST. REF.	DEBIT	CREDIT	DEBIT BALANCE
19-- Dec.	1	Balance	✓			90320

ACCOUNTS PAYABLE LEDGER

[5, 7–9, 12–14]

NAME De Chaines Electronics

ADDRESS 4350 Marvin Drive, Austin, TX 78751-8397

DATE		ITEM	POST. REF.	DEBIT	CREDIT	CREDIT BALANCE
19-- Dec.	1	Balance	✓			176100

NAME Fidelity Sound Systems

ADDRESS 1635 Victory Expressway, Dallas, TX 75206-2347

DATE		ITEM	POST. REF.	DEBIT	CREDIT	CREDIT BALANCE
19-- Dec.	1	Balance	✓			146800

NAME Gulf Sound, Ltd.

ADDRESS 6742 St. James Ave., Austin, TX 78703-1533

DATE		ITEM	POST. REF.	DEBIT	CREDIT	CREDIT BALANCE
19-- Dec.	1	Balance	✓			168790

NAME Stereo Systems, Inc.

ADDRESS 10836 Camp Dixie Blvd., Ft. Worth, TX 76119-3462

DATE		ITEM	POST. REF.	DEBIT	CREDIT	CREDIT BALANCE
19-- Dec.	1	Balance	✓			132100

ACCOUNTS PAYABLE LEDGER

NAME Westside Communications

ADDRESS 5937 West 61st Street, Austin, TX 78711-2741

DATE		ITEM	POST. REF.	DEBIT	CREDIT	CREDIT BALANCE
19-- Dec.	1	Balance	✓			110100

[14]

[14]

Perfect Score. 37	Name ______	
Deduct........ __	Date ______	Class ______
Your Score .... __	Checked by ______	

UNIT A — Analyzing Bad Debts Expense and Valuation of Accounts Receivable

DIRECTIONS: Place a check mark (√) in the proper Answers column to show whether each of the following statements is true or false.

	Answers: True	Answers: False	For Scoring
0. Businesses collect all of their accounts receivable		√	**0.** √
1. The longer a customer's account is overdue, the more likely the account will be uncollectible			**1.**
2. Risk of loss to a business occurs when it makes a sale on account			**2.**
3. A business incurs an expense when it cannot collect an account receivable			**3.**
4. The balance of a contra account is always a credit balance			**4.**
5. When the percent of charge sales method is used, the amount of uncollectible accounts is estimated			**5.**
6. When the aging accounts receivable method is used, the amount of bad debts is estimated			**6.**
7. When Allowance for Uncollectible Accounts is used, the amount of bad debts expense shown on the income statement is an estimated amount			**7.**
8. Under the percent of charge sales method, Allowance for Uncollectible Accounts is debited to write off a customer's account			**8.**
9. In writing off a customer's account, Accounts Receivable is credited			**9.**
10. When an adjusting entry for bad debts expense is recorded, Allowance for Uncollectible Accounts is debited			**10.**
11. When an adjusting entry for bad debts expense is recorded, the accounts receivable account is credited			**11.**
12. When an adjusting entry for bad debts expense is recorded, the bad debts expense account is credited			**12.**
13. After an adjusting entry for bad debts expense is posted, the bad debts expense account has a credit balance			**13.**
14. The account number 113.1 shows that the account with this number is the contra account for account 113			**14.**
15. When a contra account is listed on the balance sheet, this balance is subtracted from the balance of the related account			**15.**
16. Under the direct write-off of uncollectible accounts method when a customer's account is written off, book value of accounts receivable decreases			**16.**
17. Under the allowance method of recording uncollectible accounts when a customer's account is written off, book value of accounts receivable decreases			**17.**
18. Aging accounts to estimate uncollectible accounts is generally considered more accurate than using a percent of charge sales			**18.**
19. The aging accounts receivable method of estimating bad debts expense requires more time than other methods			**19.**
20. The value of Accounts Receivable on the balance sheet is overstated when there is no adjustment for uncollectible accounts			**20.**
21. The book value of accounts receivable is reported on an income statement			**21.**
22. The balance of Accounts Receivable in the general ledger must equal the sum of the customers' accounts in the subsidiary ledger			**22.**
23. Information used to journalize the adjustment for bad debts expense is obtained from the adjustments columns of the work sheet			**23.**

UNIT B — Accounting Terms

DIRECTIONS: Select the one term in Column I that best fits each definition in Column II. Print the letter identifying your choice in the Answers column.

Column I

A. aging accounts receivable
B. allowance method of recording losses from uncollectible accounts
C. bad debts expense
D. book value of accounts receivable
E. direct write-off of uncollectible accounts
F. schedule of accounts receivable by age
G. uncollectible accounts
H. writing off an account

Column II	Answers	For Scoring
0. Accounts receivable that cannot be collected	*G*	**0.** √
24. Analyzing accounts receivable according to when they are due		**24.**
25. Recording bad debts expense only when a customer's account is known to be uncollectible		**25.**
26. The expense caused by uncollectible accounts		**26.**
27. Crediting the estimated value of uncollectible accounts to a contra account		**27.**
28. The difference between the balance of Accounts Receivable and the estimated uncollectible accounts		**28.**
29. Canceling the balance of a customer's account because the customer does not pay		**29.**
30. A list of charge customers that shows the balances due by age of account		**30.**

UNIT C — Analyzing Uncollectible Accounts and Accounts Receivable

DIRECTIONS: For each item below, select the choice that best completes the sentence. Print the letter identifying your choice in the Answers column.

	Answers	For Scoring
0. Allowance for Uncollectible Accounts is **(A)** an asset account **(B)** a contra asset account **(C)** a liability account **(D)** a contra sales account.....	*B*	**0.** √
31. Revenue from sales on account should be recorded **(A)** at the time of sale **(B)** when payment is made **(C)** when the merchandise is delivered		**31.**
32. When Allowance for Uncollectible Accounts is used, a customer's past-due account is written off as uncollectible by **(A)** debiting Allowance for Uncollectible Accounts and crediting Accounts Receivable and the customer's account **(B)** debiting Accounts Receivable and crediting the customer's account **(C)** debiting Bad Debts Expense and crediting the customer's account		**32.**
33. When the direct write-off of uncollectible accounts method is used, a customer's account is written off by **(A)** debiting Accounts Receivable and crediting the customer's account **(B)** debiting Bad Debts Expense and crediting Accounts Receivable and the customer's account **(C)** debiting Accounts Receivable and crediting Allowance for Uncollectible Accounts .		**33.**
34. At the end of each fiscal period, the account debited to show the estimated amount of uncollectible accounts is **(A)** Bad Debts Expense **(B)** Accounts Receivable **(C)** Allowance for Uncollectible Accounts		**34.**
35. At the end of each fiscal period, the account credited to show the estimated amount of uncollectible accounts is **(A)** Bad Debts Expense **(B)** Accounts Receivable **(C)** Allowance for Uncollectible Accounts		**35.**
36. When the allowance method of recording uncollectible accounts is used and a customer's account is written off **(A)** revenues decrease **(B)** expenses increase **(C)** revenues and expenses do not change		**36.**
37. When the direct write-off of uncollectible accounts method is used and a customer's account is written off **(A)** revenues decrease **(B)** expenses increase **(C)** revenues and expenses do not change		**37.**

Name ________________ Date ________ Class ________ *DRILL 24-D 1, p. 499*

Journalizing uncollectible accounts

Transaction	General Ledger Accounts			Accounts Not Affected
	Accounts Receivable	Allowance for Uncollectible Accounts	Bad Debts Expense	
Direct Write-Off Method Used: **a.** Estimated amount of uncollectible accounts				
b. Wrote off an uncollectible account.				
Estimated Method Used: **c.** Estimated amount of uncollectible accounts at end of fiscal period.......				
d. Wrote off an uncollectible account.				

Figuring bad debts expense

DRILL 24-D 2, p. 499

Store	Method For Figuring Bad Debts Expense		
	Direct Write-Off Method	Percentage of Charge Sales Method	Aging Method
1			
2			
3			

Use blank space below for any necessary calculations.

GENERAL JOURNAL

PAGE

DATE		ACCOUNT TITLE	POST. REF.	DEBIT	CREDIT

Recording entries for bad debts expense

GENERAL JOURNAL

PAGE

DATE		ACCOUNT TITLE	POST. REF.	DEBIT	CREDIT

GENERAL JOURNAL PAGE

DATE		ACCOUNT TITLE	POST. REF.	DEBIT	CREDIT

Name ______________________ Date __________ Class __________

CHALLENGE PROBLEM 24-C, p. 501

[1, 2]

Recording entries for bad debts expense

GENERAL JOURNAL

PAGE

DATE		ACCOUNT TITLE	POST. REF.	DEBIT	CREDIT

GENERAL JOURNAL PAGE

	DATE		ACCOUNT TITLE	POST. REF.	DEBIT	CREDIT	
1							1
2							2
3							3
4							4
5							5
6							6
7							7
8							8
9							9
10							10
11							11
12							12
13							13
14							14
15							15
16							16
17							17
18							18
19							19
20							20
21							21
22							22
23							23
24							24
25							25
26							26
27							27
28							28
29							29
30							30
31							31
32							32

Perfect Score. 35	Name
Deduct..........	Date ______ Class ______
Your Score....	Checked by

STUDY GUIDE 25

UNIT A — Accounting Terms

DIRECTIONS: Select the one term in Column I that best fits each definition in Column II. Print the letter identifying your choice in the Answers column.

Column I	Column II	Answers	For Scoring
A. book value of a plant asset	**0.** Assets that will be used for a number of years in the operation of a business	*F*	**0.** ✓
B. depreciation	**1.** A decrease in value of a plant asset because of use and passage of time		**1.**
C. equipment	**2.** Plant assets such as delivery trucks, machinery, display cases, tables, typewriters, and desks		**2.**
D. estimated salvage value	**3.** The amount an owner expects to receive when a plant asset is removed from use		**3.**
E. plant asset record	**4.** An accounting form on which a business records data about each plant asset		**4.**
F. plant assets	**5.** Charging an *equal* amount of annual depreciation expense for a plant asset		**5.**
G. straight-line method of depreciation	**6.** The original cost of a plant asset minus the accumulated depreciation		**6.**

UNIT B — Analyzing Plant Assets Depreciation

DIRECTIONS: Place a check mark (✓) in the proper Answers column to show whether each of the following statements is true or false.

Statement	Answers: True	Answers: False	For Scoring
0. All land is classified as a plant asset		✓	**0.** ✓
7. The amount of plant asset depreciation is a liability			**7.**
8. A plant asset's estimated salvage value must be known to determine depreciation expense			**8.**
9. A plant asset's estimated useful life must be known to determine depreciation expense			**9.**
10. The debit balance of a plant asset account shows the book value of that asset at the end of each year			**10.**
11. The original cost minus the estimated salvage value of a plant asset equals its total amount of estimated depreciation			**11.**
12. The debit balance of the equipment account always represents the cost price of all equipment currently on hand			**12.**
13. A debit entry in the accumulated depreciation account for equipment shows the estimated decrease in value of the equipment because of depreciation			**13.**
14. After adjusting entries have been posted, the debit balance of the account Equipment shows the original cost of all equipment on hand			**14.**
15. After adjusting entries have been posted, the credit balance of Accumulated Depreciation — Equipment represents the amount of depreciation expense that has been recorded since the equipment was purchased for all equipment on hand.			**15.**
16. The difference between the balance of the accumulated depreciation and depreciation expense accounts is the book value of a plant asset			**16.**
17. Accumulated Depreciation is decreased when the related plant asset is sold			**17.**
18. Depreciation expense is recorded every year on an asset until it is discarded			**18.**

UNIT C — Examining Plant Assets and Depreciation

DIRECTIONS: For each item below, select the choice that best completes the sentence. Print the letter identifying your choice in the Answers column.

	Answers	For Scoring
0. A business uses a plant asset **(A)** to sell for a profit **(B)** to operate the business **(C)** as an investment	*B*	**0.** ✓
19. If depreciation expense is not recorded, net income will **(A)** be understated **(B)** be overstated **(C)** not be affected............................		**19.**
20. An estimate of a plant asset's useful life should be based on **(A)** FICA guidelines **(B)** a minimum of 10 years **(C)** prior experience with similar assets..		**20.**
21. An example of a plant asset is **(A)** Supplies **(B)** Delivery Equipment **(C)** Accounts Receivable.....................		**21.**
22. A factor affecting the amount of plant asset depreciation expense for a fiscal period is **(A)** original cost **(B)** accumulated depreciation **(C)** contra account **(D)** cash.		**22.**
23. The debit balance of Equipment always represents the **(A)** original cost of all equipment owned **(B)** cost of equipment bought during the past fiscal period **(C)** cost of equipment bought during the current fiscal period..................................		**23.**
24. The amount by which a plant asset depreciates is classified as **(A)** a liability **(B)** an asset **(C)** an expense..		**24.**
25. Accumulated Depreciation — Equipment is classified as **(A)** a liability account **(B)** a contra expense account **(C)** a contra asset account		**25.**
26. The annual depreciation for a plant asset with original cost of $10,000.00, estimated salvage value of $1,000.00, and estimated useful life of 10 years, using the straight-line method, is **(A)** $1,000.00 **(B)** $10,000.00 **(C)** $900.00..............................		**26.**
27. The amount appearing in a work sheet's Adjustments Debit column for Depreciation Expense — Equipment is extended to the **(A)** Balance Sheet Debit column **(B)** Income Statement Credit column **(C)** Income Statement Debit column **(D)** Balance Sheet Credit column................		**27.**
28. The amount appearing in a work sheet's Adjustments Credit column for Accumulated Depreciation — Equipment is included in the amount extended to the **(A)** Income Statement Credit column **(B)** Income Statement Debit column **(C)** Balance Sheet Credit column **(D)** Balance Sheet Debit column.....................		**28.**
29. The total accumulated depreciation of equipment appears on the work sheet in the **(A)** Income Statement Credit column **(B)** Income Statement Debit column **(C)** Balance Sheet Debit column **(D)** Balance Sheet Credit column.....................		**29.**
30. In journalizing an adjusting entry for equipment, the account debited is **(A)** Equipment **(B)** Depreciation Expense — Equipment **(C)** Accumulated Depreciation — Equipment **(D)** Cash..................................		**30.**
31. In journalizing an adjusting entry for equipment, the account credited is **(A)** Equipment **(B)** Depreciation Expense — Equipment **(C)** Accumulated Depreciation — Equipment **(D)** Cash..................................		**31.**
32. In journalizing an entry for buying new equipment for cash, the account debited is **(A)** Equipment **(B)** Depreciation Expense — Equipment **(C)** Accumulated Depreciation — Equipment **(D)** Cash..................................		**32.**
33. In journalizing an entry for buying new equipment for cash, the account credited is **(A)** Equipment **(B)** Depreciation Expense — Equipment **(C)** Accumulated Depreciation — Equipment **(D)** Cash..................................		**33.**
34. In journalizing an entry for a cash sale of equipment for book value, the account(s) debited is (are) **(A)** Equipment **(B)** Depreciation Expense — Equipment **(C)** Accumulated Depreciation — Equipment **(D)** Cash..................................		**34.**
35. In journalizing an entry for a cash sale of equipment for book value, the account(s) credited is (are) **(A)** Equipment **(B)** Depreciation Expense — Equipment **(C)** Accumulated Depreciation — Equipment **(D)** Cash..................................		**35.**

Name ________________________ Date __________ Class __________

DRILL 25-D 1, p. 515

Figuring depreciation expense

Plant Asset	Original Cost	Estimated Salvage Value	Estimated Life	Amount of Annual Depreciation
1	$ 2,850.00	$ 450.00	4 years	$
2	1,700.00	200.00	5 years	
3	900.00	none	3 years	
4	36,600.00	1,600.00	20 years	
5	17,000.00	2,400.00	8 years	
6	12,160.00	800.00	16 years	
7	2,280.00	300.00	3 years	
8	2,210.00	240.00	5 years	
9	29,280.00	1,280.00	10 years	
10	14,500.00	2,800.00	20 years	

Figuring book value of a plant asset

DRILL 25-D 2, p. 515

Plant Asset	Date Bought	Original Cost	Estimated Salvage Value	Estimated Life	(a) Total Amount of Estimated Depreciation as of 12/31/83	(b) Book Value 12/31/83
1	Jan. 1, 1979	$ 2,400.00	$150.00	5 years	$	$
2	July 1, 1979	7,150.00	550.00	10 years		
3	Dec. 31, 1979	10,725.00	825.00	15 years		
4	Jan. 1, 1980	1,865.00	245.00	20 years		
5	July 1, 1980	3,360.00	210.00	5 years		
6	Nov. 1, 1980	240.00	24.00	4 years		
7	Jan. 1, 1981	1,320.00	none	10 years		
8	April 1, 1982	2,770.00	500.00	5 years		
9	Jan. 1, 1983	2,900.00	300.00	10 years		
10	Dec. 1, 1983	428.00	50.00	7 years		

Recording the buying of plant assets

PROBLEM 25-1, p. 516

CASH PAYMENTS JOURNAL

PAGE

	DATE		ACCOUNT TITLE	CHECK NO.	POST. REF.	1 GENERAL DEBIT	2 GENERAL CREDIT	3 ACCOUNTS PAYABLE DEBIT	4 PURCHASES DISCOUNT CREDIT	5 CASH CREDIT	
1											1
2											2
3											3
4											4
5											5
6											6
7											7
8											8

Figuring depreciation expense

PROBLEM 25-2, p. 516

Plant Asset	Date Bought	Original Cost	Estimated Salvage Value	Estimated Life	Total Depreciation Expense 1983
1	Jan. 1, 1976	$5,200.00	$400.00	10 years	$
2	July 1, 1978	1,372.00	300.00	8 years	
3	July 1, 1978	1,650.00	150.00	6 years	
4	Oct. 1, 1979	2,700.00	300.00	5 years	
5	April 1, 1983	4,000.00	400.00	5 years	
6	July 1, 1983	1,734.00	150.00	6 years	

Preparing a plant asset record

PLANT ASSET RECORD

Wood Creations

Account No. ______

Item ______________________ General Ledger Account ______________________

Serial No. ______________ Description ______________________

From Whom Purchased ______________________ Cost ______________

Estimated Life ______________ Estimated Salvage or Trade-in Value ______________ Depreciation per year ______________

Disposal date ______________________ Disposal amount ______________________

Date Mo. Day Yr.	Annual Depreciation Expense	Accumulated Depreciation	Book Value

Recording work sheet adjustments and journal entries for depreciation expense [1, 2]

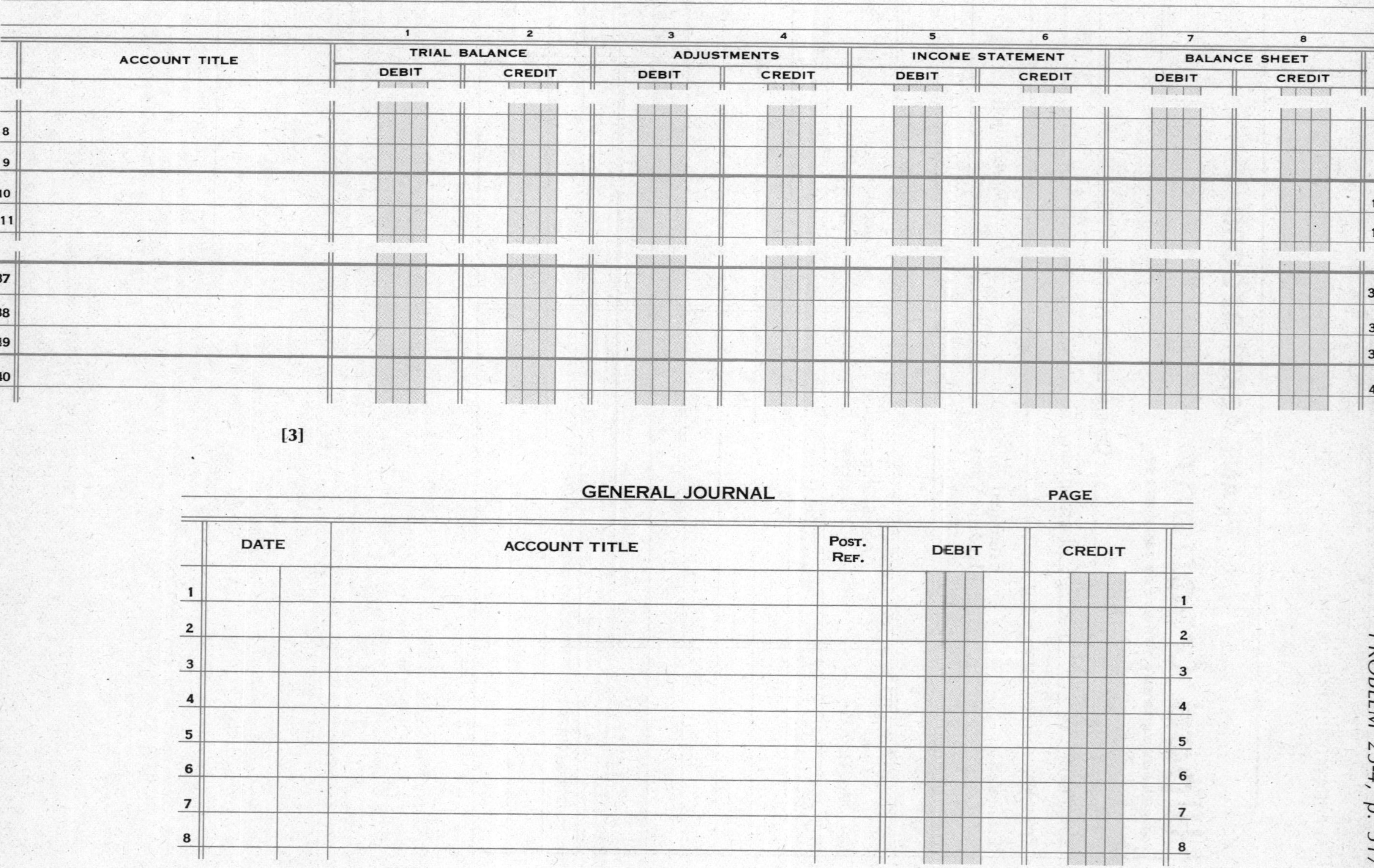

	ACCOUNT TITLE	1 TRIAL BALANCE DEBIT	2 TRIAL BALANCE CREDIT	3 ADJUSTMENTS DEBIT	4 ADJUSTMENTS CREDIT	5 INCOME STATEMENT DEBIT	6 INCOME STATEMENT CREDIT	7 BALANCE SHEET DEBIT	8 BALANCE SHEET CREDIT	
8										8
9										9
10										10
11										11
37										37
38										38
39										39
40										40

[3]

GENERAL JOURNAL PAGE

	DATE		ACCOUNT TITLE	POST. REF.	DEBIT	CREDIT	
1							1
2							2
3							3
4							4
5							5
6							6
7							7
8							8

Name ______________________ Date __________ Class __________

MASTERY PROBLEM 25-M, p. 517

[1, 2]

Figuring depreciation expense and book value of plant assets; journalizing depreciation expense and disposal of a plant asset

Plant Asset	Asset Account	Date Bought	Original Cost	Estimated Salvage Value	Estimated Life	Total Depreciation Expense 1983	Book Value 12/31/83
1	Delivery Equipment	Oct. 1, 1976	$8,000.00	$440.00	7 years	$	$
2	Delivery Equipment	July 1, 1983	7,400.00	500.00	5 years		
3	Shop Equipment	Oct. 1, 1979	1,638.00	150.00	8 years		
4	Shop Equipment	Feb. 1, 1980	2,820.00	none	10 years		
5	Shop Equipment	April 1, 1983	1,060.00	100.00	4 years		
6	Shop Equipment	July 1, 1983	1,150.00	70.00	3 years		

[3]

GENERAL JOURNAL PAGE

DATE	ACCOUNT TITLE	POST. REF.	DEBIT	CREDIT

MASTERY PROBLEM 25-M, concluded **[4]**

CASH RECEIPTS JOURNAL

PAGE

	DATE		ACCOUNT TITLE	DOC. NO.	POST. REF.	1 GENERAL DEBIT	2 GENERAL CREDIT	3 ACCOUNTS RECEIVABLE CREDIT	4 SALES CREDIT	5 SALES TAX PAYABLE CREDIT	6 CASH DEBIT	
1												1
2												2
3												3

Figuring depreciation expense using a declining-balance method *CHALLENGE PROBLEM 25-C, p. 518*

Year	Book value at beginning of year	Rate of depreciation	Annual depreciation this year	Accumulated depreciation at end of year	Book value at end of year
1982	$7,000.00	20%	$1,400.00	$1,400.00	$5,600.00
1983	5,600.00	20%	1,120.00	2,520.00	4,480.00

Perfect Score. 54 Name ______________

Deduct.......... ___ Date ______________ Class ______________

Your Score .... ___ Checked by ______________

STUDY GUIDE 26

UNIT A — Accounting Terms

DIRECTIONS: Select the one term in Column I that best fits each definition in Column II. Print the letter identifying your choice in the Answers column.

Column I

A. bank discount
B. date of a note
C. discounted note
D. dishonored note
E. interest
F. interest-bearing notes
G. interest rate of a note
H. maker of a note
I. maturity date of a note
J. maturity value
K. non-interest-bearing notes
L. notes payable
M. notes receivable
N. number of a note
O. payee of a note
P. principal of a note
Q. proceeds
R. promissory note
S. time of a note

Column II	Answers	For Scoring
0. The day a note is issued	*B*	**0.**✓
1. A note that is not paid when due		**1.**
2. A written and signed promise to pay a sum of money		**2.**
3. The person who signs a note and thus promises to make payment		**3.**
4. Promissory notes that do not contain a provision for the payment of interest		**4.**
5. The amount received for a note after the bank has deducted the bank discount		**5.**
6. An amount paid for the use of the principal of a note for a period of time		**6.**
7. The date a note is due		**7.**
8. The days, months, or years from the date of issue until a note is to be paid		**8.**
9. Promissory notes that require interest payments		**9.**
10. Promissory notes that a business gives creditors		**10.**
11. The person to whom a note is payable		**11.**
12. A note on which interest is paid in advance		**12.**
13. Promissory notes that a business accepts from customers		**13.**
14. Interest on a note collected in advance by a bank		**14.**
15. The amount a borrower promises to pay — the face of a note		**15.**
16. The principal plus the interest on a note		**16.**
17. The percentage of the principal that is paid for use of the money		**17.**
18. The number assigned by the maker to identify a specific note		**18.**

UNIT B — Examining a Promissory Note

DIRECTIONS: Each line of the promissory note at the right is identified with a capital letter. Answer each question below by printing the identifying capital letter in the Answers column.

$ A ______ B ______ 19 B
______ C ______ AFTER DATE D PROMISE TO PAY TO
THE ORDER OF ______ E ______
PAYABLE AT ______ F ______
______ G ______ DOLLARS
VALUE RECEIVED WITH INTEREST AT H
No. I DUE J ______ K ______

Which letter represents the line on which is written the:

	Answers	For Scoring
0. Time of a note?	*C*	**0.**✓
19. Maker of a note?		**19.**
20. Number of a note?		**20.**
21. Place where note is due?		**21.**
22. Interest rate of a note?		**22.**

	Answers	For Scoring
23. Principal in figures?		**23.**
24. Payee of a note?		**24.**
25. Word *I*?		**25.**
26. Maturity date of a note?		**26.**
27. Date of a note?		**27.**
28. Principal in words?		**28.**

UNIT C — Recording Notes Payable and Notes Receivable Transactions

DIRECTIONS: For each transaction below, print in the proper Answers columns the identifying letters of the accounts to be debited and credited.

Account Title

GENERAL LEDGER:
A. Accounts Payable
B. Accounts Receivable
C. Allowance for Uncollectible Accounts
D. Bad Debts Expense
E. Cash
F. Equipment
G. Interest Expense
H. Interest Income
I. Notes Payable
J. Notes Receivable

ACCTS. RECEIVABLE LEDGER:
K. Dona Konich
L. John Vargo

ACCTS. PAYABLE LEDGER:
M. Sykes Company

Transaction	Answers Debit	Answers Credit	For Scoring Debit	For Scoring Credit
0–0. Received an interest-bearing note from Dona Konich on account..........	*J*	*B,K*	0. ✓	0. ✓
29–30. Bought equipment by issuing an interest-bearing note payable in payment ..			29.	30.
31–32. Issued an interest-bearing note payable for cash			31.	32.
33–34. Discounted at 10% at the bank our non-interest-bearing note payable......			33.	34.
35–36. John Vargo dishonored his note receivable plus interest due today			35.	36.
37–38. Issued an interest-bearing note payable to Sykes Company for an extension of time on our account.............			37.	38.
39–40. Issued check in payment of note payable discounted in Transaction 33–34.			39.	40.
41–42. Received check from Dona Konich in settlement of her note and interest.....			41.	42.
43–44. Paid cash for principal and interest on an interest-bearing note payable........			43.	44.
45–46. Issued check to pay note payable and interest in Transaction 29–30...........			45.	46.

UNIT D — Analyzing Notes and Interest

DIRECTIONS: For each item below, select the choice that best completes the sentence. Print the letter identifying your choice in the Answers column.

Item	Answers	For Scoring
0. Promissory notes are used **(A)** to borrow money **(B)** to show evidence of a debt **(C)** to obtain an extension of time on an account **(D)** all of these	*D*	0.✓
47. The interest on a 6-month, 10% interest-bearing note of $1,000.00 is **(A)** $100.00 **(B)** $50.00 **(C)** $10.00 **(D)** none of these................................		47.
48. The maturity value of a 3-month, 12% interest-bearing note of $600.00 is **(A)** $600.00 **(B)** $618.00 **(C)** $672.00 **(D)** none of these............................		48.
49. The bank discount on a 2-month, non-interest-bearing note of $900.00, discounted at 9% is **(A)** $18.00 **(B)** $13.50 **(C)** $81.00 **(D)** none of these.....................		49.
50. The proceeds on a 3-month, non-interest-bearing note of $800.00, discounted at 8% is **(A)** $816.00 **(B)** $800.00 **(C)** $784.00 **(D)** none of these............................		50.
51. The maturity value of a 6-month, non-interest-bearing note of $1,000.00, discounted at 12% is **(A)** $1,060.00 **(B)** $1,000.00 **(C)** $940.00 **(D)** none of these..........		51.
52. When a note payable is issued for cash **(A)** Cash is decreased and Notes Payable is decreased **(B)** Cash is decreased and Notes Payable is increased **(C)** Cash is increased and Notes Payable is decreased **(D)** Cash is increased and Notes Payable is increased		52.
53. When cash is received in settlement of a note receivable plus interest **(A)** Cash is increased, Interest Income is increased, Notes Receivable is increased **(B)** Cash is increased, Interest Income is increased, Notes Receivable is decreased **(C)** Cash is increased, Interest Income is decreased, Notes Receivable is increased **(D)** Cash is increased, Interest Income is decreased, Notes Receivable is decreased.....		53.
54. One advantage of a note over an account receivable or account payable is **(A)** a note can be useful in a court of law as evidence of a debt **(B)** a note can be collected sooner **(C)** a note can be used to buy supplies		54.

Name ______________________ Date __________ Class __________

DRILL 26-D 1, p. 528

Recording principal, interest, and bank discount for notes payable

Trans. No.	Cash		Notes Payable		Accounts Payable		Interest Expense	
	Debit	Credit	Debit	Credit	Debit	Credit	Debit	Credit
1.	√			√				
2.								
3.								
4.								
5.								
6.								
7.								
8.								
9.								
10.								
11.								
12.								

Recording principal and interest for notes receivable

DRILL 26-D 2, p. 529

Trans. No.	Cash		Notes Receivable		Accounts Receivable		Interest Income	
	Debit	Credit	Debit	Credit	Debit	Credit	Debit	Credit
1.			√			√		
2.								
3.								
4.								
5.								
6.								
7.								
8.								

[1]

GENERAL JOURNAL

PAGE

DATE		ACCOUNT TITLE	POST. REF.	DEBIT	CREDIT

[1, 2]

CASH RECEIPTS JOURNAL

PAGE

	DATE		ACCOUNT TITLE	DOC. NO.	POST. REF.	1 GENERAL DEBIT	2 GENERAL CREDIT	3 ACCOUNTS RECEIVABLE CREDIT	4 SALES CREDIT	5 SALES TAX PAYABLE CREDIT	6 CASH DEBIT	
1												1
2												2
3												3
4												4
5												5
6												6

[1, 2]

CASH PAYMENTS JOURNAL

PAGE

	DATE		ACCOUNT TITLE	CHECK NO.	POST. REF.	1 GENERAL DEBIT	2 GENERAL CREDIT	3 ACCOUNTS PAYABLE DEBIT	4 PURCHASES DISCOUNT CREDIT	5 CASH CREDIT	
1											1
2											2
3											3
4											4
5											5
6											6
7											7
8											8
9											9
10											10
11											11
12											12

Recording notes receivable and interest [1]

GENERAL JOURNAL

PAGE

	DATE		ACCOUNT TITLE	POST. REF.	DEBIT	CREDIT	
1							1
2							2
3							3
4							4
5							5
6							6
7							7
8							8
9							9
10							10
11							11

[1, 2]

CASH RECEIPTS JOURNAL

PAGE

						1	2	3	4	5	6	
	DATE		ACCOUNT TITLE	DOC. NO.	POST. REF.	GENERAL		ACCOUNTS RECEIVABLE CREDIT	SALES CREDIT	SALES TAX PAYABLE CREDIT	CASH DEBIT	
						DEBIT	CREDIT					
1												1
2												2
3												3
4												4
5												5
6												6
7												7
8												8

Recording notes, interest, and bank discount [1, 2]

CASH RECEIPTS JOURNAL

PAGE

	DATE		ACCOUNT TITLE	DOC. NO.	POST. REF.	1 GENERAL DEBIT	2 GENERAL CREDIT	3 ACCOUNTS RECEIVABLE CREDIT	4 SALES CREDIT	5 SALES TAX PAYABLE CREDIT	6 CASH DEBIT	
1												1
2												2
3												3
4												4
5												5
6												6
7												7
8												8
9												9

[1, 2]

CASH PAYMENTS JOURNAL

PAGE

	DATE		ACCOUNT TITLE	CHECK NO.	POST. REF.	1 GENERAL DEBIT	2 GENERAL CREDIT	3 ACCOUNTS PAYABLE DEBIT	4 PURCHASES DISCOUNT CREDIT	5 CASH CREDIT	
1											1
2											2
3											3
4											4
5											5
6											6
7											7
8											8
9											9

[1]

GENERAL JOURNAL

PAGE

DATE		ACCOUNT TITLE	POST. REF.	DEBIT	CREDIT

Name ______________________ Date __________ Class __________

CHALLENGE PROBLEM 26-C, p. 531

[1]

Recording notes, interest, and bank discount

GENERAL JOURNAL PAGE

	DATE		ACCOUNT TITLE	POST. REF.	DEBIT	CREDIT	
1							1
2							2
3							3
4							4
5							5
6							6
7							7
8							8
9							9
10							10
11							11
12							12
13							13
14							14
15							15
16							16
17							17
18							18
19							19
20							20
21							21
22							22
23							23
24							24
25							25
26							26
27							27
28							28
29							29
30							30
31							31
32							32

[1, 2]

CASH RECEIPTS JOURNAL

PAGE

	DATE	ACCOUNT TITLE	DOC. NO.	POST. REF.	1 GENERAL DEBIT	2 GENERAL CREDIT	3 ACCOUNTS RECEIVABLE CREDIT	4 SALES CREDIT	5 SALES TAX PAYABLE CREDIT	6 CASH DEBIT	
1											1
2											2
3											3
4											4
5											5
6											6
7											7

[1, 2]

CASH PAYMENTS JOURNAL

PAGE

	DATE	ACCOUNT TITLE	CHECK NO.	POST. REF.	1 GENERAL DEBIT	2 GENERAL CREDIT	3 ACCOUNTS PAYABLE DEBIT	4 PURCHASES DISCOUNT CREDIT	5 CASH CREDIT	
1										1
2										2
3										3
4										4
5										5
6										6
7										7
8										8
9										9
10										10
11										11

Perfect Score. 69 Name ____________________

Deduct.......... ___ Date ______________ Class ______________

Your Score.... ___ Checked by ____________________

UNIT A — Examining End-of-Fiscal-Period Work for a Corporation

DIRECTIONS: Place a check mark (√) in the proper Answers column to show whether each of the following statements is true or false.

	Answers: True	Answers: False	For Scoring
0. Financial information about a corporation is needed by a number of people	√		**0.** √
1. Work sheets for corporations differ in many ways from work sheets for partnerships			**1.**
2. Both partnerships and corporations use accounts for federal income tax			**2.**
3. For a corporation, a separate capital account is kept for each owner			**3.**
4. The merchandise inventory balance shown in a trial balance is the ending inventory for a fiscal period			**4.**
5. Federal income tax is an expense of a corporation			**5.**
6. The account Federal Income Tax is a liability			**6.**
7. A statement of stockholders' equity is prepared for a corporation but not for a partnership			**7.**
8. A corporation's balance sheet reports financial progress during a fiscal period...			**8.**
9. Income from operations is the income earned only from normal business activities			**9.**
10. Net sales is reported in the Operating Revenue section of an income statement.			**10.**
11. Net purchases is reported in the Operating Expenses section of an income statement........			**11.**
12. Reporting net income before and after federal income tax is unique to corporation income statements........			**12.**
13. Operating revenue less cost of merchandise sold equals gross profit on operations			**13.**
14. Gross profit on operations plus operating expenses equals income from operations			**14.**
15. Income from operations plus other revenue less other expenses equals net income or net loss before federal income tax			**15.**
16. A statement of stockholders' equity contains a capital stock section and a retained earnings section			**16.**
17. All information necessary to prepare a statement of stockholders' equity is obtained from a work sheet			**17.**
18. A corporation's capital stock plus retained earnings always equals total assets..			**18.**
19. A corporation's balance sheet is prepared from information on a work sheet and an equity statement........			**19.**
20. The Current Assets section of a balance sheet is listed immediately below the Plant Assets section........			**20.**
21. Examples of current liabilities are accounts payable and FICA tax payable			**21.**
22. The book value of equipment is shown on a balance sheet in the Plant Assets section			**22.**
23. No income can be distributed to stockholders except by formal action of a corporation's board of directors			**23.**
24. A declared dividend is classified as a stockholders' equity........			**24.**
25. The source document for recording declaration of a dividend is a check stub			**25.**

UNIT B — Accounting Terms

DIRECTIONS: Select the one term in Column I that best fits each definition in Column II. Print the letter identifying your choice in the Answers column.

Column I

A. board of directors
B. capital stock
C. current assets
D. current liabilities
E. declaring a dividend
F. dividends
G. long-term liabilities
H. net purchases
I. net sales
J. retained earnings
K. share of stock
L. statement of stockholders' equity
M. stockholder

Column II	Answers	For Scoring
0. Total sales less sales returns and allowances	*I*	**0.✓**
26. A financial statement showing changes in a corporation's ownership for a fiscal period		**26.**
27. Cash and assets readily exchanged for cash or consumed within a year		**27.**
28. Liabilities owed for more than a year		**28.**
29. Action by a board of directors to distribute corporate earnings to stockholders		**29.**
30. Each unit of ownership in a corporation		**30.**
31. Total shares of ownership in a corporation		**31.**
32. Total purchases less purchases returns and allowances and purchases discount		**32.**
33. Earnings distributed to stockholders		**33.**
34. Liabilities due within a short time, usually within a year		**34.**
35. A group of persons elected by the stockholders to manage a corporation		**35.**
36. An owner of one or more shares of a corporation		**36.**
37. An amount earned by a corporation and not yet distributed to stockholders		**37.**

UNIT C — Recording End-of-Fiscal-Period Entries for a Corporation

DIRECTIONS: For each transaction below, print in the proper Answers column the identifying capital letters of the accounts to be debited and credited. Select the capital letters from the list at the left.

Account Titles

A. Accumulated Depreciation
B. Allowance for Uncollectible Accounts
C. Bad Debts Expense
D. Cash
E. Depreciation Expense
F. Dividends Payable
G. Federal Income Tax
H. Federal Income Tax Payable
I. Income Summary
J. Insurance Expense
K. Merchandise Inventory
L. Purchases
M. Purchases Discount
N. Prepaid Insurance
O. Retained Earnings
P. Sales
Q. Sales Returns and Allowances
R. Supplies
S. Supplies Expense

Transactions	Answers Debit	Answers Credit	For Scoring Debit	For Scoring Credit
0–0. Make adjustment for supplies used	*S*	*R*	**0.✓**	**0.✓**
38–39. Make adjustment for Prepaid Insurance expired			**38.**	**39.**
40–41. Close the purchases discount account			**40.**	**41.**
42–43. Make adjustment for actual income tax owed			**42.**	**43.**
44–45. Close the income summary account (net income balance)			**44.**	**45.**
46–47. Close the depreciation expense account			**46.**	**47.**
48–49. Make adjustment for beginning inventory			**48.**	**49.**
50–51. Close the sales account			**50.**	**51.**
52–53. Make adjustment for depreciation			**52.**	**53.**
54–55. Make adjustment for bad debts for the period			**54.**	**55.**
56–57. Make adjustment for ending inventory			**56.**	**57.**
58–59. Close the purchases account			**58.**	**59.**
60–61. Close the bad debts expense account			**60.**	**61.**
62–63. Close the federal income tax account			**62.**	**63.**
64–65. Close the sales returns and allowances account			**64.**	**65.**
66–67. Declared stockholders' dividend			**66.**	**67.**
68–69. Paid cash for dividends declared			**68.**	**69.**

Name ______________________ Date __________ Class __________

DRILL 27-D 1, p. 554

Analyzing adjustments on a work sheet

Adjustment No.	Work Sheet Adjustment	
	(a) Account Debited	(b) Account Credited
1.	*Income Summary*	*Merchandise Inventory*
2.		
3.		
4.		
5.		
6.		
7.		
8.		
9.		

Drill 27-D 2 is on page 398.

DRILL 27-D 3, p. 555

Analyzing closing entries

Closing Entry No.	Closing Entry	
	(a) Account Debited	(b) Account Credited
1.	*Income Summary*	*Delivery Expense*
2.		
3.		
4.		
5.		
6.		
7.		
8.		
9.		
10.		
11.		
12.		

Classifying assets, liabilities, and stockholders' equity accounts on a balance sheet

DRILL 27-D 2, p. 554

Account No.	Current Assets	Contra Acct. of a Current Asset	Plant Assets	Contra Acct. of a Plant Asset	Current Liability	Long-Term Liability	Stockholders' Equity
1.	√						
2.							
3.							
4.							
5.							
6.							
7.							
8.							
9.							
10.							
11.							
12.							
13.							
14.							
15.							
16.							
17.							
18.							
19.							
20.							

Preparing a work sheet

Melody Shop

Work Sheet

For Year Ended December 31, 19--

	ACCOUNT TITLE	1 Trial Balance Debit	2 Trial Balance Credit	3 Adjustments Debit	4 Adjustments Credit	5 Income Statement Debit	6 Income Statement Credit	7 Balance Sheet Debit	8 Balance Sheet Credit	
1	Cash	5190600								1
2	Notes Receivable	212000								2
3	Accounts Receivable	3370800								3
4	Allowance for Uncollectible Accounts		22000							4
5	Merchandise Inventory	14578000								5
6	Supplies	468200								6
7	Prepaid Insurance	888000								7
8	Delivery Equipment	1430000								8
9	Accum. Depr.--Delivery Equipment		420000							9
10	Office Equipment	777000								10
11	Accum. Depr.--Office Equipment		156000							11
12	Store Equipment	3290000								12
13	Accum. Depr.--Store Equipment		486000							13
14	Notes Payable		100000							14
15	Accounts Payable		1512000							15
16	Employees Income Tax Payable		93000							16
17	Federal Income Tax Payable									17
18	FICA Tax Payable		108100							18
19	Sales Tax Payable		379200							19
20	Unemployment Tax Payable--Federal		2200							20
21	Unemployment Tax Payable--State		8600							21
22	Hospital Insurance Premium Payable		31800							22
23	U. S. Savings Bonds Payable		5000							23
24	United Way Donations Payable		2000							24
25	Dividends Payable									25

Continue this work sheet on the next page.

(continued)

	ACCOUNT TITLE	1 TRIAL BALANCE DEBIT	2 TRIAL BALANCE CREDIT	3 ADJUSTMENTS DEBIT	4 ADJUSTMENTS CREDIT	5 INCOME STATEMENT DEBIT	6 INCOME STATEMENT CREDIT	7 BALANCE SHEET DEBIT	8 BALANCE SHEET CREDIT	
26	Capital Stock		15000000							26
27	Retained Earnings		6713400							27
28	Income Summary									28
29	Sales		76750000							29
30	Sales Returns and Allowances	910000								30
31	Purchases	54872200								31
32	Purchases Returns and Allowances		200000							32
33	Purchases Discount		406500							33
34	Advertising Expense	1213300								34
35	Bad Debts Expense									35
36	Delivery Expense	403200								36
37	Depr. Expense--Delivery Equipment									37
38	Depr. Expense--Office Equipment									38
39	Depr. Expense--Store Equipment									39
40	Insurance Expense									40
41	Miscellaneous Expense	1440800								41
42	Payroll Taxes Expense	709500								42
43	Rent Expense	2400000								43
44	Salary Expense	9404200								44
45	Supplies Expense									45
46	Interest Income		340400							46
47	Interest Expense	378400								47
48	Federal Income Tax	800000								48
49		102736200	102736200							49
50										50
51										51

The solution to Problem 27-1 is needed to complete Problem 27-2 and Problem 27-3.

Name ______________________ Date __________ Class __________

PROBLEM 27-2, p. 557
[1]

Preparing financial statements

The work sheet prepared in Problem 27-1 is needed to complete Problem 27-2.

Melody Shop

Income Statement

For Year Ended December 31, 19--

Continue this income statement on the next page.

[1]

Melody Shop

Income Statement (continued)

For Year Ended December 31, 19--

[2]

Melody Shop

Statement of Stockholders' Equity

For Year Ended December 31, 19--

[3]

Melody Shop

Balance Sheet

December 31, 19--

Continue this balance sheet on the next page.

[3]

Melody Shop

Balance Sheet (continued)

December 31, 19--

Recording adjusting and closing entries

PROBLEM 27-3, p. 557

[1]

The work sheet prepared in Problem 27-1 is needed to complete Problem 27-3.

GENERAL JOURNAL

PAGE

DATE		ACCOUNT TITLE	POST. REF.	DEBIT	CREDIT

Name ____________________ Date __________ Class __________

PROBLEM 27-3, concluded

[2]

GENERAL JOURNAL

PAGE

DATE		ACCOUNT TITLE	POST. REF.	DEBIT	CREDIT

PROBLEM 27-4, p. 558

[1]

GENERAL JOURNAL

PAGE

DATE		ACCOUNT TITLE	POST. REF.	DEBIT	CREDIT

[2]

CASH PAYMENTS JOURNAL

PAGE

	DATE	ACCOUNT TITLE	CHECK NO.	POST. REF.	1 GENERAL DEBIT	2 GENERAL CREDIT	3 ACCOUNTS PAYABLE DEBIT	4 PURCHASES DISCOUNT CREDIT	5 CASH CREDIT	
1										1
2										2
3										3
4										4
5										5
6										6
7										7
8										8
9										9
10										10
11										11
12										12
13										13
14										14
15										15
16										16
17										17
18										18
19										19
20										20
21										21
22										22

Preparing end-of-fiscal-period work for a corporation [1]

RSD Corporation

Work Sheet

For Year Ended December 31, 19--

	ACCOUNT TITLE	TRIAL BALANCE (1) DEBIT	TRIAL BALANCE (2) CREDIT	ADJUSTMENTS (3) DEBIT	ADJUSTMENTS (4) CREDIT	INCOME STATEMENT (5) DEBIT	INCOME STATEMENT (6) CREDIT	BALANCE SHEET (7) DEBIT	BALANCE SHEET (8) CREDIT	
1	Cash	4412010								1
2	Notes Receivable	180000								2
3	Accounts Receivable	2865380								3
4	Allowance for Uncollectible Accounts		18700							4
5	Merchandise Inventory	12391300								5
6	Supplies	399170								6
7	Prepaid Insurance	756000								7
8	Delivery Equipment	1215500								8
9	Accum. Depr.--Delivery Equipment		357000							9
10	Office Equipment	660450								10
11	Accum. Depr.--Office Equipment		132600							11
12	Store Equipment	2796500								12
13	Accum. Depr.--Store Equipment		413100							13
14	Accounts Payable		1370200							14
15	Employees Income Tax Payable		79050							15
16	Federal Income Tax Payable									16
17	FICA Tax Payable		91885							17
18	Sales Tax Payable		322320							18
19	Unemployment Tax Payable--Federal		1870							19
20	Unemployment Tax Payable--State		7310							20
21	Hospital Insurance Premium Payable		27030							21
22	U. S. Savings Bonds Payable		4450							22
23	United Way Donations Payable		1500							23
24	Dividends Payable									24
25	Capital Stock		15000000							25

Continue this work sheet on the next page.

[1]

(continued)

	ACCOUNT TITLE	1 TRIAL BALANCE DEBIT	2 TRIAL BALANCE CREDIT	3 ADJUSTMENTS DEBIT	4 ADJUSTMENTS CREDIT	5 INCOME STATEMENT DEBIT	6 INCOME STATEMENT CREDIT	7 BALANCE SHEET DEBIT	8 BALANCE SHEET CREDIT	
26	Retained Earnings		3458785							26
27	Income Summary									27
28	Sales		65237500							28
29	Sales Returns and Allowances	773500								29
30	Purchases	46641370								30
31	Purchases Returns and Allowances		170000							31
32	Purchases Discount		345520							32
33	Advertising Expense	1031300								33
34	Bad Debts Expense									34
35	Delivery Expense	342720								35
36	Depr. Expense--Delivery Equipment									36
37	Depr. Expense--Office Equipment									37
38	Depr. Expense--Store Equipment									38
39	Insurance Expense									39
40	Miscellaneous Expense	1224680								40
41	Payroll Taxes Expense	603070								41
42	Rent Expense	2040000								42
43	Salary Expense	7993570								43
44	Supplies Expense									44
45	Interest Income		289340							45
46	Interest Expense	321640								46
47	Federal Income Tax	680000								47
48		87328160	87328160							48
49										49
50										50
51										51

The form for the income statement begins on the next page.

[3]

RSD Corporation

Statement of Stockholders' Equity

For Year Ended December 31, 19--

[2]

RSD Corporation

Income Statement

For Year Ended December 31, 19--

Continue this income statement on the next page.

[2]

RSD Corporation

Income Statement (continued)

For Year Ended December 31, 19--

[4]

RSD Corporation

Balance Sheet

December 31, 19--

Continue this balance sheet on the next page.

[4]

RSD Corporation

Balance Sheet (continued)

December 31, 19--

[5]

GENERAL JOURNAL

PAGE

	DATE		ACCOUNT TITLE	POST. REF.	DEBIT	CREDIT	
1							1
2							2
3							3
4							4
5							5
6							6
7							7
8							8
9							9
10							10
11							11
12							12
13							13
14							14
15							15
16							16
17							17
18							18
19							19
20							20
21							21
22							22
23							23
24							24
25							25
26							26
27							27
28							28
29							29
30							30
31							31
32							32
33							33

[6]

GENERAL JOURNAL

PAGE

DATE		ACCOUNT TITLE	POST. REF.	DEBIT	CREDIT

Name ______________ Date ________ Class ________

MASTERY PROBLEM 27-M, continued

[7]

GENERAL JOURNAL

PAGE

DATE		ACCOUNT TITLE	POST. REF.	DEBIT	CREDIT

[8]

CASH PAYMENTS JOURNAL

PAGE

	DATE		ACCOUNT TITLE	CHECK No.	POST. REF.	1 GENERAL DEBIT	2 GENERAL CREDIT	3 ACCOUNTS PAYABLE DEBIT	4 PURCHASES DISCOUNT CREDIT	5 CASH CREDIT	
1											1
2											2
3											3
4											4
5											5
6											6
7											7
8											8
9											9
10											10
11											11
12											12
13											13
14											14
15											15
16											16
17											17
18											18
19											19
20											20
21											21
22											22

Preparing end-of-fiscal-period work for a corporation [1]

Aquarian Electronics
Work Sheet
For Year Ended December 31, 19--

	ACCOUNT TITLE	1 TRIAL BALANCE DEBIT	2 TRIAL BALANCE CREDIT	3 ADJUSTMENTS DEBIT	4 ADJUSTMENTS CREDIT	5 INCOME STATEMENT DEBIT	6 INCOME STATEMENT CREDIT	7 BALANCE SHEET DEBIT	8 BALANCE SHEET CREDIT	
1	Cash	2893720								1
2	Notes Receivable	413400								2
3	Accounts Receivable	3131636								3
4	Allowance for Uncollectible Accounts		3100							4
5	Merchandise Inventory	8633100								5
6	Supplies	177240								6
7	Prepaid Insurance	630000								7
8	Delivery Equipment	824000								8
9	Accum. Depr.--Delivery Equipment		247200							9
10	Office Equipment	482000								10
11	Accum. Depr.--Office Equipment		120500							11
12	Store Equipment	648000								12
13	Accum. Depr.--Store Equipment		194400							13
14	Notes Payable		1000000							14
15	Accounts Payable		917370							15
16	Employees Income Tax Payable		124000							16
17	Federal Income Tax Payable									17
18	FICA Tax Payable		32700							18
19	Sales Tax Payable		275116							19
20	Unemployment Tax Payable--Federal		1500							20
21	Unemployment Tax Payable--State		5800							21
22	Hospital Insurance Premium Payable		22250							22
23	Dividends Payable		750000							23
24	Capital Stock		7500000							24
25	Retained Earnings		463869							25

Continue this work sheet on the next page.

[1]

(continued)

	ACCOUNT TITLE	TRIAL BALANCE DEBIT (1)	TRIAL BALANCE CREDIT (2)	ADJUSTMENTS DEBIT (3)	ADJUSTMENTS CREDIT (4)	INCOME STATEMENT DEBIT (5)	INCOME STATEMENT CREDIT (6)	BALANCE SHEET DEBIT (7)	BALANCE SHEET CREDIT (8)	
26	Income Summary									26
27	Sales		66005340							27
28	Sales Returns and Allowances	496890								28
29	Purchases	43897850								29
30	Purchases Returns and Allowances		161740							30
31	Purchases Discount		325256							31
32	Advertising Expense	949300								32
33	Bad Debts Expense									33
34	Delivery Expense	322560								34
35	Depr. Expense--Delivery Equipment									35
36	Depr. Expense--Office Equipment									36
37	Depr. Expense--Store Equipment									37
38	Insurance Expense									38
39	Miscellaneous Expense	576320								39
40	Payroll Taxes Expense	661500								40
41	Rent Expense	1920000								41
42	Salary Expense	9462200								42
43	Supplies Expense									43
44	Interest Income		172320							44
45	Interest Expense	302745								45
46	Federal Income Tax	1900000								46
47		78322461	78322461							47
48										48
49										49
50										50
51										51

[2]

Aquarian Electronics

Income Statement

For Year Ended December 31, 19--

Continue this income statement on the next page.

[2]

Aquarian Electronics

Income Statement (continued)

For Year Ended December 31, 19--

[3]

Aquarian Electronics

Statement of Stockholders' Equity

For Year Ended December 31, 19--

[4]

Aquarian Electronics

Balance Sheet

December 31, 19--

Continue this balance sheet on the next page.

[4]

Aquarian Electronics

Balance Sheet (continued)

December 31, 19--

[5]

GENERAL JOURNAL

PAGE

DATE		ACCOUNT TITLE	POST. REF.	DEBIT	CREDIT

[6]

GENERAL JOURNAL

PAGE

DATE		ACCOUNT TITLE	POST. REF.	DEBIT	CREDIT

[7]

CASH PAYMENTS JOURNAL

PAGE

	DATE		ACCOUNT TITLE	CHECK NO.	POST. REF.	1 GENERAL DEBIT	2 GENERAL CREDIT	3 ACCOUNTS PAYABLE DEBIT	4 PURCHASES DISCOUNT CREDIT	5 CASH CREDIT	
1											1
2											2
3											3
4											4
5											5
6											6
7											7
8											8
9											9
10											10
11											11
12											12
13											13
14											14
15											15
16											16
17											17
18											18
19											19
20											20
21											21
22											22

Name ____________ Date ________ Class ________

AN ACCOUNTING CYCLE FOR A CORPORATION USING SPECIAL JOURNALS [1]

The general ledger and general journal prepared in Part A are needed to complete Part B.

Electronic Emporium

Work Sheet

For Year Ended December 31, 19--

	ACCOUNT TITLE	1 TRIAL BALANCE DEBIT	2 TRIAL BALANCE CREDIT	3 ADJUSTMENTS DEBIT	4 ADJUSTMENTS CREDIT	5 INCOME STATEMENT DEBIT	6 INCOME STATEMENT CREDIT	7 BALANCE SHEET DEBIT	8 BALANCE SHEET CREDIT	
1	Cash									1
2	Notes Receivable									2
3	Accounts Receivable									3
4	Allowance for Uncollectible Accounts									4
5	Merchandise Inventory									5
6	Supplies									6
7	Prepaid Insurance									7
8	Office Equipment									8
9	Accum. Depr.--Office Equipment									9
10	Store Equipment									10
11	Accum. Depr.--Store Equipment									11
12	Notes Payable									12
13	Accounts Payable									13
14	Employees Income Tax Payable									14
15	Federal Income Tax Payable									15
16	FICA Tax Payable									16
17	Sales Tax Payable									17
18	Unemployment Tax Payable--Federal									18
19	Unemployment Tax Payable--State									19
20	Dividends Payable									20
21	Capital Stock									21
22	Retained Earnings									22
23	Income Summary									23
24	Sales									24
25	Sales Returns and Allowances									25

Continue this work sheet on the next page.

[1]

(continued)

		1	2	3	4	5	6	7	8	
	ACCOUNT TITLE	TRIAL BALANCE		ADJUSTMENTS		INCOME STATEMENT		BALANCE SHEET		
		DEBIT	CREDIT	DEBIT	CREDIT	DEBIT	CREDIT	DEBIT	CREDIT	
26	Purchases									26
27	Purchases Returns and Allowances									27
28	Purchases Discount									28
29	Advertising Expense									29
30	Bad Debts Expense									30
31	Credit Card Fee Expense									31
32	Depr. Expense--Office Equipment									32
33	Depr. Expense--Store Equipment									33
34	Insurance Expense									34
35	Miscellaneous Expense									35
36	Payroll Taxes Expense									36
37	Rent Expense									37
38	Salary Expense									38
39	Supplies Expense									39
40	Interest Income									40
41	Interest Expense									41
42	Federal Income Tax									42
43										43
44										44
45										45
46										46
47										47
48										48
49										49
50										50
51										51

[2]

Electronic Emporium

Income Statement

For Year Ended December 31, 19--

Continue this income statement on the next page.

[2]

Electronic Emporium

Income Statement (continued)

For Year Ended December 31, 19--

[3]

Electronic Emporium

Statement of Stockholders' Equity

For Year Ended December 31, 19--

[4]

Electronic Emporium

Balance Sheet

December 31, 19--

[7]

Electronic Emporium

Post-Closing Trial Balance

December 31, 19--

ACCOUNT TITLE	DEBIT	CREDIT

Perfect Score. 50 Name ______________________

Deduct.......... ___ Date ______________ Class ______________

Your Score.... ___ Checked by ______________________

STUDY GUIDE 28

UNIT A — Accounting Terms

DIRECTIONS: Select the one term in Column I that best fits each definition given in Column II. Print the letter identifying your choice in the Answers column.

Column I	Column II	Answers	For Scoring
A. check register	0. An account in a general ledger that summarizes all the accounts in a subsidiary ledger	B	0. ✓
B. controlling account	1. A journal in which vouchers are recorded		1.
C. voucher	2. A journal used in a voucher system to record cash payments		2.
D. voucher check	3. A business form showing approval by an authorized person for a cash payment		3.
E. voucher register	4. A check with space for writing the purpose of the payment		4.
F. voucher system	5. Controlling cash payments by preparing and approving vouchers before payments are made		5.

UNIT B — Principles of a Voucher System

DIRECTIONS: Place a check mark (✓) in the proper Answers column to show whether each of the following statements is true or false.

Statement	Answers True	Answers False	For Scoring
0. A voucher system is frequently used for controlling cash payments when several persons are authorized to approve cash payments	✓		0. ✓
6. The first major step in using a voucher system is obtaining approval for payment of a voucher			6.
7. A verified invoice is used to prepare a voucher			7.
8. A voucher register replaces a purchases journal			8.
9. A separate voucher is usually prepared for each purchase invoice			9.
10. A check number is written in the voucher register when a voucher is recorded			10.
11. Vouchers are filed in an unpaid vouchers file by voucher number			11.
12. Vouchers are prepared from information on checks			12.
13. A voucher is the source document for each entry in a voucher register			13.
14. The total of the Vouchers Payable Credit column of a voucher register is posted to a general ledger account			14.
15. When a voucher system is used, each voucher is paid by check			15.
16. If a discount is allowed for prompt payment of a voucher, the amount of the discount is recorded in the check register as a credit to Purchases Discount			16.
17. When a Bank Deposits column and a Bank Balance column are on a check register, it is necessary to keep a record of deposits and the bank balance on check stubs			17.
18. When a business makes a deposit to its checking account, the amount of the deposit is subtracted from the previous amount in the Bank Balance column			18.
19. A voucher system eliminates all posting to customers' accounts			19.
20. When merchandise is returned under a voucher system, the old voucher should be canceled and a new voucher should be prepared for the amount still owed			20.
21. The paid vouchers file and unpaid vouchers file of a voucher system replace the accounts payable ledger			21.
22. Vouchers are filed in the paid vouchers file by due dates			22.
23. Amounts can be entered in the General columns of a voucher register when there is not an appropriate account in the general ledger			23.
24. Information from a payroll register is used in preparing a payroll voucher			24.

UNIT C — Recording Voucher Transactions

DIRECTIONS: In Answers Column 1, print the abbreviation for the register in which each transaction is to be recorded. In columns 2 and 3, print the letters identifying the accounts to be debited and credited for each transaction.

CR — check register　　VR — voucher register

Account Titles

A. Cash
B. Delivery Expense
C. Purchases
D. Purchases Discount
E. Purchases Returns and Allowances
F. Supplies
G. Vouchers Payable

Transactions	Answers 1 Reg.	Answers 2 Dr.	Answers 3 Cr.	For Scoring 1 Reg.	For Scoring 2 Dr.	For Scoring 3 Cr.
0–0–0. Purchased merchandise on account	*VR*	*C*	*G*	**0.✓**	**0.✓**	**0.✓**
25–26–27. Bought supplies on account				**25.**	**26.**	**27.**
28–29–30. Paid voucher less discount				**28.**	**29.**	**30.**
31–32–33. Issued debit memorandum for return of merchandise purchased, $100.00. Canceled Voucher No. 28 ($300.00) and issued new Voucher No. 30				**31.**	**32.**	**33.**
34–35–36. Received a statement for delivery expenses				**34.**	**35.**	**36.**
37–38–39. Paid voucher; no discount				**37.**	**38.**	**39.**

UNIT D — Analyzing Procedures of a Voucher System

DIRECTIONS: For each item below, select the choice that best completes the sentence. Print the letter identifying your choice in the Answers column.

	Answers	For Scoring
0. A principal reason for using a voucher system is **(A)** to place accounting controls on the asset cash **(B)** to keep a record of accounts payable **(C)** to increase the work of accountants	*A*	**0.✓**
40. The source document for an entry in a voucher register is **(A)** debit memorandum **(B)** voucher **(C)** voucher check		**40.**
41. The total amount of each voucher is recorded in a voucher register in the **(A)** Vouchers Payable Credit column **(B)** Purchases Debit column **(C)** General Credit column		**41.**
42. The only items recorded in a voucher register that need to be posted individually are those entered in the **(A)** Vouchers Payable Credit column **(B)** Purchases Debit column **(C)** General columns		**42.**
43. Totals of the special columns of a voucher register are posted to the **(A)** general ledger **(B)** accounts payable ledger **(C)** accounts receivable ledger		**43.**
44. To show that an amount recorded in a voucher register's General Debit or Credit column has been posted, write in the voucher register's Post. Ref. column the **(A)** voucher check number **(B)** invoice date **(C)** account number		**44.**
45. Each check written is recorded in a check register as a debit to **(A)** Vouchers Payable **(B)** Purchases **(C)** Cash		**45.**
46. Each check written is recorded in a check register as a credit to **(A)** Vouchers Payable **(B)** Purchases **(C)** Cash		**46.**
47. The source document for an entry in a check register to record payment of a voucher is **(A)** an invoice duplicate **(B)** a voucher duplicate **(C)** a voucher check duplicate		**47.**
48. When a voucher is paid, write in a voucher register's Paid columns the **(A)** date and check number **(B)** date and account number **(C)** account number and check number		**48.**
49. The Bank Deposits and Bank Balance columns should be totaled and ruled **(A)** monthly **(B)** yearly **(C)** never		**49.**
50. When a payroll is recorded in a voucher register, Vouchers Payable is credited for the **(A)** amount of salary expense **(B)** net payroll amount to be paid to the employees **(C)** total amount of withholding taxes		**50.**

Name ____________________ Date __________ Class __________

Analyzing transactions using a voucher register

Trans. No.	Name of Amount Column Used in Voucher Register	
	(a) For Amount Debited	(b) For Amount Credited
1.	*Supplies Debit*	*Vouchers Payable Credit*
2.		
3.		
4.		
5.		
6.		
7.		
8.		
9.		
10.		

Trans. or Activity No.	Vouchers Payable Debit	Purchases Discount Credit	Cash Credit	Bank	
				Deposits	Balance
1.	√		√		√
2.					
3.					
4.					
5.					
6.					
7.					
8.					
9.					

Name ____________________ Date __________ Class __________

PROBLEM 28-1, p. 583
[1, 2]

Preparing a voucher

Vchr. No. ________ Date ________ Due Date ________

To ______________________________

Address ______________________________
Street

____
City State ZIP

ACCOUNTS DEBITED	AMOUNT	
PURCHASES		
SUPPLIES		
ADVERTISING EXPENSE		
DELIVERY EXPENSE		
INSURANCE EXPENSE		
MISCELLANEOUS EXPENSE		
PAYROLL TAXES EXPENSE		
RENT EXPENSE		
SALARY EXPENSE		
TOTAL DEBITS		

ACCOUNTS CREDITED	AMOUNT	
VOUCHERS PAYABLE		
EMPLOYEES INC. TAX PAY. – FED.		
EMPLOYEES INC. TAX PAY. – STATE		
FICA TAX PAYABLE		
TOTAL CREDITS		

Voucher Approved by ______________________________

Recorded in Voucher
Register Page ____________ by ____________

Paid { Date ______________________________
Check No. ________ Amount $ ________
Approved by ______________________________ }

Vchr. No. ________ Date ________ Due Date ________

To ______________________________

Address ______________________________
Street

____
City State ZIP

ACCOUNTS DEBITED	AMOUNT	
PURCHASES		
SUPPLIES		
ADVERTISING EXPENSE		
DELIVERY EXPENSE		
INSURANCE EXPENSE		
MISCELLANEOUS EXPENSE		
PAYROLL TAXES EXPENSE		
RENT EXPENSE		
SALARY EXPENSE		
TOTAL DEBITS		

ACCOUNTS CREDITED	AMOUNT	
VOUCHERS PAYABLE		
EMPLOYEES INC. TAX PAY. – FED.		
EMPLOYEES INC. TAX PAY. – STATE		
FICA TAX PAYABLE		
TOTAL CREDITS		

Voucher Approved by ______________________________

Recorded in Voucher
Register Page ____________ by ____________

Paid { Date ______________________________
Check No. ________ Amount $ ________
Approved by ______________________________ }

Vchr. No. ________ Date ________ Due Date ________

To ______________________________

Address ______________________________
Street

____
City State ZIP

ACCOUNTS DEBITED	AMOUNT	
PURCHASES		
SUPPLIES		
ADVERTISING EXPENSE		
DELIVERY EXPENSE		
INSURANCE EXPENSE		
MISCELLANEOUS EXPENSE		
PAYROLL TAXES EXPENSE		
RENT EXPENSE		
SALARY EXPENSE		
TOTAL DEBITS		

ACCOUNTS CREDITED	AMOUNT	
VOUCHERS PAYABLE		
EMPLOYEES INC. TAX PAY. – FED.		
EMPLOYEES INC. TAX PAY. – STATE		
FICA TAX PAYABLE		
TOTAL CREDITS		

Voucher Approved by ______________________________

Recorded in Voucher
Register Page ____________ by ____________

Paid { Date ______________________________
Check No. ________ Amount $ ________
Approved by ______________________________ }

[1, 2]

PAGE

VOUCHER REGISTER

DATE		PAYEE	VCHR. NO.	PAID		VOUCHERS PAYABLE CREDIT
				DATE	CK. NO.	1

[1, 2]

FOR MONTH OF   19   PAGE

2	3	4			5	6
DISTRIBUTION			GENERAL			
PURCHASES DEBIT	DELIVERY EXPENSE DEBIT	SUPPLIES DEBIT	ACCOUNT	POST REF.	DEBIT	CREDIT

The voucher register prepared in Problem 28-2 is needed to complete Problem 28-3.

The voucher register prepared in Problem 28-2 is needed to complete Problem 28-3.

Recording cash transactions in a check register [1, 3]

CHECK REGISTER

PAGE

	DATE		PAYEE	CK. NO.	VCHR. NO.	1 VOUCHERS PAYABLE DEBIT	2 PURCHASES DISCOUNT CREDIT	3 CASH CREDIT	4 BANK DEPOSITS	5 BANK BALANCE	
1											1
2											2
3											3
4											4
5											5
6											6
7											7
8											8
9											9
10											10
11											11
12											12
13											13
14											14
15											15
16											16
17											17
18											18
19											19
20											20
21											21
22											22
23											23

Preparing payroll vouchers

Vchr. No. __________ Date __________ Due Date __________

To ______________________________

Address ______________________________
Street

____
City State ZIP

ACCOUNTS DEBITED	AMOUNT	
PURCHASES		
SUPPLIES		
ADVERTISING EXPENSE		
DELIVERY EXPENSE		
INSURANCE EXPENSE		
MISCELLANEOUS EXPENSE		
PAYROLL TAXES EXPENSE		
RENT EXPENSE		
SALARY EXPENSE		
TOTAL DEBITS		

ACCOUNTS CREDITED	AMOUNT	
VOUCHERS PAYABLE		
EMPLOYEES INC. TAX PAY. – FED.		
EMPLOYEES INC. TAX PAY. – STATE		
FICA TAX PAYABLE		
TOTAL CREDITS		

Voucher Approved by ______________________

Recorded in Voucher
Register Page __________ by __________

Paid { Date ______________________
Check No. __________ Amount $ __________
Approved by ______________________ }

The inside of this voucher is on the next page.

VOUCHER

Vchr.
No. ________ Date __________________ 19____ Terms ____________ Due __________________ 19______

To ____

Address ____

City ______________________________ State __________________ Zip ______________

For the following: Attach all invoices or other papers permanently to voucher.

DATE	VOUCHER DETAILS	AMOUNT

Vchr. No. __________ Date __________ Due Date __________

To ______________________________

Address ______________________________
Street

____
City State ZIP

ACCOUNTS DEBITED	AMOUNT	
PURCHASES		
SUPPLIES		
ADVERTISING EXPENSE		
DELIVERY EXPENSE		
INSURANCE EXPENSE		
MISCELLANEOUS EXPENSE		
PAYROLL TAXES EXPENSE		
RENT EXPENSE		
SALARY EXPENSE		
TOTAL DEBITS		

ACCOUNTS CREDITED	AMOUNT	
VOUCHERS PAYABLE		
EMPLOYEES INC. TAX PAY. – FED.		
EMPLOYEES INC. TAX PAY. – STATE		
FICA TAX PAYABLE		
TOTAL CREDITS		

Voucher Approved by ______________________________

Recorded in Voucher Register Page __________ by __________

Paid { Date ______________________________
Check No. __________ Amount $ __________
Approved by ______________________________ }

The inside of this voucher is on the next page.

VOUCHER

Vchr.
No._______ Date________________ 19____ Terms__________ Due_______________ 19____

To ____

Address _____________________________________

City ____________________ State _______________ Zip __________

For the following: Attach all invoices or other papers permanently to voucher.

DATE	VOUCHER DETAILS	AMOUNT

Recording purchases returns and allowances and payroll transactions in a voucher system [1, 2]

CHECK REGISTER

PAGE

	DATE	PAYEE	CK. NO.	VCHR. NO.	1 VOUCHERS PAYABLE DEBIT	2 PURCHASES DISCOUNT CREDIT	3 CASH CREDIT	4 BANK DEPOSITS	5 BANK BALANCE	
1										1
2										2
3										3
4										4
5										5
6										6
7										7
8										8
9										9
10										10
11										11
12										12
13										13
14										14
15										15
16										16
17										17
18										18
19										19
20										20
21										21
22										22
23										23

[1, 2]

PAGE

VOUCHER REGISTER

DATE		PAYEE	VCHR. NO.	PAID		1
				DATE	CK. NO.	VOUCHERS PAYABLE CREDIT

[1, 2]

FOR MONTH OF 19 PAGE

	2	3	4			5	6	
	DISTRIBUTION			GENERAL				
	PURCHASES DEBIT	DELIVERY EXPENSE DEBIT	SUPPLIES DEBIT	ACCOUNT	POST REF.	DEBIT	CREDIT	
1								1
2								2
3								3
4								4
5								5
6								6
7								7
8								8
9								9
10								10
11								11
12								12
13								13
14								14
15								15
16								16
17								17
18								18
19								19
20								20
21								21
22								22
23								23
24								24
25								25
26								26
27								27
28								28
29								29
30								30
31								31
32								32
33								33
34								34
35								35

[1, 2]

PAGE

VOUCHER REGISTER

DATE		PAYEE	VCHR. NO.	PAID		1
				DATE	CK. NO.	VOUCHERS PAYABLE CREDIT

Name ____________________ Date __________ Class __________

MASTERY PROBLEM 28-M, continued

[1, 2]

FOR MONTH OF 19 PAGE

	2	3	4			5	6	
	DISTRIBUTION			GENERAL				
	PURCHASES DEBIT	DELIVERY EXPENSE DEBIT	SUPPLIES DEBIT	ACCOUNT	POST REF.	DEBIT	CREDIT	
1								1
2								2
3								3
4								4
5								5
6								6
7								7
8								8
9								9
10								10
11								11
12								12
13								13
14								14
15								15
16								16
17								17
18								18
19								19
20								20
21								21
22								22
23								23
24								24
25								25
26								26
27								27
28								28
29								29
30								30
31								31
32								32
33								33
34								34
35								35

[1, 2]

CHECK REGISTER

PAGE

	DATE		PAYEE	CK. NO.	VCHR. NO.	1 VOUCHERS PAYABLE DEBIT	2 PURCHASES DISCOUNT CREDIT	3 CASH CREDIT	4 BANK DEPOSITS	5 BANK BALANCE	
1											1
2											2
3											3
4											4
5											5
6											6
7											7
8											8
9											9
10											10
11											11
12											12
13											13
14											14
15											15
16											16
17											17
18											18
19											19
20											20
21											21
22											22
23											23

Recording purchase invoices at the net amount in a voucher system [1–3]

CHECK REGISTER

PAGE

	DATE		PAYEE	CK. NO.	VCHR. NO.	1 VOUCHERS PAYABLE DEBIT	2 DISCOUNTS LOST DEBIT	3 CASH CREDIT	4 BANK DEPOSITS	5 BANK BALANCE	
1											1
2											2
3											3
4											4
5											5
6											6
7											7
8											8
9											9
10											10
11											11
12											12
13											13
14											14
15											15
16											16
17											17
18											18
19											19
20											20
21											21
22											22
23											23

[2, 3]

PAGE

VOUCHER REGISTER

DATE		PAYEE	VCHR. NO.	PAID		1
				DATE	CK. NO.	VOUCHERS PAYABLE CREDIT

[2, 3]

FOR MONTH OF 19 PAGE

2	3	4			5	6
DISTRIBUTION			GENERAL			
PURCHASES DEBIT	DELIVERY EXPENSE DEBIT	SUPPLIES DEBIT	ACCOUNT	POST REF.	DEBIT	CREDIT

Extra form

CHECK REGISTER

PAGE

	DATE		PAYEE	CK. No.	VCHR. No.	1 VOUCHERS PAYABLE DEBIT	2 PURCHASES DISCOUNT CREDIT	3 CASH CREDIT	4 BANK DEPOSITS	5 BANK BALANCE	
1											1
2											2
3											3
4											4
5											5
6											6
7											7
8											8
9											9
10											10
11											11
12											12
13											13
14											14
15											15
16											16
17											17
18											18
19											19
20											20
21											21
22											22
23											23

Perfect Score. 41 | Name ______

Deduct......... ___ | Date ______ Class ______

Your Score.... ___ | Checked by ______

STUDY GUIDE 29

UNIT A — Accounting Terms

DIRECTIONS: Select the one term in Column I that best fits each definition in Column II. Print the letter identifying your choice in the Answers column.

Column I	*Column II*	Answers	For Scoring
A. cash over	**0.** A check with space for writing the purpose of the payment	*F*	**0.** ✓
B. cash short	**1.** An amount of cash kept on hand and used for making small payments		**1.**
C. petty cash	**2.** A petty cash on hand amount more than a recorded amount		**2.**
D. petty cash record	**3.** A form on which petty cash receipts and payments are recorded		**3.**
E. petty cash voucher	**4.** A petty cash on hand amount less than a recorded amount.		**4.**
F. voucher check	**5.** A form showing proof of petty cash payments		**5.**

UNIT B — Examining a Petty Cash System

DIRECTIONS: Place a check mark (√) in the proper Answers column to show whether each of the following statements is true or false.

Statement	Answers True	Answers False	For Scoring
0. Good cash control requires that businesses deposit all cash receipts in a bank account	√		**0.** √
6. Using a petty cash fund generally increases the number of checks that must be written			**6.**
7. Petty cash should be available to all employees to make small expenditures			**7.**
8. The amount in a petty cash fund should be sufficient to last for a period of time, usually a month			**8.**
9. The account Cash is placed immediately after the account Petty Cash in a general ledger			**9.**
10. A petty cash fund should be kept in a bank account			**10.**
11. Petty cash should be kept separate from all other cash			**11.**
12. Each time a petty cash payment is made, a petty cash voucher is prepared			**12.**
13. The petty cash vouchers plus cash in the petty cash box should equal the original amount of the petty cash fund			**13.**
14. Petty cash is always replenished at the end of each fiscal period			**14.**
15. Petty cash vouchers in a petty cash box represent transactions that must be journalized and posted			**15.**
16. If a petty cash fund is not replenished at the end of each fiscal period, the balance sheet is not an accurate statement of assets			**16.**
17. The steps taken to replenish a petty cash fund at the end of a fiscal period are the same as those followed to replenish it when the fund is low			**17.**
18. Credit entries on a voucher prepared to replenish a petty cash fund include each account in the petty cash record's Distribution of Payments columns			**18.**
19. An error in making change generally is the reason cash in the petty cash box is more than the cash balance shown in the petty cash record			**19.**
20. Any balance in a cash short and over account is closed to Income Summary at the end of a fiscal period			**20.**
21. To make payments from petty cash, businesses using a cash payments journal must follow different procedures than businesses using a voucher system			**21.**

UNIT C — Analyzing a Petty Cash System

DIRECTIONS: For each item below, select the choice that best completes the sentence. Print the letter identifying your choice in the Answers column.

Question	Answers	For Scoring
0. The petty cash account is classified as (A) an asset (B) a liability (C) an expense	*A*	**0.** ✓
22. An entry to establish a petty cash fund includes a debit to (A) Cash (B) Miscellaneous Expense (C) Petty Cash (D) Vouchers Payable.		**22.**
23. An entry to establish a petty cash fund includes a credit to (A) Income Summary (B) Petty Cash (C) Vouchers Payable (D) Miscellaneous Expense		**23.**
24. An entry to establish a petty cash fund is recorded in a (A) cash receipts journal (B) general journal (C) purchases journal (D) voucher register		**24.**
25. When using a voucher system, an entry to record a check for establishing a petty cash fund includes a debit to (A) Cash (B) Petty Cash (C) Miscellaneous Expense (D) Vouchers Payable.		**25.**
26. An entry to record a check for establishing a petty cash fund includes a credit to (A) Cash (B) Petty Cash (C) Miscellaneous Expense (D) Vouchers Payable.		**26.**
27. An entry to record a check for establishing a petty cash fund is recorded in a (A) check register (B) general journal (C) petty cash record (D) voucher register		**27.**
28. A petty cash voucher shows (A) an account number (B) the balance of the petty cash account (C) the signature of the person to whom payment is made (D) the name of the journal to which the amount is posted		**28.**
29. A petty cash record is usually a (A) journal (B) general ledger (C) subsidiary ledger (D) supplementary record		**29.**
30. When a payment is made from petty cash for supplies, the amount is entered in the petty cash record (A) Supplies and Payments columns (B) Supplies and Receipts columns (C) Supplies and Other Payments columns (D) Supplies and Explanation columns.		**30.**
31. The sum of the Distribution of Payments columns of a petty cash record must be equal to the (A) Receipts column total (B) Payments column total (C) Vouchers Payable column total (D) Cash column total		**31.**
32. An entry to replenish a petty cash fund includes a debit to (A) Cash (B) Petty Cash (C) Equipment (D) Miscellaneous Expense		**32.**
33. A voucher register entry to replenish a petty cash fund includes a credit to (A) Cash (B) Petty Cash (C) Vouchers Payable (D) Miscellaneous Expense.		**33.**
34. When a petty cash fund is replenished, the balance of the petty cash account (A) is increased (B) remains the same (C) is decreased		**34.**
35. When a petty cash fund is replenished a voucher is prepared for the amount paid out (A) plus cash short (B) less cash short (C) without regard for cash short		**35.**
36. When an amount is paid from a petty cash fund, the petty cash account balance (A) is increased (B) remains the same (C) is decreased		**36.**
37. A cash short and over account is classified as (A) an asset (B) a liability (C) other revenue or expense		**37.**
38. A debit balance in Cash Short and Over indicates that cash overages have been (A) more than cash shortages (B) about the same as cash shortages (C) less than cash shortages		**38.**
39. A credit balance in Cash Short and Over indicates that cash overages have been (A) more than cash shortages (B) about the same as cash shortages (C) less than cash shortages		**39.**
40. A Cash Short and Over debit balance is reported on an income statement as (A) Sales (B) Cost of Merchandise Sold (C) Other Revenue (D) Other Expenses		**40.**
41. A Cash Short and Over credit balance is reported on an income statement as (A) Sales (B) Cost of Merchandise Sold (C) Other Revenue (D) Other Expenses		**41.**

Name ______________________ Date __________ Class __________

Replenishing a petty cash fund

March 31 entry

Supplies

Delivery Expense

Miscellaneous Expense

Advertising Expense

Vouchers Payable

May 31 entry

Supplies

Delivery Expense

Miscellaneous Expense

Advertising Expense

Vouchers Payable

April 30 entry

Supplies

Delivery Expense

Miscellaneous Expense

Advertising Expense

Vouchers Payable

June 30 entry

Supplies

Delivery Expense

Miscellaneous Expense

Advertising Expense

Vouchers Payable

PROBLEM 29-1, p. 599

[1]

PAGE

VOUCHER REGISTER

DATE		PAYEE	VCHR. NO.	PAID		1
				DATE	CK. NO.	VOUCHERS PAYABLE CREDIT

PROBLEM 29-1, continued

[2]

CHECK REGISTER

PAGE

DATE		PAYEE	CK. NO.	VCHR. NO.	1	2	3	4	5
					VOUCHERS PAYABLE DEBIT	PURCHASES DISCOUNT CREDIT	CASH CREDIT	BANK	
								DEPOSITS	BALANCE

[1]

FOR MONTH OF 19 PAGE

DISTRIBUTION			GENERAL			
2	3	4			5	6
PURCHASES DEBIT	DELIVERY EXPENSE DEBIT	SUPPLIES DEBIT	ACCOUNT	POST REF.	DEBIT	CREDIT

Extra form

CHECK REGISTER PAGE

				1	2	3	4	5
							BANK	
DATE	PAYEE	CK. NO.	VCHR. NO.	VOUCHERS PAYABLE DEBIT	PURCHASES DISCOUNT CREDIT	CASH CREDIT	DEPOSITS	BALANCE

[3]

PETTY CASH RECORD

MONTH OF PAGE

	DATE	EXPLANATION	PETTY CASH VCHR. NO.	RECEIPTS	PAYMENTS	DISTRIBUTION OF PAYMENTS					
						SUPPLIES	DELIVERY EXPENSE	MISC. EXPENSE	OTHER PAYMENTS		
									ACCOUNT	AMOUNT	
1											1
2											2
3											3
4											4
5											5
6											6
7											7
8											8
9											9
10											10
11											11
12											12
13											13
14											14
15											15
16											16
17											17
18											18
19											19
20											20
21											21
22											22
23											23
24											24
25											25

The petty cash record prepared in Problem 29-1 is needed to complete Problem 29-2.

Name ____________ Date ________ Class ________

PROBLEM 29-2, p. 600

[4]

Replenishing a petty cash fund

Vchr. No. ________ Date ________ Due Date ________

To ________________

Address ________________
Street

____
City State ZIP

ACCOUNTS DEBITED	AMOUNT	
PURCHASES		
SUPPLIES		
ADVERTISING EXPENSE		
DELIVERY EXPENSE		
INSURANCE EXPENSE		
MISCELLANEOUS EXPENSE		
PAYROLL TAXES EXPENSE		
RENT EXPENSE		
SALARY EXPENSE		
TOTAL DEBITS		

ACCOUNTS CREDITED	AMOUNT	
VOUCHERS PAYABLE		
EMPLOYEES INC. TAX PAY. – FED.		
EMPLOYEES INC. TAX PAY. – STATE		
FICA TAX PAYABLE		
TOTAL CREDITS		

Voucher Approved by ________________

Recorded in Voucher Register Page ________ by ________

Paid { Date ________________
Check No. ________ Amount $ ________
Approved by ________________ }

[6]

CHECK REGISTER

PAGE

	DATE		PAYEE	CK. NO.	VCHR. NO.	1 VOUCHERS PAYABLE DEBIT	2 PURCHASES DISCOUNT CREDIT	3 CASH CREDIT	4 BANK DEPOSITS	5 BANK BALANCE	
1											1
2											2
3											3
4											4
5											5
6											6

PROBLEM 29-2, continued
[5]

PAGE VOUCHER REGISTER

	DATE		PAYEE	VCHR. NO.	PAID DATE	PAID CK. NO.	1 VOUCHERS PAYABLE CREDIT	
1								1
2								2
3								3
4								4
5								5
6								6
7								7
8								8
9								9
10								10
11								11
12								12
13								13
14								14

Problem 29-3 is on page 469.

MASTERY PROBLEM 29-M, p. 601
[1, 6]

Establishing and replenishing a petty cash fund

PAGE VOUCHER REGISTER

	DATE		PAYEE	VCHR. NO.	PAID DATE	PAID CK. NO.	1 VOUCHERS PAYABLE CREDIT	
1								1
2								2
3								3
4								4
5								5
6								6
7								7
8								8
9								9
10								10
11								11
12								12
13								13
14								14

Name ______________ Date ________ Class ________

PROBLEM 29-2, concluded

[5]

FOR MONTH OF 19 PAGE

	2	3	4			5	6	
	DISTRIBUTION			GENERAL				
	PURCHASES DEBIT	DELIVERY EXPENSE DEBIT	SUPPLIES DEBIT	ACCOUNT	POST REF.	DEBIT	CREDIT	
1								1
2								2
3								3
4								4
5								5
6								6
7								7
8								8
9								9
10								10
11								11
12								12
13								13
14								14

MASTERY PROBLEM 29-M, continued

[1, 6]

FOR MONTH OF 19 PAGE

	2	3	4			5	6	
	DISTRIBUTION			GENERAL				
	PURCHASES DEBIT	DELIVERY EXPENSE DEBIT	SUPPLIES DEBIT	ACCOUNT	POST REF.	DEBIT	CREDIT	
1								1
2								2
3								3
4								4
5								5
6								6
7								7
8								8
9								9
10								10
11								11
12								12
13								13
14								14

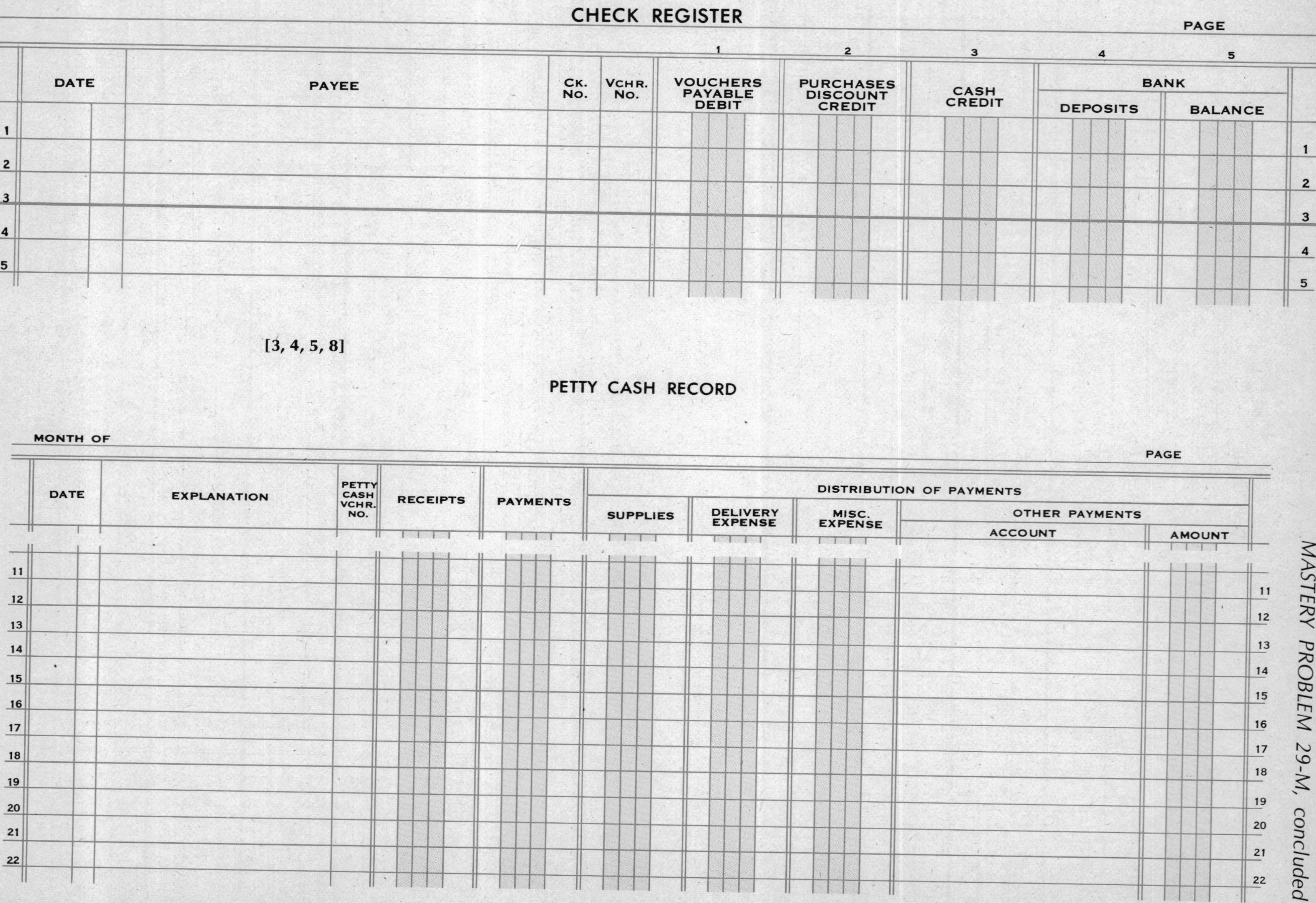
[2, 7]
CHECK REGISTER
PAGE
DATE
PAYEE
CK. NO.
VCHR. NO.
1
VOUCHERS PAYABLE DEBIT
2
PURCHASES DISCOUNT CREDIT
3
CASH CREDIT
4
5
BANK
DEPOSITS
BALANCE
[3, 4, 5, 8]
PETTY CASH RECORD
MONTH OF
PAGE
DATE
EXPLANATION
PETTY CASH VCHR. NO.
RECEIPTS
PAYMENTS
DISTRIBUTION OF PAYMENTS
SUPPLIES
DELIVERY EXPENSE
MISC. EXPENSE
OTHER PAYMENTS
ACCOUNT
AMOUNT

Establishing and replenishing a petty cash fund using a cash payments journal [1, 3]

CASH PAYMENTS JOURNAL

PAGE

	DATE	ACCOUNT TITLE	CHECK NO.	POST. REF.	1 GENERAL DEBIT	2 GENERAL CREDIT	3 ACCOUNTS PAYABLE DEBIT	4 PURCHASES DISCOUNT CREDIT	5 CASH CREDIT	
1										1
2										2
3										3
4										4
5										5
6										6
7										7
8										8
9										9
10										10
11										11
12										12
13										13
14										14
15										15
16										16
17										17
18										18
19										19
20										20
21										21
22										22

[1, 8]

PAGE

VOUCHER REGISTER

	DATE		PAYEE	VCHR. NO.	PAID DATE	PAID CK. NO.	1 VOUCHERS PAYABLE CREDIT	
1								1
2								2
3								3
4								4
5								5
6								6
7								7

[2, 9]

CHECK REGISTER

PAGE

	DATE		PAYEE	CK. NO.	VCHR. NO.	1 VOUCHERS PAYABLE DEBIT	2 PURCHASES DISCOUNT CREDIT	3 CASH CREDIT	4 BANK DEPOSITS	5 BANK BALANCE	
1											1
2											2
3											3
4											4
5											5
6											6
7											7
8											8
9											9
10											10
11											11
12											12
13											13
14											14
15											15
16											16
17											17
18											18
19											19
20											20
21											21
22											22
23											23
24											24
25											25

[1, 8]

FOR MONTH OF 19 PAGE

	2	3	4			5	6	
	DISTRIBUTION			GENERAL				
	PURCHASES DEBIT	DELIVERY EXPENSE DEBIT	SUPPLIES DEBIT	ACCOUNT	POST REF.	DEBIT	CREDIT	
1								1
2								2
3								3
4								4
5								5
6								6
7								7

[7]

Vchr. No. ______ Date ______ Due Date ______

To ______

Address ______
Street

______
City State ZIP

ACCOUNTS DEBITED	AMOUNT	
PURCHASES		
SUPPLIES		
ADVERTISING EXPENSE		
DELIVERY EXPENSE		
INSURANCE EXPENSE		
MISCELLANEOUS EXPENSE		
PAYROLL TAXES EXPENSE		
RENT EXPENSE		
SALARY EXPENSE		
TOTAL DEBITS		

ACCOUNTS CREDITED	AMOUNT	
VOUCHERS PAYABLE		
EMPLOYEES INC. TAX PAY. – FED.		
EMPLOYEES INC. TAX PAY. – STATE		
FICA TAX PAYABLE		
TOTAL CREDITS		

Voucher Approved by ______

Recorded in Voucher Register Page ______ by ______

Paid { Date ______
Check No. ______ Amount $ ______
Approved by ______ }

[3–6, 10]

PETTY CASH RECORD

MONTH OF PAGE

DATE		EXPLANATION	PETTY CASH VCHR. NO.	RECEIPTS	PAYMENTS	DISTRIBUTION OF PAYMENTS				
						SUPPLIES	DELIVERY EXPENSE	MISC. EXPENSE	OTHER PAYMENTS	
									ACCOUNT	AMOUNT

Perfect Score. 34 Name ____________________

Deduct.......... ___ Date ____________ Class ____________

Your Score.... ___ Checked by ____________________

STUDY GUIDE 30

UNIT A — Accounting Terms

DIRECTIONS: Select the one term in Column I that best fits each definition in Column II. Print the letter identifying your choice in the Answers column.

Column I

A. gross profit method of estimating inventory
B. merchandise inventory
C. periodic inventory
D. perpetual inventory
E. stock ledger
F. stock record

Column II	Answers	For Scoring
0. An itemized list showing the value of goods on hand for sale to customers	*B*	**0.** ✓
1. A form used to show kind of merchandise, quantity received, quantity sold, and balance on hand		**1.**
2. Merchandise inventory determined by counting, weighing, or measuring items of merchandise on hand		**2.**
3. Estimating inventory by using previous years' percent of gross profit on operations		**3.**
4. A file of stock records for all merchandise on hand		**4.**
5. Merchandise inventory determined by keeping a continuous record of increases, decreases, and balance on hand....		**5.**

UNIT B — Analyzing Lifo and Fifo Inventory Methods

DIRECTIONS: For each item below, select the choice that best completes the sentence. Print the letter identifying your choice in the Answers column.

	Answers	For Scoring
0. The lifo method is based on the idea that the merchandise purchased last is the merchandise **(A)** sold first **(B)** sold last	*A*	**0.** ✓
6. The fifo method is based on the idea that the merchandise purchased first is the merchandise **(A)** sold first **(B)** sold last		**6.**
7. When the lifo method of inventory valuation is used, quantities of merchandise are priced at the **(A)** average costs **(B)** earliest costs **(C)** most recent costs........		**7.**
8. When the fifo method of inventory valuation is used, quantities of merchandise are priced at the **(A)** average costs **(B)** earliest costs **(C)** most recent costs........		**8.**
9. In a year of rising prices, the inventory method that gives the lowest possible value for ending inventory is **(A)** fifo **(B)** lifo		**9.**
10. In a year of rising prices, the inventory method that gives the highest possible value for ending inventory is **(A)** fifo **(B)** lifo		**10.**
11. In a year of falling prices, the inventory method that gives the lowest possible value for ending inventory is **(A)** fifo **(B)** lifo		**11.**
12. In a year of falling prices, the inventory method that gives the highest possible value for ending inventory is **(A)** fifo **(B)** lifo....................		**12.**
13. Cost information is as follows: Beginning inventory 20 kits at $20.00; Purchases during year 20 kits at $30.00; Ending inventory 25 kits. Under the *fifo* method, ending inventory is **(A)** $500.00 **(B)** $550.00 **(C)** $700.00 **(D)** $750.00 ((E) none of these........		**13.**
14. Cost information is as follows: Beginning inventory 20 kits at $20.00; Purchases during year 20 kits at $30.00; Ending inventory 25 kits. Under the *lifo* method, ending inventory is **(A)** $500.00 **(B)** $550.00 **(C)** $700.00 **(D)** $750.00 **(E)** none of these........		**14.**

Items 13 and 14 cost information:

	Units	Unit cost
Beginning inventory	20 kits	$20.00
Purchases during year	20 kits	$30.00
Ending inventory	25 kits	

DIRECTIONS: Place a check mark (√) in the proper Answers column to show whether each of the following statements is true or false.

Statement	Answers: True	Answers: False	For Scoring
0. Businesses frequently choose a fiscal period that ends when inventory is at a low point	√		**0.** √
15. A minimum inventory balance is the amount of merchandise that will last until additional merchandise can be received from suppliers			**15.**
16. A perpetual inventory stock record always shows quantity and value of the merchandise on hand			**16.**
17. Book inventory is the same as periodic inventory			**17.**
18. The sale of merchandise provides the major source of revenue for a merchandising business			**18.**
19. A perpetual inventory is sometimes known as a physical inventory			**19.**
20. Net income of a business can be decreased by maintaining a merchandise inventory that is larger than needed			**20.**
21. Net income of a business is not decreased by maintaining a merchandise inventory that is smaller than needed			**21.**
22. A perpetual inventory usually is used when management desires up-to-date information about the inventory each day			**22.**
23. A perpetual inventory usually is prepared at the end of the month			**23.**
24. A periodic inventory should be taken at least once a year even when perpetual inventory records are kept			**24.**
25. Inventory errors may be detected by comparing periodic inventory records with perpetual inventory records			**25.**
26. Special cash registers may be used to update a perpetual inventory			**26.**
27. The lower of cost or market rule states that when the cost is lower than the current market price, use the market price to value an inventory			**27.**
28. The lower of cost or market rule states that when the market price is lower than the cost, use the market price to value an inventory			**28.**
29. If market value of an inventory declines and the lower of cost or market method is used, a loss is recognized when the merchandise is sold			**29.**
30. The gross profit method of estimating inventory makes possible the preparation of monthly income statements without taking periodic inventory			**30.**
31. A business must obtain approval from the Internal Revenue Service to change its inventory pricing method			**31.**
32. The first step in figuring an estimated ending merchandise inventory is to determine the value of merchandise available for sale			**32.**
33. An estimated inventory is not completely accurate			**33.**
34. Estimated gross profit on sales is figured by dividing net sales for the period by net purchases			**34.**

Name ______________________ Date __________ Class __________

DRILL 30-D 1, p. 613

[1–3]

Determining the quantities of merchandise on hand using perpetual inventory

Increases		Decreases		Balance
Date	Quantity	Date	Quantity	Quantity
May 1				*136*

Determining cost of inventory using the fifo and lifo methods

PROBLEM 30-1, p. 614

[1, 3]

fifo method

Model	No. of Units on Hand	Unit Cost	Inventory Value December 31
A36	*24*	*20 @ $41* *4 @ 40*	*$980*
		TOTAL *fifo* VALUE	

lifo method

[2, 3]

Model	No. of Units on Hand	Unit Cost	Inventory Value December 31
		TOTAL *lifo* VALUE	

[3] The method of pricing that resulted in the lower total amount for the inventory is ____________

[1–4]

Determining valuation of inventory at lower of cost or market

1	2	3	4	5	6
Item	No. of Units on Hand	Unit Cost	Current Unit Market Price	Unit Price to be Used	Value at Lower of Cost or Market
				TOTAL ENDING INVENTORY	

Estimating the value of inventory using the gross profit method

PROBLEM 30-3, p. 615

[1]

STEP 1

Beginning inventory, January 1	$
Plus net purchases for January	
Equals value of merchandise available for sale for January	$

STEP 2

Net sales for January	$
Less estimated gross profit on operations	
Equals estimated cost of merchandise sold	$

STEP 3

Merchandise available for sale	$
Less estimated cost of merchandise sold	
Equals estimated ending merchandise inventory	$

[2]

Name ______________________ Date __________ Class __________

MASTERY PROBLEM 30-M, p. 616

[1, 3]

Determining cost of inventory using the fifo and lifo methods

fifo method

Model	No. of Units on Hand	Unit Cost	Inventory Value December 31
		TOTAL *fifo* VALUE ▸	

lifo method

[2, 3]

Model	No. of Units on Hand	Unit Cost	Inventory Value December 31
		TOTAL *lifo* VALUE ▸	

[3] The method of pricing that resulted in the lower total amount for the inventory is __________

Determining cost of inventory using the lifo method with perpetual inventory

Date	Increases			Decreases			Balance		
	No. of Units	Unit Cost	Total Cost	No. of Units	Unit Cost	Total Cost	No. of Units	Unit Cost	Total Cost
June 1							*50*	*$20.00*	*$1,000.00*
2	*20*	*$22.00*	*$440.00*				*50* *20*	*20.00* *22.00*	*1,440.00*
6				*20* *5*	*$22.00* *20.00*	*$540.00*	*45*	*20.00*	*900.00*